GOLDEN LEGACY
ILLUSTRATED HISTORY MAGAZINE

The Saga of
TOUSSAINT L'OUVERTURE
and The Birth of Haiti

Vol. 1

© FITZGERALD PUB. Co. Inc. 1966

...AND SO THE TWO MEN UNDERTOOK THE TASK OF GIVING THE YOUNG TOUSSAINT AN EDUCATION AFTER THEIR DAY'S CHORES WERE DONE...

HIS FATHER TAUGHT HIM THE USE OF HERBS - AFRICAN MEDICINE - WHICH HAD BEEN PASSED ON TO HIM BY HIS FATHER

THERE WERE OTHER LESSONS TOUSSAINT HAD TO LEARN THOUGH... AS HE GREW UP IT BECAME APPARENT THAT HE DIDN'T HAVE NATURAL STRENGTH

PAPA, WON'T I EVER GROW AS STRONG AS YOU ARE?

WE'RE NOT ALL BUILT THE SAME, BUT THROUGH HARD WORK WE CAN OVERCOME MOST THINGS... - LIKE YOU, BORN SMALL, CAN BUILD YOURSELF UP - YOU, BORN A SLAVE, CAN SOMEDAY BE FREE

TOUSSAINT NEVER FORGOT THAT LESSON. HE WORKED HARD ON BUILDING HIS BODY AND BECAME OUTSTANDING AMONG THE YOUNG SLAVES IN PHYSICAL FEATS AS WELL AS INTELLIGENCE.

TOUSSAINT AGAIN!

BY 1790 TOUSSAINT WAS KNOWN AND RESPECTED BY BLACK AND WHITE THROUGHOUT THE COUNTRYSIDE. HE HAD STARTED TO GREY AT THE TEMPLES AND HAD SETTLED DOWN TO A QUIET FAMILY LIFE... WHEN THE GREAT SLAVE REVOLT WAS LAUNCHED

NOT TO BE OVERLOOKED IS THE FACT THAT THOUSANDS OF MILES AWAY IN THE MOTHER COUNTRY, FRANCE, THE REVOLUTION WAS IN FULL SWING AND WORDS LIKE LIBERTY! FREEDOM! AND JUSTICE! WERE HEARD EVERY DAY IN CONVERSATION. THE SLAVES, TOO, HEARD THESE CONVERSATIONS AND THE WORDS: LIBERTY! FREEDOM! AND JUSTICE!!

TOUSSAINT'S MASTER WAS CALLED TO THE CAPITAL, LE CAP, AS WERE ALL WHITES, TO DECIDE ON A COURSE OF ACTION...

TOUSSAINT, MON AMI I LEAVE MY FAMILY AND MY LAND IN YOUR HANDS.

IF ANYTHING HAPPENS TO ME AND I DON'T RETURN, LOOK AFTER THEM FOR ME TOUSSAINT

FEAR NOT, SIR

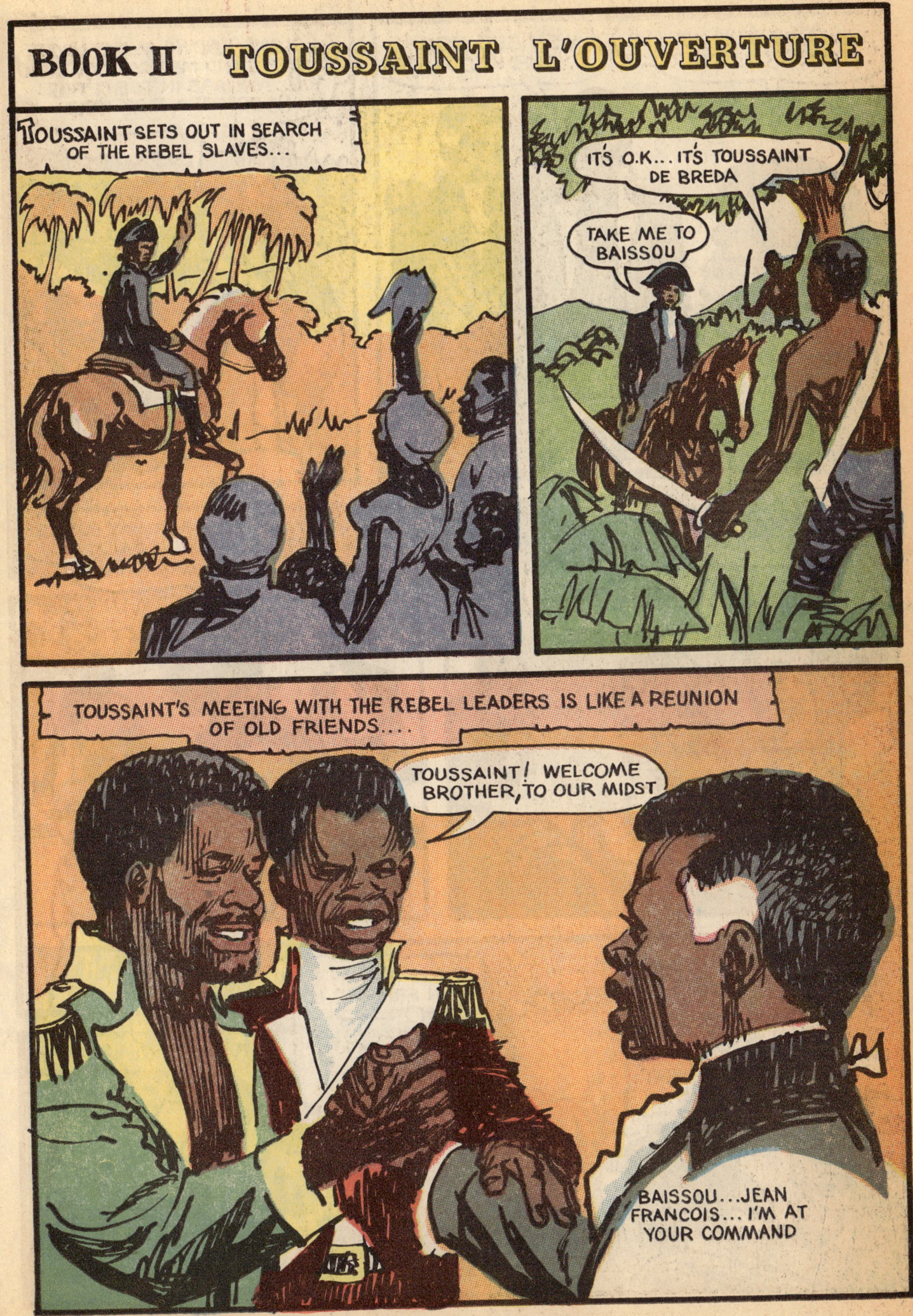

With 600 crack troops at his command, Toussaint bargains with the Spanish as an independent leader...

"On behalf of the King of Spain, I welcome you to our ranks"

Always distrustful of the colonist powers, Toussaint viewed this alliance as just another step towards his ultimate goal...

"For the present these Spanish devils can be a great help to us, Dessalines..."

"Given the chance, any one of them would have us back in chains... With the aid of God and our swords we must see that they don't succeed"

"The grave before the chains again!"

"I take an oath to that!"

Dessalines... ex-slave, trusted and devoted lieutenant... destined to fulfill Toussaint's dream.

"And now to work"

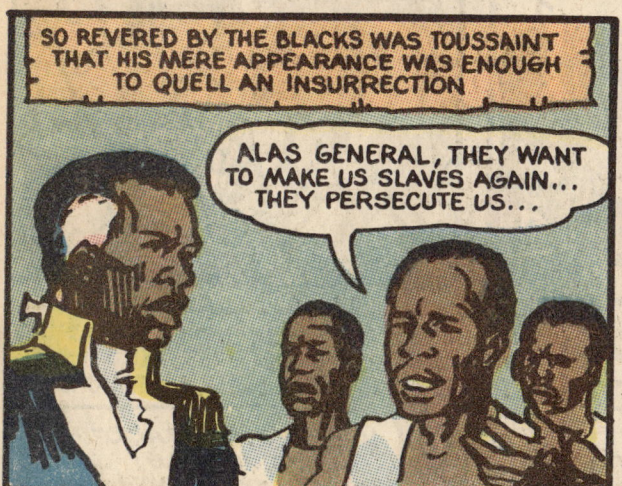

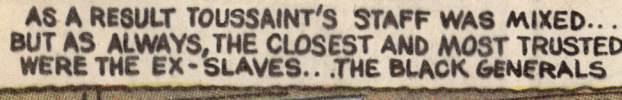

"MY STAY IN THAT CELL WAS NOT ALL BAD... IT GAVE ME TIME TO THINK. I MUST HAVE A LONG TALK WITH YOU, MON AMI"

LAVEAUX MAKES AN OFFER...

"THIS MULATTO REVOLT WAS JUST A POWER PLAY — TO GET CONCESSIONS, BUT I KNOW AS WELL AS THEY DO THAT YOU AND YOUR BLACK ARMY HOLD THE KEY HERE IN SAN DOMINGO"

"ALL THE ELEMENTS IN THE POWER STRUGGLE HERE FAIL TO TAKE INTO ACCOUNT THE FULL IMPORT OF THE BLACKS... THOSE WRETCHES SEE THIS ISLAND AS A PLUM, UP FOR GRABS — AND THE BLACKS AS MERELY A PART OF THE PLUM"

"BUT OF COURSE YOU, TRUSTED FRIEND OF THE BLACKS, DON'T HOLD TO THIS VIEW"

"EXACTLY, TOUSSAINT, AND I BELIEVE THE TIME IS RIGHT TO MAKE THIS MOVE I'VE THOUGHT ABOUT FOR SOME TIME... AS GOVERNOR OF SAN DOMINGO AND REPRESENTATIVE OF THE REPUBLIC OF FRANCE, I OFFER YOU THE POSTS OF ASSISTANT GOVERNOR AND COMMANDER-IN-CHIEF OF THE ARMIES OF SAN DOMINGO."

"**WHERE IS THE LEADER?**" — TOUSSAINT MOVES CLOSER TO HIS DESTINY — JUST 6 YEARS AFTER JOINING THE SLAVE REVOLT TOUSSAINT IS OFFERED THE SECOND HIGHEST POSITION IN THE COUNTRY

IT IS A LOGICAL SITUATION — YOU ARE THE POWER HERE — THIS WAY THEY MUST ACKNOWLEDGE THAT... SAY YOU'LL ACCEPT, MON AMI...

I ACCEPT!

ON MAY 2nd, 1797 TOUSSAINT, THE FORMER SLAVE, IS SWORN IN

Now in a position to direct the course of the island... Toussaint, believing in the principles of the French Revolution, set about to bring San Domingo even closer to France by expelling first the Spanish and then the British, from the island, for he recognized their ultimate goal of restoring SLAVERY!

In the campaigns against the Spanish Toussaint gains victory after victory through brilliant strategy

Toussaint scores 7 victories in 7 days as he sweeps the British out of Port-au-Prince

Toussaint's triumphant entry into Port-au-Prince was comparable to the receptions given to the conquering Roman armies that he'd read about.

Meanwhile, in San Domingo, Toussaint does more than roll up military victories.. he issues proclamations on freedom, encourages agricultural development, advocates the education of the blacks. Realizing the great need of the ex-slaves, he sends his two sons to France along with many other young people for a higher education. San Domingo prospers as Toussaint's powerful army maintains the peace

Laveaux is replaced as governor by Sonthonax who is more militantly pro-black than some of the richer free blacks

My first act as governor is to give you a free hand at running this island. It's only fair that a black man head a nation built on black bodies

Sonthonax goes so far as to suggest annihilation of all the whites in San Domingo

But that is unwise — we still need them, at least until we have enough blacks trained to take over.
If you have a horse he can help you plow your fields, you can ride him.... if you kill him, what good is he?

NAPOLEON IGNORES ALL CORRESPONDENCE FROM TOUSSAINT. FURIOUS BECAUSE TOUSSAINT ADDRESSES HIM AS AN EQUAL: "TO THE GREATEST GENERAL IN THE EAST FROM THE GREATEST GENERAL IN THE WEST...". NAPOLEON DECIDES TO WAIT UNTIL ALL HIS EUROPEAN CAMPAIGNS ARE COMPLETED BEFORE HE TURNS HIS FULL ATTENTION TO SAN DOMINGO AND TOUSSAINT

BY 1801 NAPOLEON HAD FINISHED THE WAR WITH ENGLAND AND AT LAST FREE TO TURN AWAY FROM EUROPE..

SEND FOR MY BROTHER-IN-LAW, LECLERC... NOW WE'LL ATTEND TO THIS INSOLENT SLAVE, TOUSSAINT!

FIRST OFFER THEM ANYTHING THEY WANT, TRY TO LAND WITHOUT A BATTLE... GAIN THEIR CONFIDENCE, ONCE YOU HAVE ESTABLISHED A FOOTHOLD ON THE ISLAND... ATTACK! *CRUSH THEM!* CAPTURE THAT SLAVE AND HIS GENERALS... SHOOT THEM! — INSTILL FEAR AND RESPECT IN THOSE BLACKS.... *GET THEM BACK ON THE PLANTATIONS!!*

ON SEPT. 18, 1801 AN ARMARDA SETS OUT FOR SAN DOMINGO WITH 24,000 TROUPS FRESH FROM VICTORIES IN EGYPT AND EUROPE...

TOUSSAINT PONDERS... HE HAD FAITH IN THE *PRINCIPLES* OF FRANCE.... SHOULD HE FIGHT AGAINST A COUNTRY BASED ON THE CREED OF EQUALITY AND JUSTICE?

I MUST PREPARE FOR THE WORST

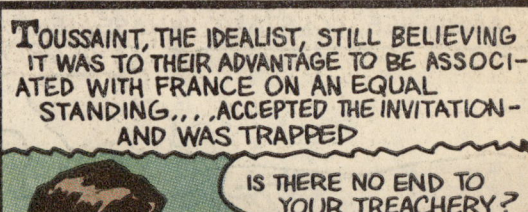

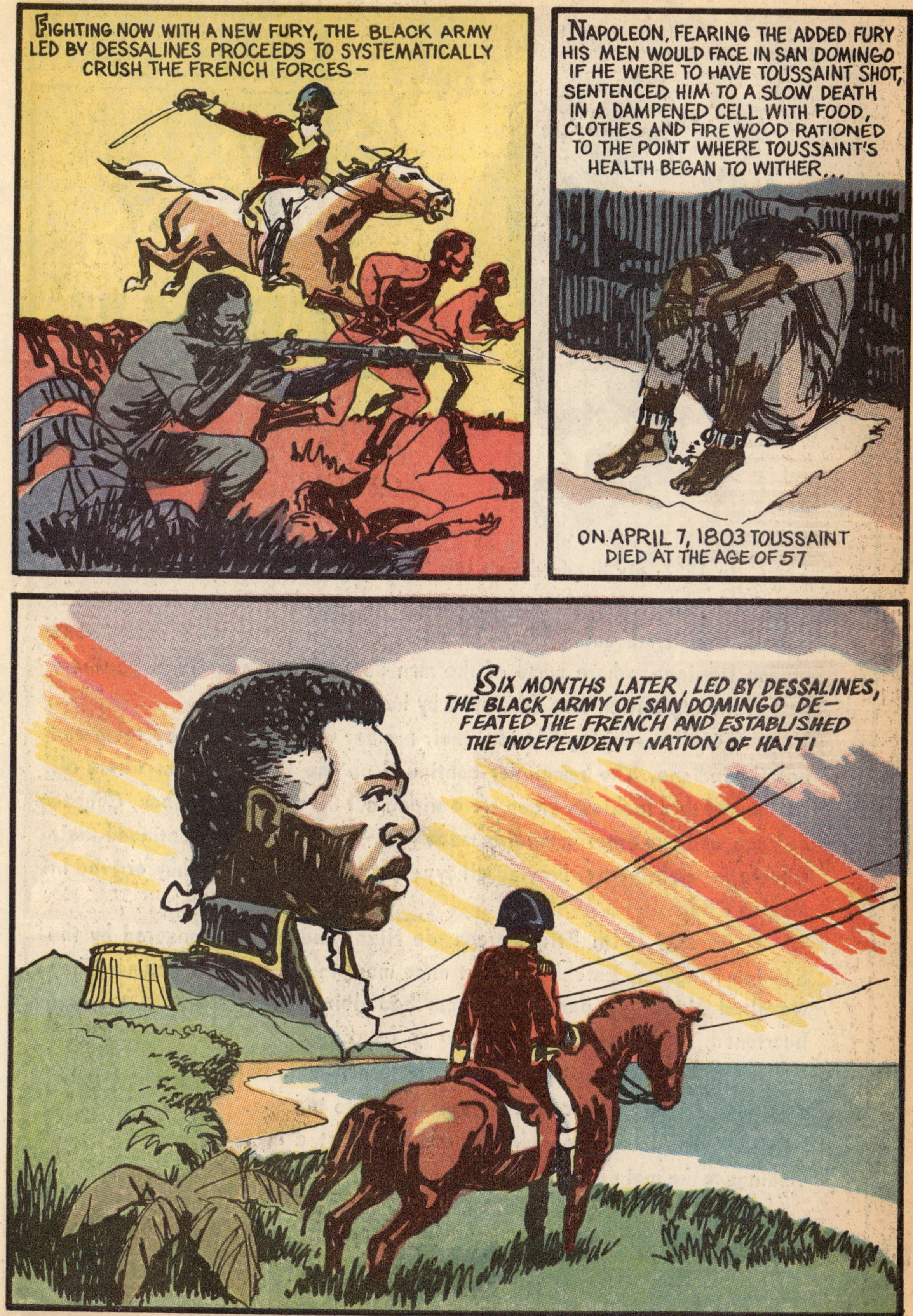

ESTEBAN

(Discoverer of Arizona)

In 1527, six hundred men left Spain, sponsored by King Charles, in search of gold in the Americas. Among them was the adventurous Morrocan Negro, named Esteban. Led by Cabeza de Vaca, they stopped for provisions at San Domingo, where some of the men deserted, then on to Cuba where part of the expedition was destroyed by hurricaine.

Finally reaching Florida, their number was cut in half by fever and hostile indians. The remainder continued up the Florida coast where all but four of this luckless group were wiped out by a storm. Esteban, Cabeza de Vaca, and two other Spaniards made their way ashore and continued their travels for eight years, braving all types of hardships, until they arrived in Mexico City.

In 1539, with Friar Marcos de Niza, and again sponsored by the Spanish Kingdom, Esteban set out once more in search of a fortune. They travelled North over deserts and scorched plains until, exhausted and disheartened, the group decided not to go on. Esteban, wanting to continue, led a small party over the blazing hot desert lands until he came upon a most unusual sight, an adobe village of Pueblo indians.

Before advancing further, Esteban sent a messenger to report his findings to the main party. This area is known today as the state of Arizona.

Unfortunately, before the main party could reach Esteban, they were met by a few of his survivors. The Pueblo indians had attacked and massacred Esteban and most of his group. Friar Marcos de Niza and the remainder of the expedition returned to Mexico City with the news of Esteban's great discovery.

DR. CHARLES DREW
1904–1950
(Pioneer in Blood Research)

Dr. Drew's leap to world–wide fame during 1940 was based primarily on his personal mastery of the blood plasma theory, which he eminently helped to perfect at McGill University, Canada, in the late thirties.

Dr. Charles Drew was born in Washington, D.C. He received his degree at Amherst College, in Massachusetts. While there he was an outstanding athlete, being captain of the track team. He was a teacher and athletics coach at Morgan College in Baltimore before going to McGill University in Canada to finish his medical training. While there he mastered the blood plasma theory. He set up the first bank in England and was called upon by the United States Government to take charge of blood conservation. As a result of his work millions of lives were saved throughout the world.

In 1942 Dr. Drew was awarded the Spingarn Medal in recognition of his contributions to Negro progress. In 1950 Dr. Drew was killed in an automobile accident while driving to a conference at Tuskegee. At the time of his untimely death he was a member of the College of Surgeons, chief surgeon and chief of staff at Freedmen's Hospital, Washington, D.C.

REFERENCES

Current Biography, 1950
Negro Yearbook, 1940
"Who's Who in Colored America" 1950, pp. 163-164
"Great Negroes Past and Present." By Russell L. Adams. Chicago, 1964. Page 61.

GOLDEN LEGACY
ILLUSTRATED HISTORY SERIES

1. Toussaint L'Overture
2. Harriet Tubman
3. Crispus Attucks
4. Benjamin Banneker
5. Matthew Henson
6. Alexander Dumas
7. Frederick Douglass Part I
8. Frederick Douglass Part II
9. Robert Smalls
10. Joseph Cinque
11. White, Wilkins & Marshall
12. Black Cowboys
13. Dr. Martin Luther King
14. Alexander Pushkin
15. Ancient African Kingdoms
16. Black Inventors

"We hope you will read, enjoy and benefit from our endeavors."

You may order GOLDEN LEGACY for your school, church, relatives, yourself-----or merely as a gift for a friend!

GOLDEN LEGACY is available in soft or hard cover editions.

Send Orders To: Fitzgerald Pub. Co., Inc.
  442 Wolf Hill Road
  Dix Hills, N.Y. 11746

Payment must accompany all orders in check or money order.

Softcover Edition: $24.00   Hardcover Edition: $45.00

GOLDEN LEGACY
ILLUSTRATED HISTORY MAGAZINE

The Saga of
HARRIET TUBMAN
"The Moses of Her People"

Vol. 2

© FITZGERALD PUB. Co. Inc. 1967

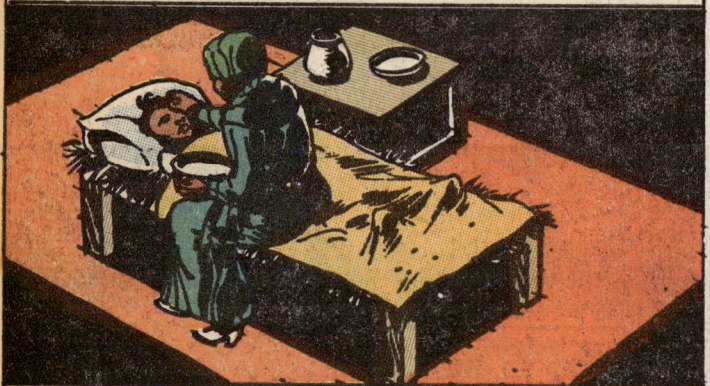

Harriet became so strong that even the men were amazed at the things she could do.

Her owner decided to "rent" her to a local farmer because he needed extra money.

"You're getting a good buy, she works hard."

This man turned out to be even more cruel than her "master", driving his slaves long before sunrise until after sunset.

This bad treatment was too much for Harriet who still suffered pain from her head injury. She collapsed, and was sent back to her master.

While she lay helpless, he tried to sell her.

"I tell you she's a bargain at a hundred. That fool farmer I rented her to just worked her too hard.. in a few days—"

"Never mind I'm not gonna pay that kind of money out."

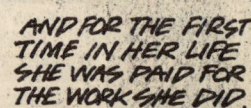

"I WILL NOT REST UNTIL **ALL** MY FAMILY ARE FREE!"

TO GET MONEY FOR HER PLAN, HARRIET DID BAKING AND WASHING AFTER HER DAYS WORK.

AND SHE MADE MANY FRIENDS IN THE CITY OF PHILADELPHIA.

"I PLAN TO RETURN SOUTH AND BRING MY FAMILY TO FREEDOM."

"AND WE WILL HELP YOU HARRIET, WE WILL TAKE YOU TO PEOPLE WHO WANT TO AID OUR CAUSE."

"THIS IS HARRIET TUBMAN. SHE HAS ESCAPED FROM SLAVERY, AND PLANS TO RETURN TO THE SOUTH TO HELP MORE OF HER PEOPLE TO GET OUT."

"SPLENDID! WE, THE **SOCIETY OF FRIENDS*** WILL HELP YOU, WITH MONEY AND THE NAMES OF OTHER FRIENDS ALONG YOUR ROUTE. THEY WILL AID YOU IN WHATEVER WAY THEY CAN."

"THEY WILL HIDE AND FEED YOU."

*THE SOCIETY OF FRIENDS — MORE POPULARLY KNOWN AS QUAKERS, — HAD ESCAPED FROM RELIGIOUS PERSECUTION AND WERE ACTIVE AGAINST THE EVILS OF SLAVERY.

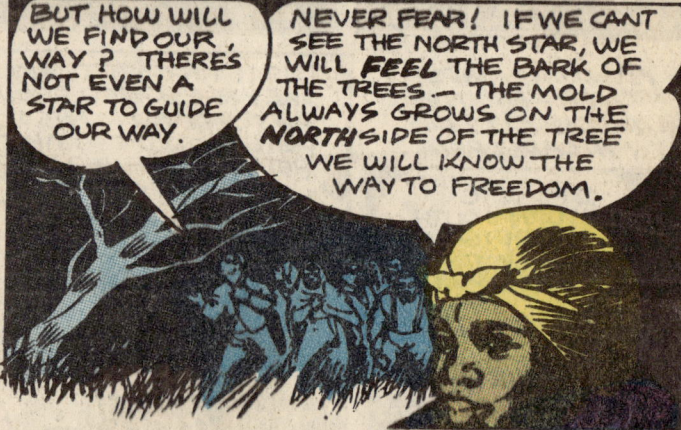

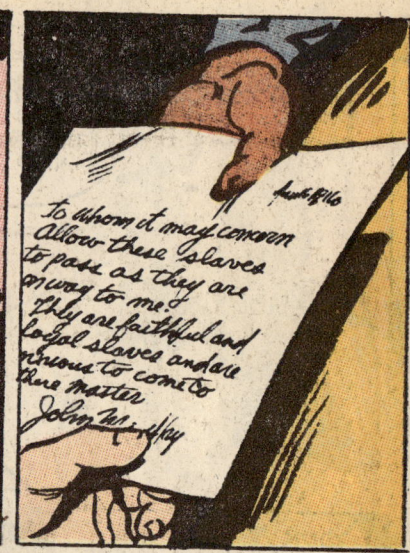

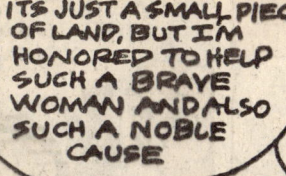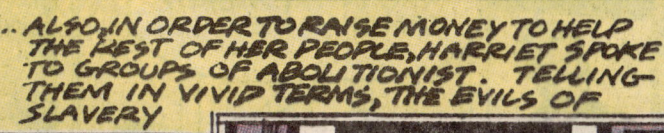

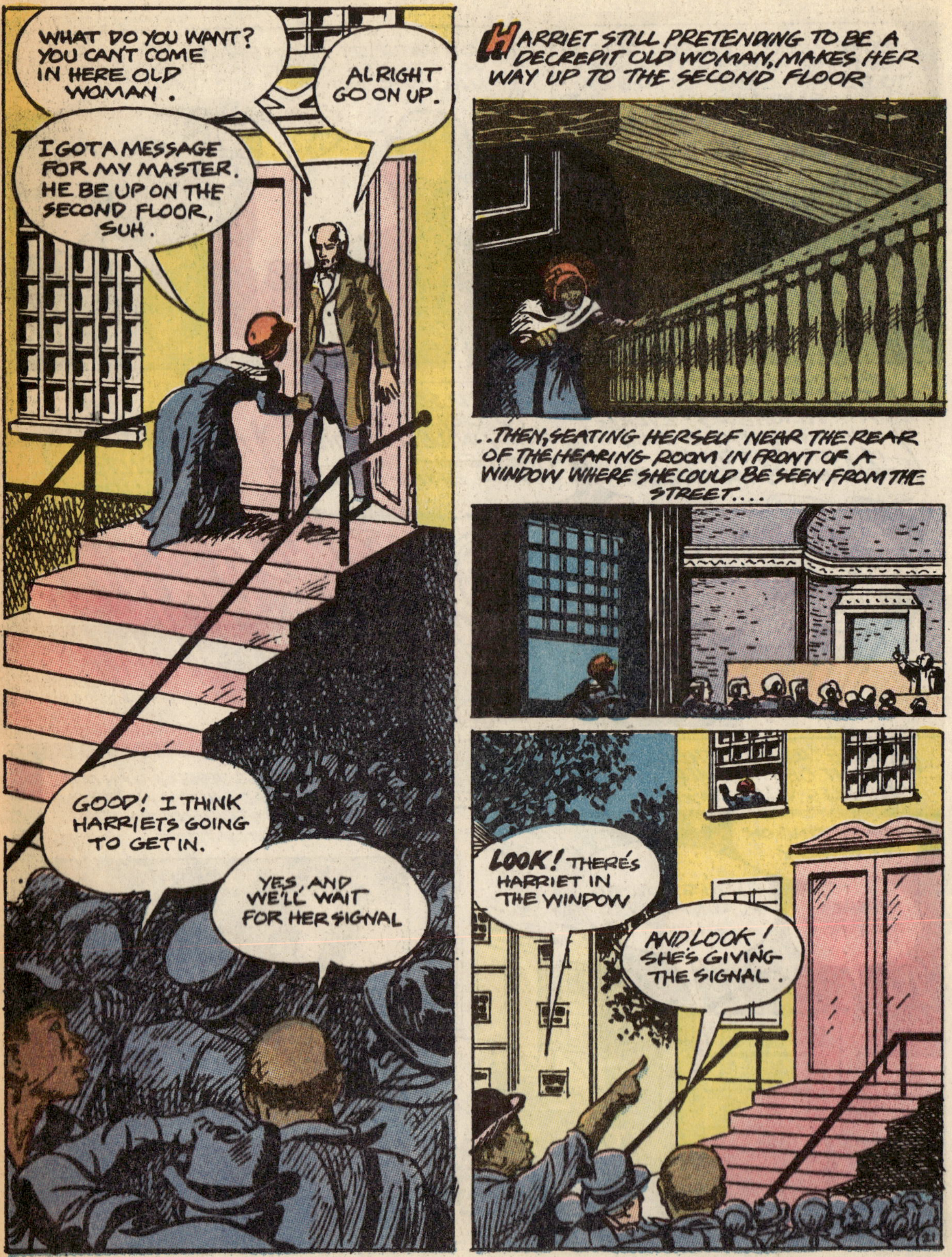

WHEN THE CIVIL WAR BEGAN, HARRIET BECAME A NURSE FOR THE UNION ARMIES. LATER, AS A MILITARY SCOUT AND INVALUABLE INTELLIGENCE AGENT, SHE PENETRATED THE ENEMY'S LINES MANY TIMES AND ESCAPED WITHOUT INJURY BUT NOT WITHOUT EXTREME HAZARD.

AT FORT WAGNER SHE ORGANIZED A GROUP OF NINE NEGRO SCOUTS AND RIVER PILOTS AND, WITH COLONEL MONTGOMERY, **LED** A UNION RAIDING PARTY OF THREE GUNBOATS AND 150 NEGRO TROOPS UP THE COMBAHEE RIVER....

BOSTON JULY 10, 1863. RESULTS OF THAT RAID WERE REPORTED BY THE BOSTON **COMMONWEALTH**

LISTEN HERE! IT SAYS "UNDER THE GUIDANCE OF A **BLACK WOMAN** THEY DASHED INTO THE REBELS COUNTRY, STRUCK A BOLD AND EFFECTIVE BLOW, DESTROYING MILLIONS OF DOLLARS WORTH OF GOODS, AND STRIKING TERROR INTO THE HEART OF THE SOUTH, BRINGING OUT NEAR 800 SLAVES AND THOUSANDS OF DOLLARS WORTH OF PROPERTY" NOW THAT **IS** A SETBACK FOR THE REBS!

HARRIET TUBMAN LIVED FOR ALMOST FIFTY YEARS AFTER THE END OF A WAR SHE HELPED TO WIN. SHE WAS NEAR A HUNDRED YEARS OLD WHEN SHE DIED IN 1913 SO PASSED THE MOST FAMOUS "**CONDUCTOR**" ON THE UNDERGROUND RAILROAD WHO ONCE SAID, PROUDLY "I NEVER RUN MY TRAIN OFF THE TRACK, AND I NEVER **LOST** A PASSENGER."

THE END

DANIEL HALE WILLIAMS

1856 – 1931
(FIRST SUCCESSFUL OPERATION ON THE HUMAN HEART)

Perhaps it was the words of Daniel Hale Williams' father, "We...must cultivate our minds", or Frederick Douglass' advice "The only way you can succeed is to override the obstacles in your way. By the power that is within you, do what you hope to do", that inspired him to the greatness he later achieved in the medical profession.

Williams had been a shoemaker's apprentice, barber, musician, and a student of law. He finally decided on medicine as a career while in his early twenties in Janesville, Wisconsin.

After his graduation from Northwestern University in 1883 he was retained as an instructor, an unusual honor in those days. He later became one of the founders of the Interracial Provident Hospital and the first Negro nurses and interne training school in the United States. Dr. Williams was also one of the founders of the National Medical Association and became its first Vice-President.

In 1893, the year of his greatest achievement, he became the first man to successfully operate on the human heart. Dr. Williams was appointed by President Grover Cleveland to head the Freedmen's Hospital in Washington, D.C., where he founded another nurses training school, and became a charter member and Fellow of the American College of Surgeons.

He performed many daring and history-making operations before his death on August 4, 1931 in Idlewild, Michigan. Time cannot dim the greatness we've found in Dr. Danial Hale Williams.

IRA ALDRIDGE

1807 – 1867
(WORLD FAMOUS ACTOR)

By hurling stones and taunts from the seats of Bleecker Street's African Grove in the New York of the 1820's, rowdies were able to force the closure of the African Company's Shakespearian and classical theater. But not before one of the world's most widely acclaimed actors was lured by the magic of the stage.

His name was Ira Aldridge. He was born the grandson of a Senegalese chieftain, and the son of a non-slave Presbyterian pastor.

Disturbed by Ira's attraction to the theater, the elder Aldridge sent the teenaged boy off to the University of Glasgow, in Scotland, where he was a scholastic success.

But soon, young Ira was in London playing Othello at the Royalty Theater before he was twenty, then to Coburg and Sadler's Wells, and on to Covent Garden in 1833, where he again played Othello.

While in Dublin, he was asked by Irish actor Edmond Kean to perform Othello to Kean's Iago. They became a two-year touring triumph and fast friends.

He went on to perform in all of the major cities of Europe, eventually receiving the Order of Chevalier from the King of Prussia; an invitation from the King of Sweden for special performances in Stockholm; the Cross of Leopold from the Czar of Russia.

After forty years of stardom, he died in 1867 while on tour in Poland. He is presently honored with an Ira Aldridge Memorial Chair at the Shakespeare Memorial Theater at Stratford-on-Avon, in England.

BISHOP JAMES AUGUSTINE HEALY
1830 – 1900
(FIRST NEGRO CATHOLIC BISHOP)

Though the times and laws were difficult to overcome James Healy managed, through his brilliance and hard work, to reach great heights in the Catholic church.

He attended school in Montreal and Paris before graduating from Holy Cross College in Massachusetts. He also received a degree from Georgetown, graduating at the head of his class.

In 1854, Father Healy was appointed pastor of one of Boston's largest churches. Later, in 1866, he assumed the very important position of Secretary and Chancellor of the diocese. Then, in 1875, Healy was appointed Bishop of Portland, Maine, becoming America's first Negro Catholic Bishop.

Bishop James Augustine Healy, after working tirelessly for many years for the poor of his parish, died in 1900 of a heart attack.

JEAN BAPTISTE POINTE DU SABLE

1745 – 1818
(FOUNDER OF CHICAGO)

Jean Baptiste Pointe Du Sable was born in San Domingo and educated in France. After returning home, he worked for his father, a coffee dealer, until he grew restless and left for New Orleans in the family's schooner, Suzanne.

Suzanne, named after his mother, was destroyed in a hurricane off the Florida coast and Du Sable was rescued by a Danish ship en route to New Orleans. In New Orleans, without identification papers, Du Sable was fearful of being claimed as a runaway slave so he travelled north to Illinois where he met and married an Indian girl.

In Illinois, Du Sable purchased a farm on which he, his wife, and her relatives remained for about one year when he left to locate a site on which to build a trading post. Du Sable travelled to an unsettled area at the southern end of Lake Michigan and the northern bank of the Chicago river where, in 1772, he built a trading post. The trading post soon became so successful servicing travellers to and from Canada that he built a home, several other buildings, and sent for his family.

As Du Sable's business increased, others moved into the area which gradually grew into one of America's largest cities, Chicago. Jean Baptiste Pointe Du Sable was one of America's great pioneers and, today, near the Michigan Avenue bridge is a plaque indicating the site of his home. Other plaques honoring him are owned by the Chicago Historical Society and can be found in Chicago's Du Sable High School

As the March moon began to shed its rays upon the dusty New England streets, a small band of men armed with sticks and stones gathered outside the Boston Custom House of 1770. The citizens had long been enraged over the unfair policies of England, the mother country. The presence of English Red Coats to enforce these laws only served to increase their anger.

"The way to get rid of these soldiers is to attack the main guard! Strike at the root! This is the nest!", cried a tall, strapping Negro seaman, named Crispus Attucks, who had escaped from slavery twenty years before. As the guns of the panic-stricken soldiers went off — there lay Crispus, "The first to defy and the first to die", one of five who were killed in the first skirmish in America's fight for freedom, known today as the Boston massacre.

From then on, a memorial service was held every March 5th at Boston's Old South Meeting House until the War for American Independence officially began.

Though it was not the general rule to include Negroes in military service, as many patriots did not welcome arming them, nevertheless, 5,000 served America and the ideal of liberty and equality.

In the battles at Bunker Hill, Brandywine, Newport, and every major conflict, Negroes are credited with outstanding acts of heroism.

When the War of 1812 broke out between the British and America, many black men enlisted. Free men to further the cause of freedom for themselves and all men, and slaves to gain their personal freedom. General Stonewall Jackson had this to say of their performance "...The American nation shall applaud your valor as your General now praises your ardor." Nevertheless, when the war ended many found themselves forced back into slavery.

In the Civil War Negroes represented one-fourth of the Union Navy and more than 190,000 served in the Union Army. They fought in over 400 battles and more than 38,000 lost their lives to preserve the Union.

Secretary of War Stanton, in a letter to President Lincoln, dated February 8, 1864, wrote "...They have proved themselves among the bravest of the brave, performing deeds of daring and shedding their blood with a heroism unsurpassed by soldiers of any other race." Among the many awards they received were several Congressional Medals of Honor.

Black men, too, have fought and died, and continue to fight and die, for the right of all people to life, liberty, and the pursuit of happiness.

GOLDEN LEGACY
ILLUSTRATED HISTORY SERIES

1. Toussaint L'Overture
2. Harriet Tubman
3. Crispus Attucks
4. Benjamin Banneker
5. Matthew Henson
6. Alexander Dumas
7. Frederick Douglass Part I
8. Frederick Douglass Part II
9. Robert Smalls
10. Joseph Cinque
11. White, Wilkins & Marshall
12. Black Cowboys
13. Dr. Martin Luther King
14. Alexander Pushkin
15. Ancient African Kingdoms
16. Black Inventors

"We hope you will read, enjoy and benefit from our endeavors."

You may order GOLDEN LEGACY for your school, church, relatives, yourself-----or merely as a gift for a friend!

GOLDEN LEGACY is available in soft or hard cover editions.

Send Orders To: Fitzgerald Pub. Co., Inc.
442 Wolf Hill Road
Dix Hills, N.Y. 11746

Payment must accompany all orders in check or money order.

Softcover Edition: $24.00   Hardcover Edition: $45.00

THE YEAR IS 1770... THE BRITISH SHIP, ROMMEY, HEADS FOR THE HARBOR OF BOSTON, MASSACHUSETTS.

GOSH!! IT'S AMERICA!! BOSTON!

WHOA THERE SON! NOT SO FAST! YOU'LL FALL OVERBOARD!

BOSTON FEBRUARY 1770...

ATTUCKS! CRISPUS ATTUCKS! WELL, LOOK WHAT THE WINDS BLEW IN. WHERE HAVE YOU BEEN ALL THIS TIME?

TOMMY MEET MY OLD SHIPMATE MISTER CARR. CARR, HAS THERE BEEN MUCH TROUBLE SINCE I WAS LAST HERE?

TOMMY, THE PEOPLE FOLLOWED CRISPUS, THIS BIG MAN WHO SEEMED TO COME FROM NOWHERE, WAS READY AND WILLING TO FIGHT FOR AMERICA AND HER INDEPENDENCE...

ONE OTHER LEADER WHO BELIEVED AS ATTUCKS DID, WAS JAMES OTIS...

"WORDS ARE A WASTE AT A TIME LIKE THIS. ACTION MUST BE TAKEN! THE STATE OF BOSTON IS THE SAME AS IF WAR HAD BEEN DECLARED!"

"MR. OTIS IS RIGHT. STAND UP AND FIGHT FOR YOUR RIGHTS."

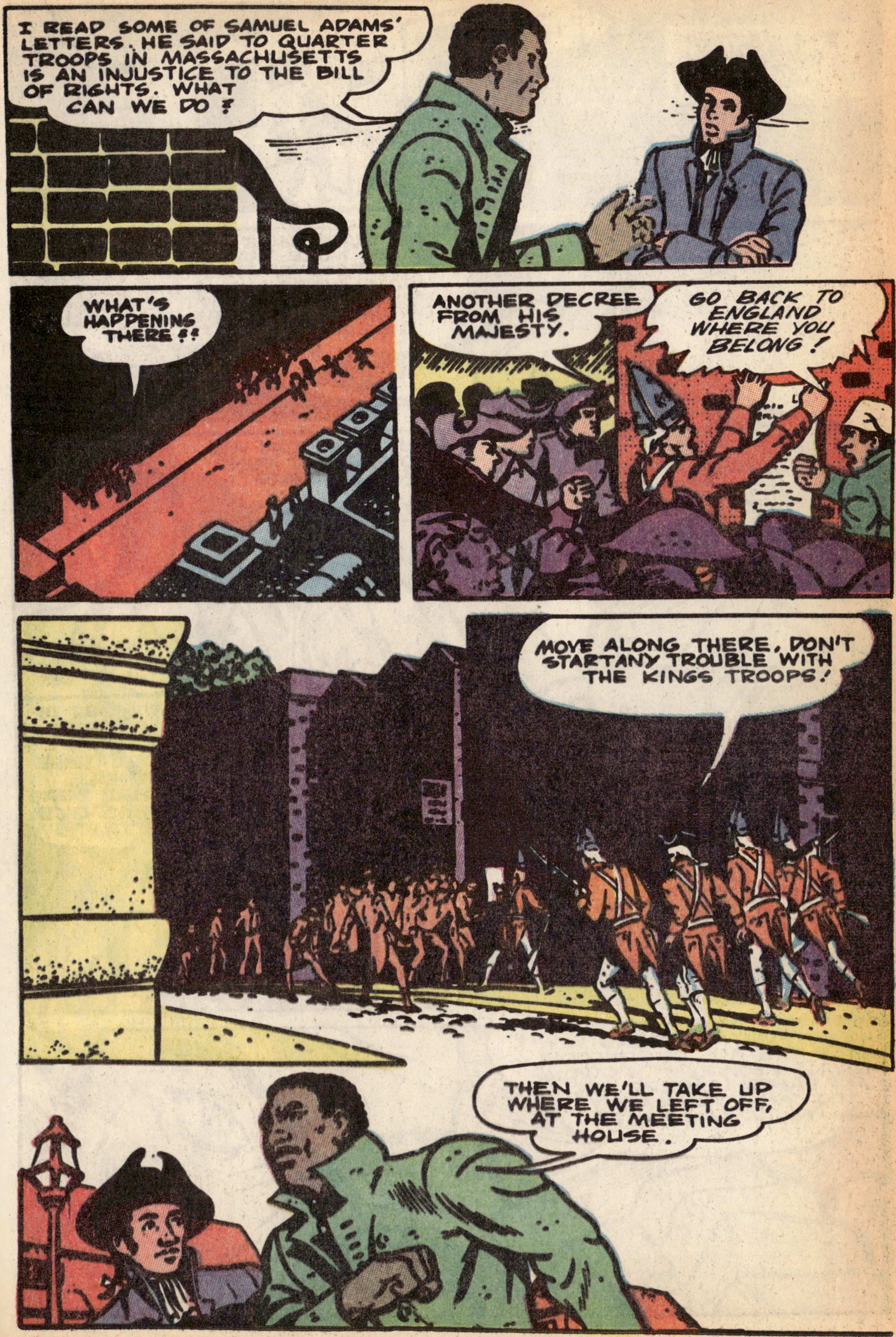

THE MEETING HOUSE MARCH 1770...

TWO YEARS AGO I SPOKE HERE. NO ONE KNOWS MORE THAN I DO ABOUT THE PRIVILEGES OF FREEDOM. I WAS SOLD INTO SLAVERY WHEN I WAS JUST A YOUNG BOY. I COULDN'T SEE ONE MAN OWNING ANOTHER AGAINST HIS WILL. THE SAME THING APPLIES TO OUR COUNTRY!

BUT WHAT CAN WE DO AGAINST GUNS AND BAYONETS?

WE CAN FIGHT! BAYONETS WON'T STOP THE WILL OF FREEDOM LOVING PEOPLE. WITH STRONG AND EAGER LEADERS WE, TOO, CAN HAVE AN ARMY! WE, TOO, CAN FIGHT!

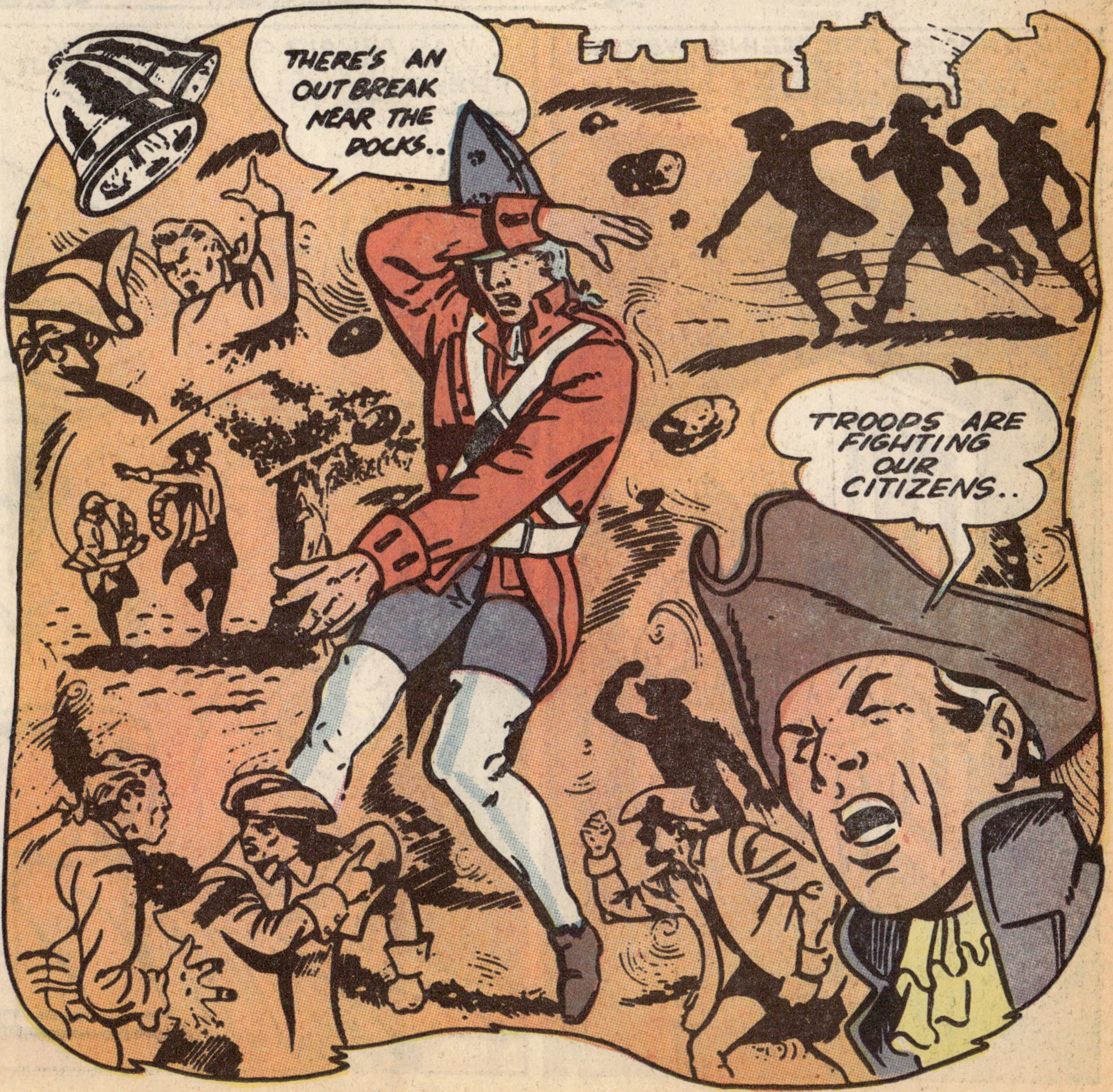

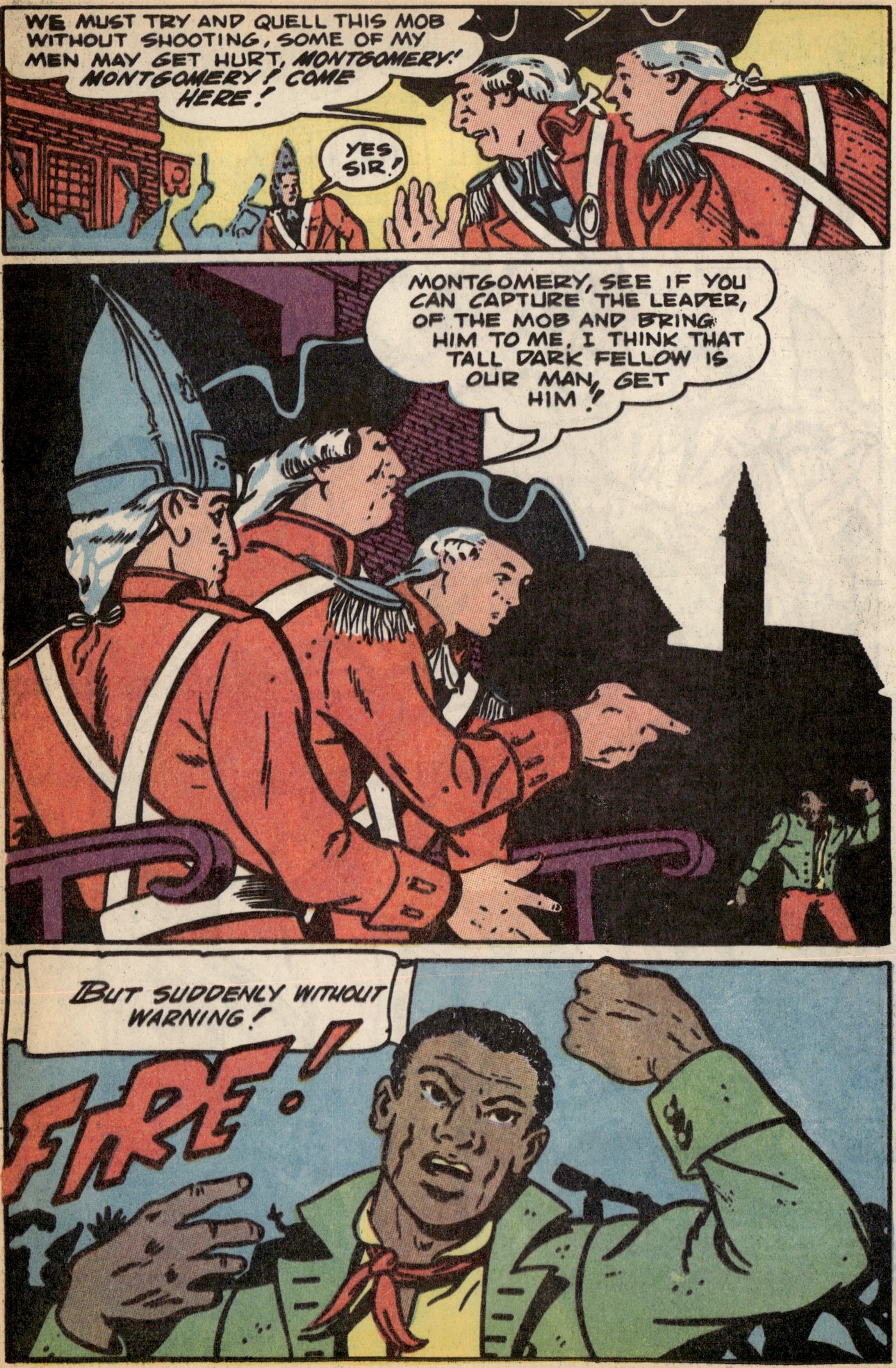

DEBORAH GANNETT

The only woman to actually enlist and serve in the Continental Army was a Negro. Her name was Deborah Sampson of Plymouth, Massachusetts. At twenty-two she cut her hair, dressed in men's clothing, and, as Robert Shurtliff, joined the army. She fought bravely for over a year. Wounded by saber and musket, she tended her own wounds to avoid discovery. Finally detected, she journeyed back to Massachusetts, Married Benjamin Gannett and had three children.

The General Court of Massachusetts has an order in its offical records of January 20, 1792, relating her story. It says in part:

"Whereas, it appears to this court that the said Deborah Gannett enlisted under the name of Robert Shurtliff, in Captain Webb's company, in the Fourth Massachusetts Regiment, on May 20, 1782, and did actually perform the duty of a soldier, in the late army of the United States, to the 23rd day of October, 1783, for which she has received no compensation; and

"Whereas, it further appears that the said Deborah exhibited an extraordinary instance of female heroism, by discharging the duties of a faithful, gallant soldier, and at the same time preserving the virtue and chastity of her sex unsuspected and unblemished and was discharged from the service with a fair and honorable character; therefore,

"Resolved, that the Treasurer of this Commonwealth be, and he hereby is, directed to issue his note to the said Deborah for the sum of thirty-four pounds, bearing interest from October 23, 1783."

JAMES ARMISTEAD

As the Revolutionary War moved into Virginia in 1781, Major General Marquis de Lafayette was placed in command of 1,200 New England and New Jersey soldiers. James Armistead, a Virginia slave, became a spy in the service of Lafayette.

James Armistead was responsible for delivering instructions to other spies in Portsmouth, Virginia, and for picking up bits of information while loitering around British camps. "He completely fooled the British and saved Lafayette's army from defeat."

Lafayette wrote that Armistead "properly acquitted himself with important communications I gave him" and "his intelligence from the enemy's camp was industriously collected and faithfully delivered."

According to the Virginia Legislature, James Armistead was freed in 1786 because "...at the peril of his own life he found means to frequent the British camps, and thereby faithfully executed important commissions entrusted to him by the Marquis" and "kept open a channel of the most useful information to the army of the State."

Returning to his home in New Kent County, Virginia, in 1816, Armistead purchased forty acres of land. In 1819, the Virginia Legislature awarded him one hundred dollars and a yearly sum of forty dollars.

In 1824, Lafayette made a return visit to America. It was as a celebrated and important citizen that James Armistead greeted his former French comrade.

PETER SALEM

(1750 – 1816)

Peter Salem, the Minuteman, toughened in the Battles of Lexington and Concord, and in the stormy assaults on Fort Ticonderoga, was now a part of the First Massachusetts Regiment. With this group he helped the Colonists defend Breed's and Bunker Hills.

During the historic Battle of Bunker Hill, the British Commander, Major Pitcairn, jumped up and shouted, "The day is ours!" But he spoke too soon as Peter Salem fired a fatal round, downing the Major. In the following seven years, he fought in many other engagements, including "our biggest victory in open battle", the Battle of Saratoga.

Peter Salem was a slave, freed to enlist in the service of America. He was born in Framingham, Massachusetts in 1750. A basket-maker by trade, he moved to Leicester, Massachusetts after the war, and in 1783 married Katy Benson. They later returned to his home town of Framingham where he died, August 16, 1816.

In 1882, the citizens of Framingham collected funds to place a memorial stone over his grave.

Peter Salem is pictured in John Trumbull's painting of The Battle of Bunker Hill, located in The Capitol at Washington, D.C.

His Leicester home has been turned into a historical shrine by The Daughters of the American Revolution, who honored his heroism in 1909. A large boulder situated in the stone fence by the roadside is inscribed: "Here lived Peter Salem, a Negro soldier of the Revolution."

JAMES FORTEN

From two generations of free Pennsylvania Negroes came James Forten, born in Philadelphia on September 2, 1766.

When James was nine years old his father died, so the boy left school to support his family. But America was soon at war and the patriotic lad was anxious to enlist. With his mother's consent, he signed aboard the ship Royal Louis as a powder boy. Twenty black and two hundred white sailors manned this ship captained by Stephen Decatur.

On one voyage, the ship was captured by a British war vessel, and young James was taken prisoner with the rest of the crew.

In time, James and the ship captain's son grew to be friends. The captain, impressed with the powder boy, offered to take him to England for an education. But the brave youth replied, "I am here as a prisoner for the liberties of my country!" and he would not betray those freedoms which were so important for his people to gain in this struggle.

Negro prisoners-of-war were rarely exchanged — they were more often sold back into slavery in the West Indies. Fortunately for James Forten, he was released in a general exchange of prisoners. He returned to Philadelphia and, in time, earned a fortune as a sail manufacturer. He was a major contributor to the work and paper of the abolitionist, William Lloyd Garrison — becoming one of the "greatest pioneer Negro abolitionists" in the country.

GOLDEN LEGACY
ILLUSTRATED HISTORY SERIES

1. Toussaint L'Overture
2. Harriet Tubman
3. Crispus Attucks
4. Benjamin Banneker
5. Matthew Henson
6. Alexander Dumas
7. Frederick Douglass Part I
8. Frederick Douglass Part II
9. Robert Smalls
10. Joseph Cinque
11. White, Wilkins & Marshall
12. Black Cowboys
13. Dr. Martin Luther King
14. Alexander Pushkin
15. Ancient African Kingdoms
16. Black Inventors

"We hope you will read, enjoy and benefit from our endeavors."

You may order GOLDEN LEGACY for your school, church, relatives, yourself------or merely as a gift for a friend!

GOLDEN LEGACY is available in soft or hard cover editions.

Send Orders To: Fitzgerald Pub. Co., Inc.
442 Wolf Hill Road
Dix Hills, N.Y. 11746

Payment must accompany all orders in check or money order.

Softcover Edition: $24.00   Hardcover Edition: $45.00

BEN WORKED HARD... READING EVERYTHING, MEASURING, TAKING THE WATCH APART CAREFULLY...

..AND SKETCHING ITS PARTS...

ENLARGING THEM AND CARVING EVERY PIECE BUT THE SOUNDING DEVICE, OUT OF WOOD....

..UNTIL HE BUILT HIS OWN CLOCK THAT CHIMED!

YOU'RE A GENIUS, DEAR BEN! TRULY A GENIUS!

BENJAMIN DECIDED TO GO TO PHILADELPHIA TO GET INFORMATION ON THE COMING REVOLUTION....

WHILE THERE, HE HELPED BUILD CANNONS THAT WERE USED IN THE WAR....

HOWDY, YOU'RE A STRANGER HERE?

YES, BEN BANNEKER BY NAME.. OF MARYLAND!

AND YOURS!

RICHARD, RICHARD ALLEN, AS SOON AS I'M A FREE MAN!

RICHARD ALLEN PAID 2,000 DOLLARS FOR HIS FREEDOM AND YEARS LATER FOUNDED THE AFRICAN METHODIST FREEDOM CHURCH..

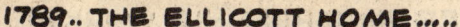

1789.. THE SURVEYORS WORKING NEAR THE POTOMAC RIVER AREA....

WHERE SHALL WE LOCATE THIS STRUCTURE?

THERE'S A GOOD PLOT BETWEEN THE EAST POTOMAC AND ROCK CREEK. I'LL SKETCH IT FOR YOU!

FROM THEN ON, BANNEKER WAS ONE OF THE TWO OR THREE SURVEYORS WHO WORKED CLOSELY WITH L'ENFANT, THE CHIEF ENGINEER.

I'VE COMPLAINED TO THE COMMISSIONERS THAT L'ENFANT DOESN'T INCLUDE US IN THE WORK ON THE PLANS.

L'ENFANT BOSSES THE JOB BUT BANNEKER DOES ALL THE WORK.

WITHIN THREE DAYS BANNEKER RETURNED WITH THE PLANS FOR WASHINGTON, D.C. AND CONSTRUCTION GOT UNDER WAY...

NOW TO RETURN HOME AND FINISH MY ALMANAC..

JAMES McHENRY WROTE THE INTRODUCTION FOR BANNEKER'S ALMANAC AND STATED IT WAS A WORK OF GENIUS.....

"THE EDITORS... FEEL THEMSELVES GRATIFIED IN PRESENTING... WHAT MUST BE CONSIDERED AN EXTRAORDINARY EFFORT OF GENIUS... CALCULATED BY A DESCENDENT OF AFRICA... I CONSIDER THIS NEGRO AS A FRESH PROOF THAT THE POWERS OF THE MIND ARE DISCONNECTED WITH THE COLOUR OF THE SKIN."

CONGRATULATIONS BEN, ON YOUR FINE ALMANAC. THEY HAIL YOU EVEN IN EUROPE!

PRESIDENT JEFFERSON SENT MY ALMANAC TO THE ACADEMY OF SCIENCES IN PARIS.

YES, AND PRIME MINISTER WILLIAM PITT HAS PLACED YOUR NAME IN THE RECORDS OF ENGLAND'S PARLIAMENT.

WALTER E. WASHINGTON
'MAYOR' OF WASHINGTON, D.C.

On September 29, 1967, Walter E. Washington was sworn in as the Commissioner of our nation's Capital and thereby became the first black 'Mayor' of a major American city.

Washington was born April 15, 1915 in Dawson, Georgia, and was raised in Jamestown, N.Y. In 1938, he received his Bachelor's degree in Public Administration from Howard University and attended American University's Graduate School

In 1941, he joined the staff of the National Capital Housing Authority and rose steadily to become its Chairman in 1961. During that time he gained a Law degree by attending Howard University at night and was admitted to practice before the Supreme Court.

Walter Washington also served his community as the President of the Washington Urban League and later became the Chairman of the New York City Housing Authority.

The United States Congress, through the House and Senate District Committees, controls many of the affairs of the district. However, the appointment of 'Mayor' Washington as the District's chief executive by President Johnson and the President's reorganization plan have given the citizens of Washington renewed hope of realizing 'home rule'. 'Mayor' Washington is an excellent administrator and, with the new powers of his office, faces the difficult tasks that confront him with optimism and a desire to administer programs for the good of all people.

BISHOP RICHARD ALLEN

(FEBRUARY 14, 1760 – MARCH 22, 1831)

FOUNDER OF THE AFRICAN METHODIST EPISCOPAL (A.M.E.) CHURCH

Richard Allen was born into slavery in Philadelphia on February 14, 1760. He was attracted to the Ministry at the age of seventeen and became a minister when he reached twenty. One of Allen's first converts was his slavemaster who, thereafter, permitted his slaves to purchase their freedom.

Richard Allen was ordained a minister in the Methodist Church by Bishop Francis Asbury and given assignments to preach at many white churches.

In 1787. Rev. Allen and Rev. Absalom Jones withdrew from the St. George Methodist Church because of the restrictions placed upon black worshippers. They established The Free African Society which, by January 1816, grew into into the African Methodist Episcopal Church. The A.M.E. Church is now the oldest and one of the largest black religious denominations in the United states with nearly two million members and six thousand churches.

During the "War of 1812" Bishop Allen and James Forten organized 2,500 free black men to help defend Philadelphia against the British.

In 1830, Bishop Allen organized and presided over the first national convention of black people. The convention was held annually and sought to acquire all of the rights and privileges enjoyed by other citizens.

Bishop Richard Allen presided over the African Methodist Episcopal Church until his death on March 22nd, 1831, and today, this vast religious body is a monument to his memory.

GOLDEN LEGACY
ILLUSTRATED HISTORY SERIES

1. Toussaint L'Overture
2. Harriet Tubman
3. Crispus Attucks
4. Benjamin Banneker
5. Matthew Henson
6. Alexander Dumas
7. Frederick Douglass Part I
8. Frederick Douglass Part II
9. Robert Smalls
10. Joseph Cinque
11. White, Wilkins & Marshall
12. Black Cowboys
13. Dr. Martin Luther King
14. Alexander Pushkin
15. Ancient African Kingdoms
16. Black Inventors

"We hope you will read, enjoy and benefit from our endeavors."

You may order GOLDEN LEGACY for your school, church, relatives, yourself-----or merely as a gift for a friend!

GOLDEN LEGACY is available in soft or hard cover editions.

Send Orders To: Fitzgerald Pub. Co., Inc.
442 Wolf Hill Road
Dix Hills, N.Y. 11746

Payment must accompany all orders in check or money order.

Softcover Edition: $24.00   Hardcover Edition: $45.00

GOLDEN LEGACY
ILLUSTRATED HISTORY MAGAZINE

THE LIFE OF MATTHEW HENSON

Vol. 5

© FITZGERALD PUB. Co. Inc. 1969

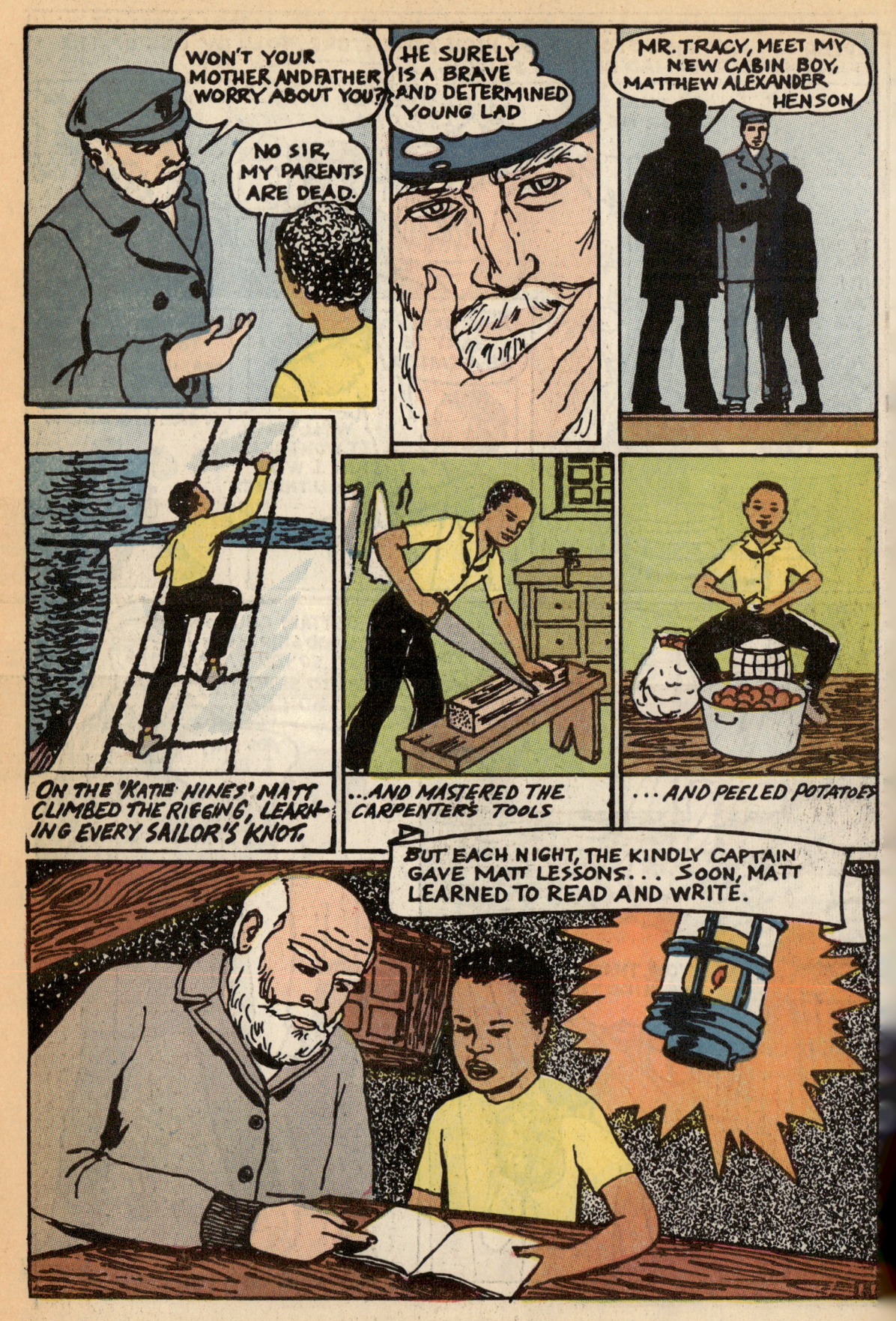

PEARY'S LEG HEALED THAT WINTER... AND IN THE SPRING, HE CROSSED THE NORTHERN RIM OF GREENLAND, PROVING THAT IT WAS INDEED AN ISLAND. WITH THIS VICTORY, THE PEARY PARTY RETURNED TO NEW YORK. PEARY VOWED TO RETURN AND REACH THE NORTH POLE.

BACK IN THE STATES, PEARY GAVE LECTURES ON THEIR ARCTIC EXPERIENCES TO RAISE MONEY FOR FURTHER EXPLORATIONS. MATTHEW HENSON ELECTRIFIED AUDIENCES BY COMING ON STAGE IN FURS, COMPLETE WITH SLED AND ESKIMO DOGS.

"LADIES AND GENTLEMEN, MY ASSISTANT MATTHEW HENSON!"

"WILL YOU LOOK AT HENSON, HE HANDLES THOSE DOGS LIKE AN ESKIMO."

"DID YOU HEAR, HE CALLED HENSON HIS ASSISTANT."

"YES, BUT THE NEWSPAPERS CALLED HENSON ONLY A SERVANT."

AFTER A PERFORMANCE

"SAY, THAT'S LT. SCAPTEC OVER THERE. I THINK I'LL SHOW HIM I'VE GOT ALL MY FINGERS AND TOES"

"MATT, I NEVER THOUGHT YOU HAD A CHANCE TO WIN THIS, BUT AFTER HEARING WHAT YOU WENT THROUGH, I'D SAY YOU SURE EARNED IT."

RETURNING TO THE NORTH, THE PEARY PARTY FACED TERRIBLE ARCTIC STORMS WHICH SENT SOME OF THE SLEDS CRASHING DOWN GLACIERS. MOST OF THE MEN WERE SNOWBLINDED AND CRIPPLED WITH FROZEN HANDS AND FEET. THE GROUP HAD TO TURN BACK TO CAMP. PEARY WAS VERY DESPONDENT.

MATT, I DON'T KNOW HOW WE CAN GO ON, THE MEN ARE IN BAD SHAPE

WELL, LIEUTENANT, I'M WILLING TO STAY FOR ANOTHER WINTER AND TRY AGAIN.

WHEN THE SUPPLY SHIP 'FALCON' CAME IN AUGUST, EVERY MAN LEFT EXCEPT PEARY, LEE, AND HENSON.

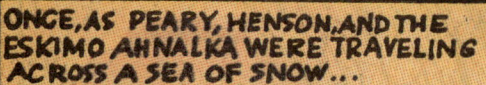
ONCE, AS PEARY, HENSON, AND THE ESKIMO AHNALKA WERE TRAVELING ACROSS A SEA OF SNOW...

HENSON HAD FALLEN INTO A DEEP CREVASSE IN THE SNOW. A SMALL OUTCROPPING OF ICE IN THE PIT HALTED HIS FALL... ANY WRONG MOVE WOULD PLUNGE HIM INTO AN ICY GRAVE, FOREVER.

THE SURFACE SUDDENLY GAVE WAY BENEATH HENSON'S FEET.
WOOSH

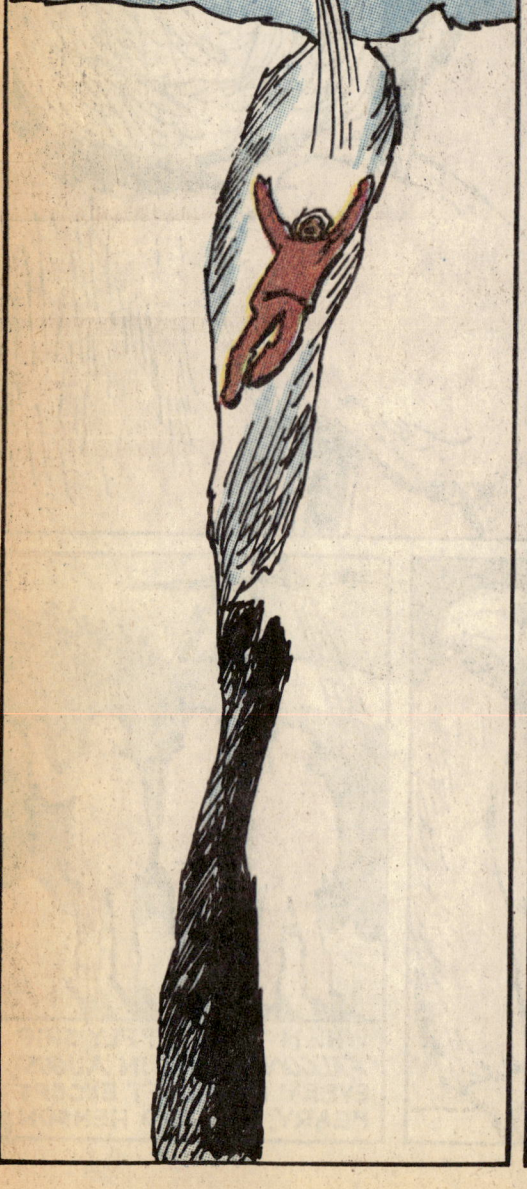

HENSON REMAINED CALM AND PLANNED HOW TO GET OUT.

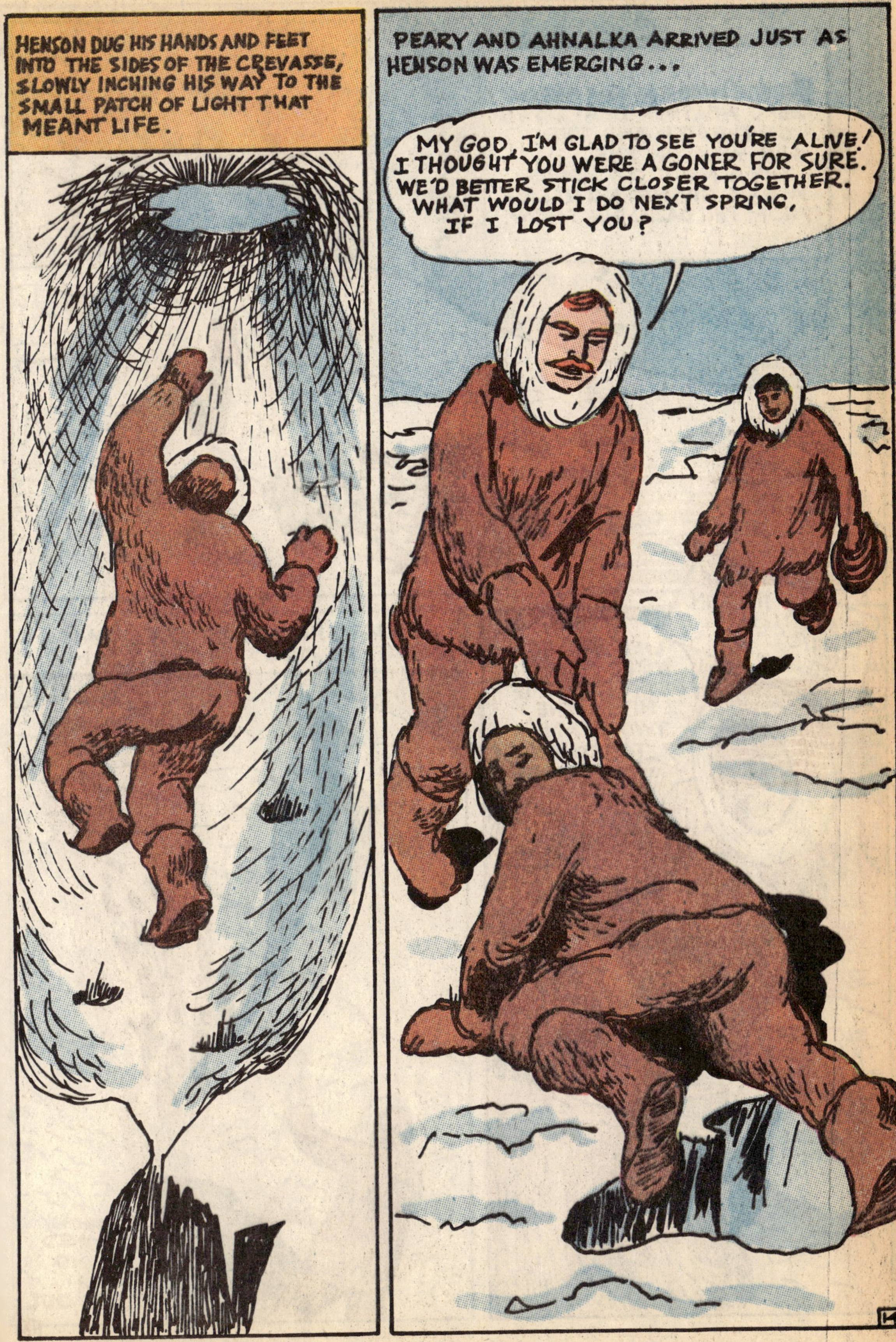

VERY SOON, THE TWO MEN HAD BROUGHT DOWN ALL THE MUSK-OXEN EXCEPT FOR ONE COW, STILL TRYING TO PROTECT THE CALVES.

PEARY FIRED HIS LAST SHOT AT THE ANIMAL BUT MISSED, HITTING ONE OF THE CALVES.

CRACK

INFURIATED, THE ANIMAL CHARGED AFTER PEARY

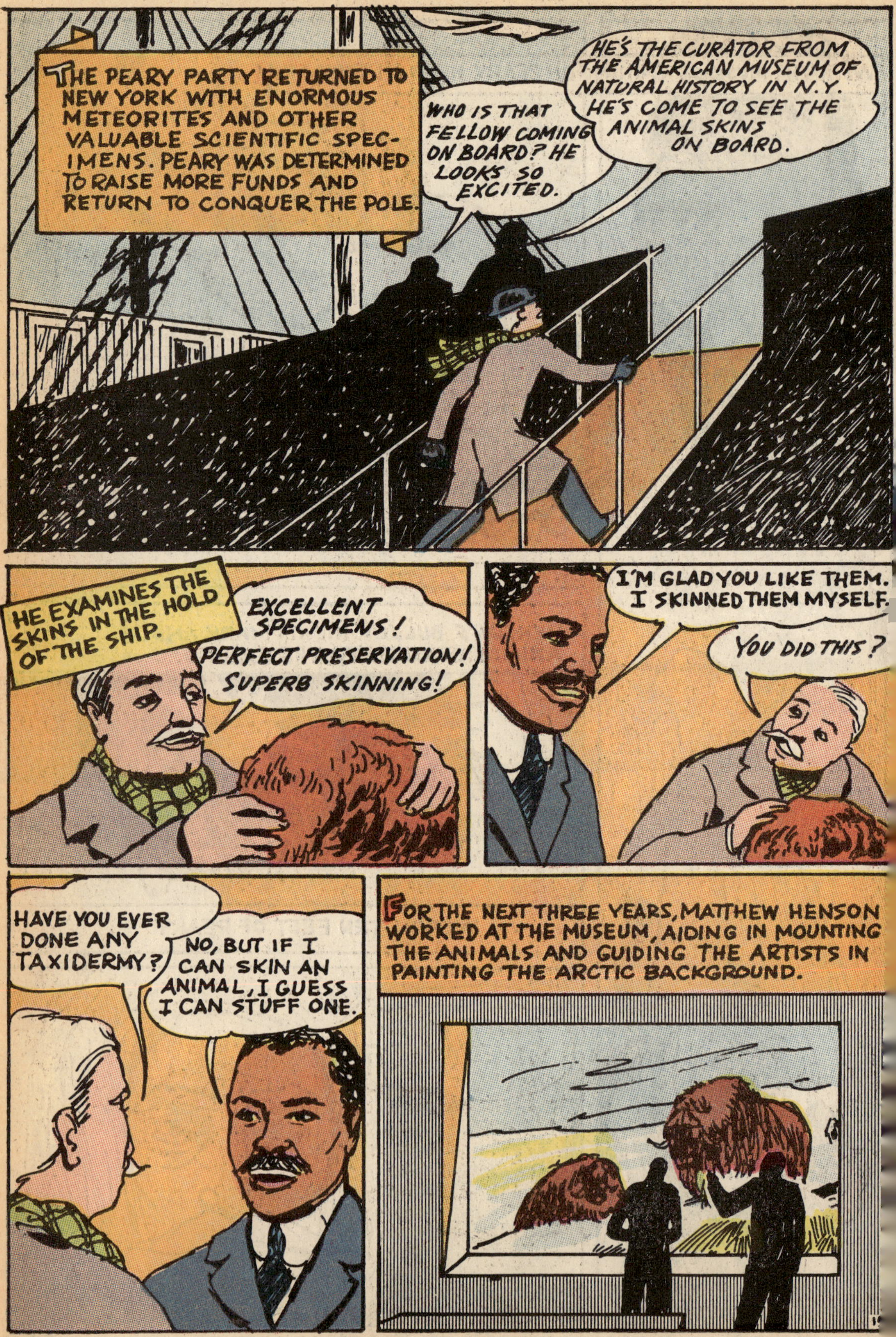

AFTER THEY RETURNED TO N.Y., HENSON DECIDED TO SEE THE U.S. AND TOOK A JOB ON THE RAILROAD AS A PULLMAN PORTER. ON HIS TRIPS THROUGH THE SOUTH, HE SAW THE TERRIBLE TREATMENT OF AFRO-AMERICANS BY RACISTS, HE TOO WAS ATTACKED WITH A SHOTGUN.

IN N.Y., AT A DINNER PARTY GIVEN IN HIS HONOR AT THE HOME OF HIS FRIEND, MR. GARDNER, IN HARLEM

YES I DO!... AND I LONG TO BE BACK IN THE ARCTIC WHERE A MAN IS JUDGED ON MERIT AND NOT THE COLOR OF HIS SKIN.

DO YOU THINK YOU'LL EVER REACH THE NORTH POLE?

WHAT ARE THE ESKIMOS REALLY LIKE?

MATT, HERE'S TO YOUR SUCCESS... IF YOU REACH THE POLE, IT WILL MEAN A LOT TO OUR PEOPLE!

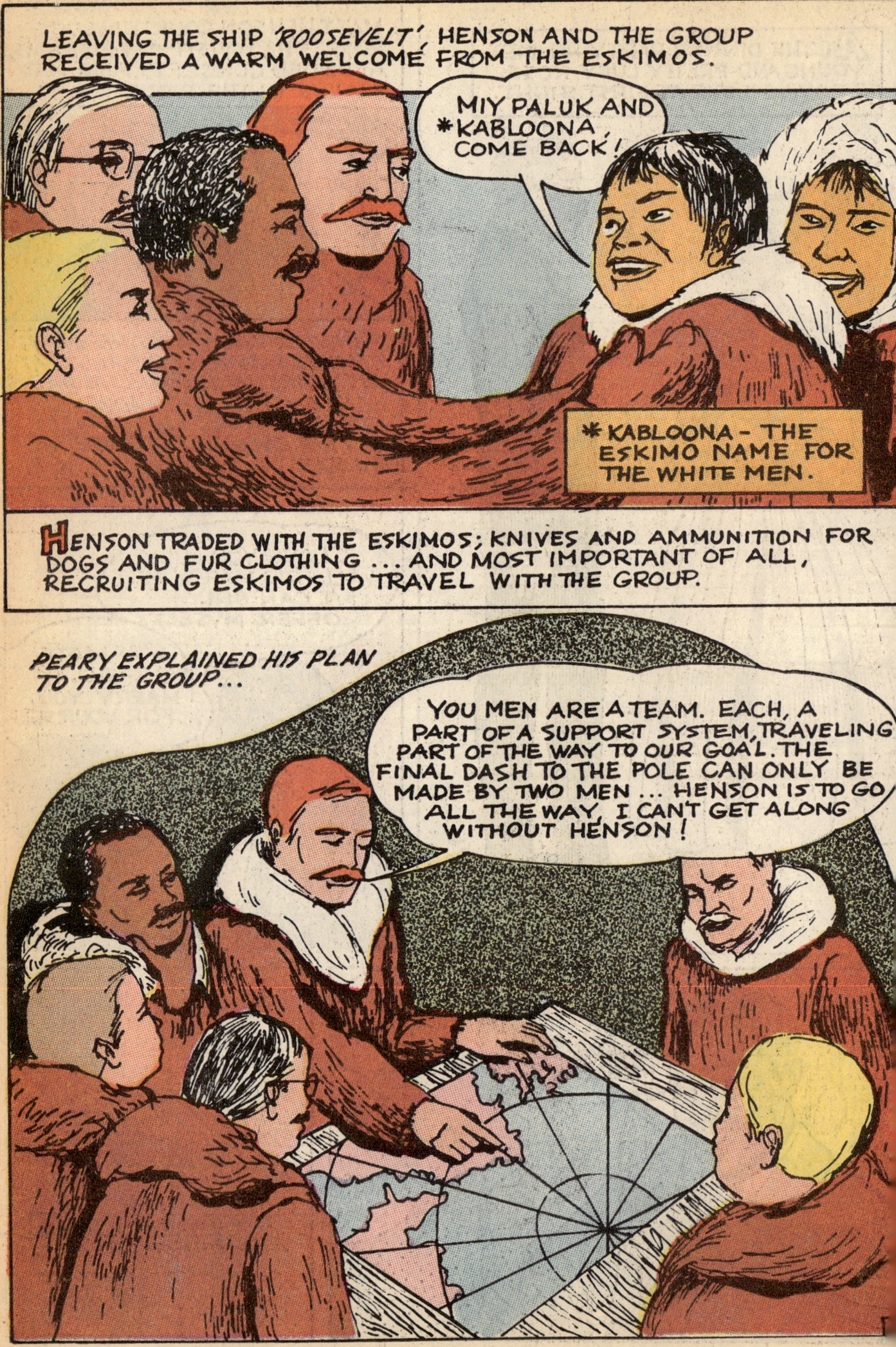

They had traveled a little over 300 miles from the ship. Bob Bartlett was the last of the supporting party to leave Peary and Henson...

"Peary is very tired. We've done all we can... The rest is up to you... History will be made in the next few days. Good luck, Matt!"

"Thanks, Bob."

Peary, Henson, and four Eskimos started on the last 133 miles to the Pole.

Time and temperature became the most important factors. Rising temperatures were causing the ice to crack everywhere... If they were to reach the Pole and return alive, they had to travel at top speed.

"MATT, THE SEXTANT SAYS OUR POSITION IS 89 DEGREES, 25 MINUTES... THE NORTH POLE IS 35 MILES AWAY!"

HENSON AND THE ESKIMO OOTAH WERE IN THE LEAD. MATT WAS DRIVING HIS SLED ACROSS VERY THIN ICE WHEN SUDDENLY...

THE ICE BROKE UNDER HIM, EXPOSING THE CRUEL ARCTIC WATERS.

IN A FEW MOMENTS MATT WAS PULLED DOWN BY THE FRIGID WATER THAT WAS FILLING HIS BOOTS.

WHEN HE THOUGHT IT WAS ALL OVER, HE FELT STRONG ARMS LIFTING HIM.

... OOTAH HAD PULLED HIM TO SAFETY!

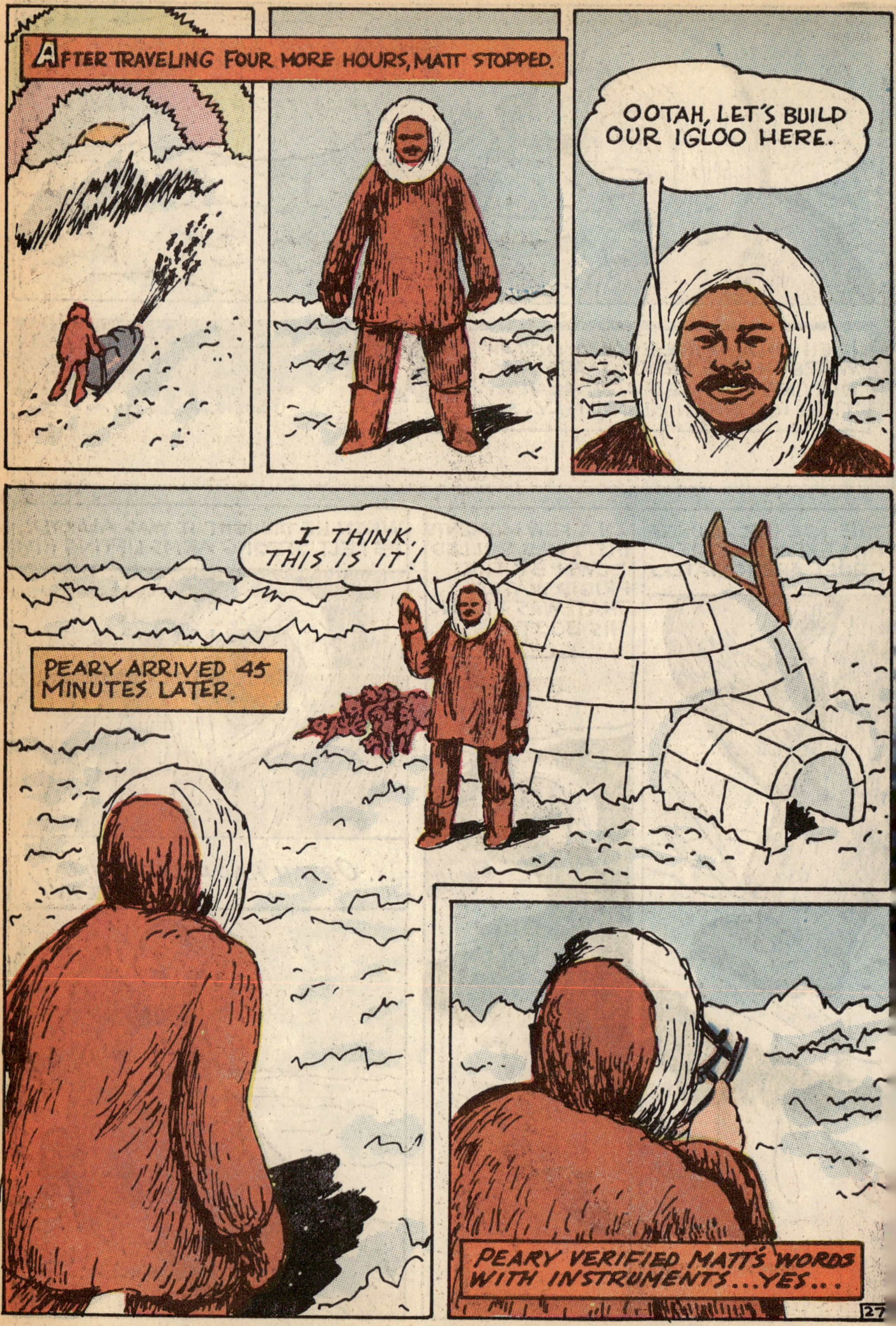

KATHERINE G. JOHNSON
SPACE SCIENTIST

In collaboration with another mathematician, Ted Skopinski, Mrs. Johnson devised the method that the National Aeronautics and Space Administration uses to "project at all times where an astronaut in flight is with respect to the earth." This report enabled the astronauts to return from outer space to a specific area on earth!

The report is entitled "Determination of Azimuth Angle at Burnout for Placing a Satellite Over a Selected Earth Position" and is one of a number of technical reports to which Mrs. Johnson has contributed.

Mrs. Katherine G. Johnson was born August 26, 1918, at White Sulphur Springs, West Virginia. She received her Bachelor of Science degree summa cum laude from West Virginia State College in 1937 and taught high school mathematics for eight years.

Since 1953, she has been a member of the science staff of NASA's Langley Research Center working on, and developing, mathematical techniques used for spacecraft navigation.

Mrs. Johnson received the NASA Lunar Orbiter Project Group Achievement award for her work associated with Lunar Orbiter. The highly successful Lunar Orbiter program produced five successful photographic flights within a single year and returned to earth highly detailed knowledge of the entire moon.

HIRAM R. REVELS
(1822-1901)

Hiram R. Revels, the first black man to serve in the U.S. Senate, was born free in Fayetteville, North Carolina. Senator Revels was elected from the state of Mississippi and, on February 25, 1870, filled the seat vaby Senator Jefferson Davis.

Unable to obtain an education in the state of his birth, Revels received his education in Indiana and attended Knox College in Illinois. He was ordained a minister in the African Methodist Episcopal Church and served as a pastor in the Northwest Territory, Kentucky and Tennessee.

When the Civil War began, Revels helped organize the first two black regiments in Maryland and while there, served as a school principal. During the war, he served as a chaplain and as a provost marshal in the Union Army.

At the end of his service in the U.S. Senate, Revels became the president of Alcorn University and the editor of a religious journal. After a lifetime of dedicated service, Hiram R. Revels died on January 16, 1901.

GOLDEN LEGACY
ILLUSTRATED HISTORY SERIES

1. Toussaint L'Overture
2. Harriet Tubman
3. Crispus Attucks
4. Benjamin Banneker
5. Matthew Henson
6. Alexander Dumas
7. Frederick Douglass Part I
8. Frederick Douglass Part II
9. Robert Smalls
10. Joseph Cinque
11. White, Wilkins & Marshall
12. Black Cowboys
13. Dr. Martin Luther King
14. Alexander Pushkin
15. Ancient African Kingdoms
16. Black Inventors

"We hope you will read, enjoy and benefit from our endeavors."

You may order GOLDEN LEGACY for your school, church, relatives, yourself-----or merely as a gift for a friend!

GOLDEN LEGACY is available in soft or hard cover editions.

Send Orders To: Fitzgerald Pub. Co., Inc.
442 Wolf Hill Road
Dix Hills, N.Y. 11746

Payment must accompany all orders in check or money order.

Softcover Edition: $24.00   Hardcover Edition: $45.00

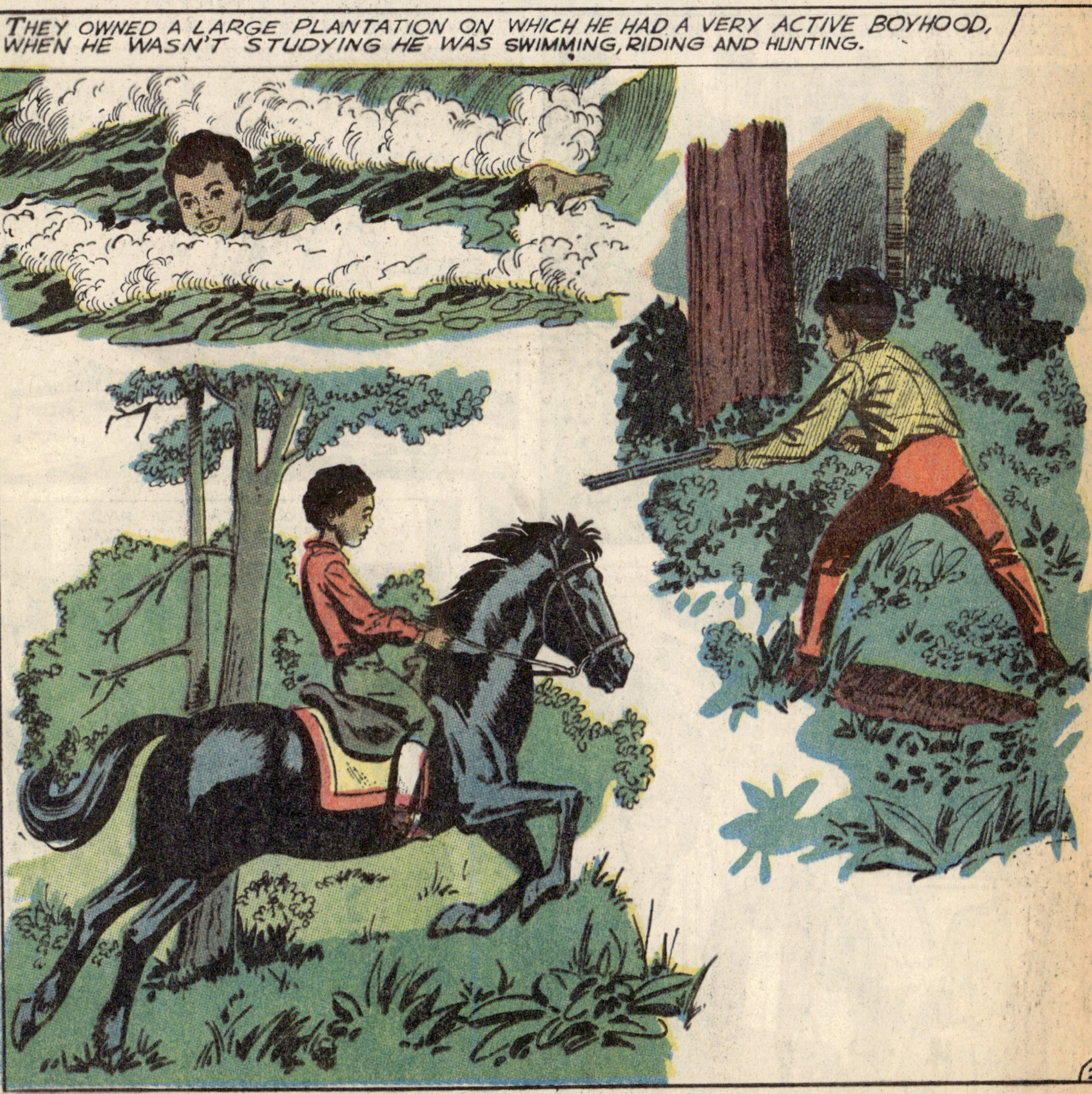

THEN HIS MOTHER DIED.

HE AND HIS FATHER LIVED IN THE WEST INDIES 8 YEARS LONGER.

....THEN RETURNED TO FRANCE!

DURING THE NEXT THREE YEARS THOMAS BECAME VERY POPULAR!
"A VERY HANDSOME YOUNG MAN!"

THOMAS WAS GENEROUS AND KINDHEARTED, BUT ALSO QUICK TO RESENT INSULTS...

...AND HAD MANY DUELS, ONCE WINNING THREE IN A SINGLE DAY.

ANGERED BY HIS FATHER'S PLAN TO REMARRY, THOMAS DECIDES TO LEAVE HOME.

I'LL ENLIST IN THE ARMY!

HIS FATHER ONCE SERVED AS A COLONEL AND WAS AGAINST HIS ENLISTING AS A COMMON SOLDIER. SO THOMAS REJECTED NAME AND TITLE AND TOOK ANOTHER THAT BECAME IMMORTAL...THAT OF HIS MOTHER...**DUMAS!!!**

Thomas-Alexander Dumas soon became well known for his feats of strength and bravery!

While on a mission he found himself cut off from his group and facing 13 of the enemy...
TRAPPED!

Charging the enemy, Dumas fought with such fury...
WAK!

...that fear overtook them and...
"SURRENDER OR DIE!"

...they surrendered!

At the camp the commander commends Dumas for his bravery!
FOR SERVICE BEYOND THE CALL OF DUTY, YOU ARE PROMOTED TO THE RANK OF SERGEANT-MAJOR!

Times were very hard in France during this period! People were starving...

...and the storming and capture of the Bastille marked the beginning of the French Revolution!

During the Revolution, many black men came from the West Indies to fight for liberty and equality!

They fought in a regiment known as "The Black Legion" under the command of Colonel St. Georges, known as one of the best swordsmen of his time!

"Welcome to our regiment, Lt. Dumas!"

"Thank you, Colonel!"

Dumas' fame increased as he continued to perform acts of bravery!

AFTER THE FRENCH ARMY FAILED TO CAPTURE MT. CENIS, GENERAL DUMAS TOOK COMMAND!

DUMAS STUDIED THE AREA FOR 5 DAYS...

THE ENEMY HAD THREE SIDES OF MT. CENIS HEAVILY ARMED AND HAD TURNED THE FRENCH BACK SEVERAL TIMES!

THE FOURTH SIDE APPEARED TO BE PROTECTED BY NATURE!

"IN A MONTH MT. CENIS WILL BE OURS!"

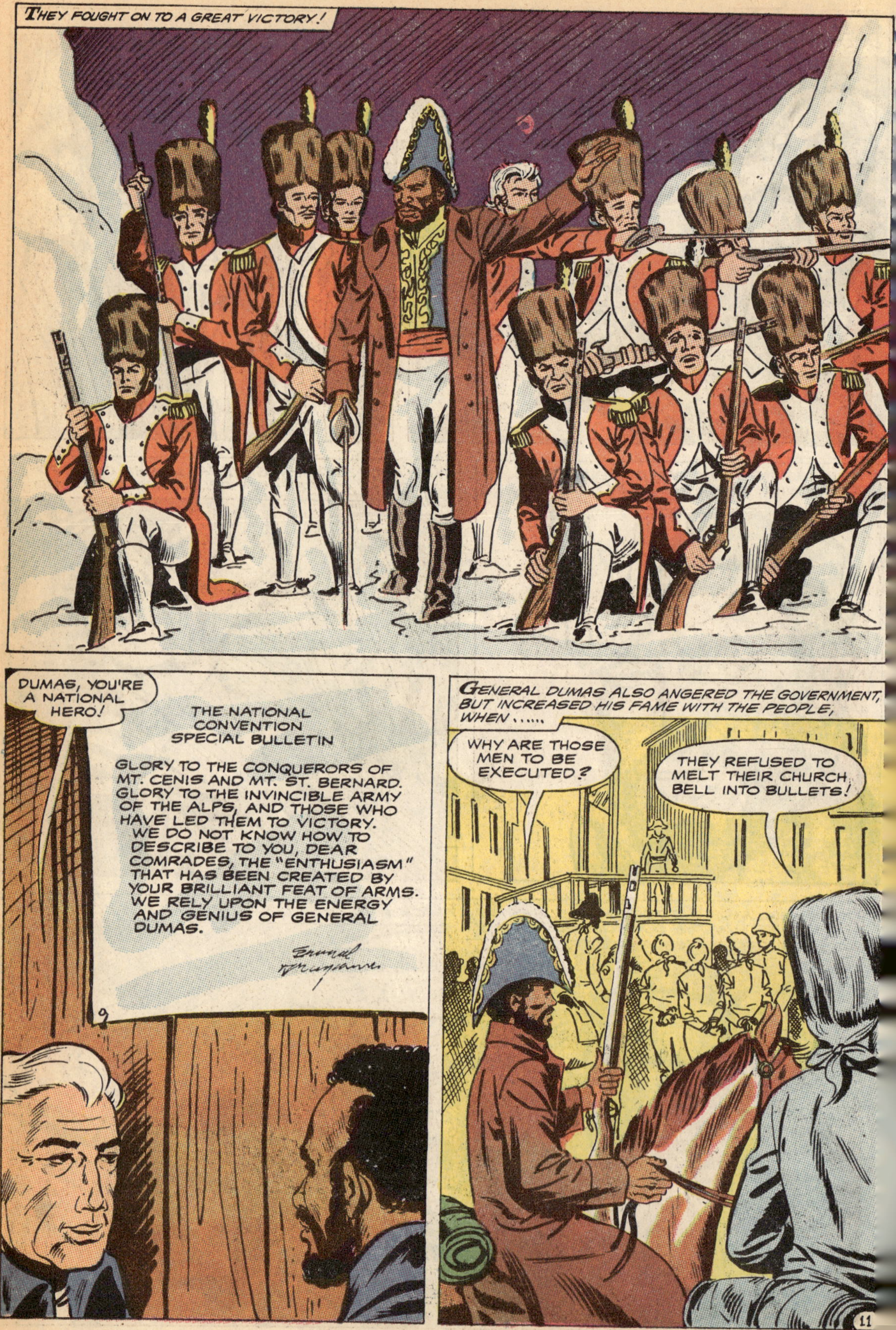

BUT THE SHIP IS OLD AND LEAKY, AND THEY SAILED TOWARDS NAPLES...
HEAD FOR SHORE, WE'RE SINKING!

NAPLES WAS AT WAR WITH THE FRENCH AND WHEN THEY LANDED...
YOU'RE WISE TO SURRENDER!

WHILE A PRISONER OF WAR, SEVERAL ATTEMPTS WERE MADE TO POISON GENERAL DUMAS!

MEANWHILE, NAPOLEON RETURNED TO FRANCE AND TOOK OVER THE GOVERNMENT!

Dumas came to Paris to become a writer, but needed a job to support himself!

"So you're the son of the great General Dumas, of course I'll help!"

The general found Dumas a job as a clerk in the office of the Duke of Orleans, who later became the King of France!

At night he studied...

...and wrote!

...and learned from his visits to the theater!

"I must see that!"

Tonight "HAMLET" STARRING—

After five years of study and hard work, Dumas wrote Henry III! This play was a great success! The Duke of Orleans and 30 princes and princesses were among the first night's audience!

BRAVO! BRAVO! DUMAS!

This great success was followed by an even greater one, his play 'Christine'!

DUMAS IS A GENIUS! LONG LIVE DUMAS!

...which led to still greater success, the play 'Anthony'!

DUMAS, YOU AMAZE ME!

THANK YOU, VICTOR!

...and during these years, Dumas received his greatest gift--a son, Alexander Dumas II!

Alexander Dumas became one of the world's greatest writers and in the years that followed, wrote several hundred books!

Three Musketeers

The Man in the Iron Mask

The Corsican Brothers

The Count of Monte Cristo

Many of Dumas' stories, although written in France over 100 years ago, are as popular in America today as any stories ever written here!

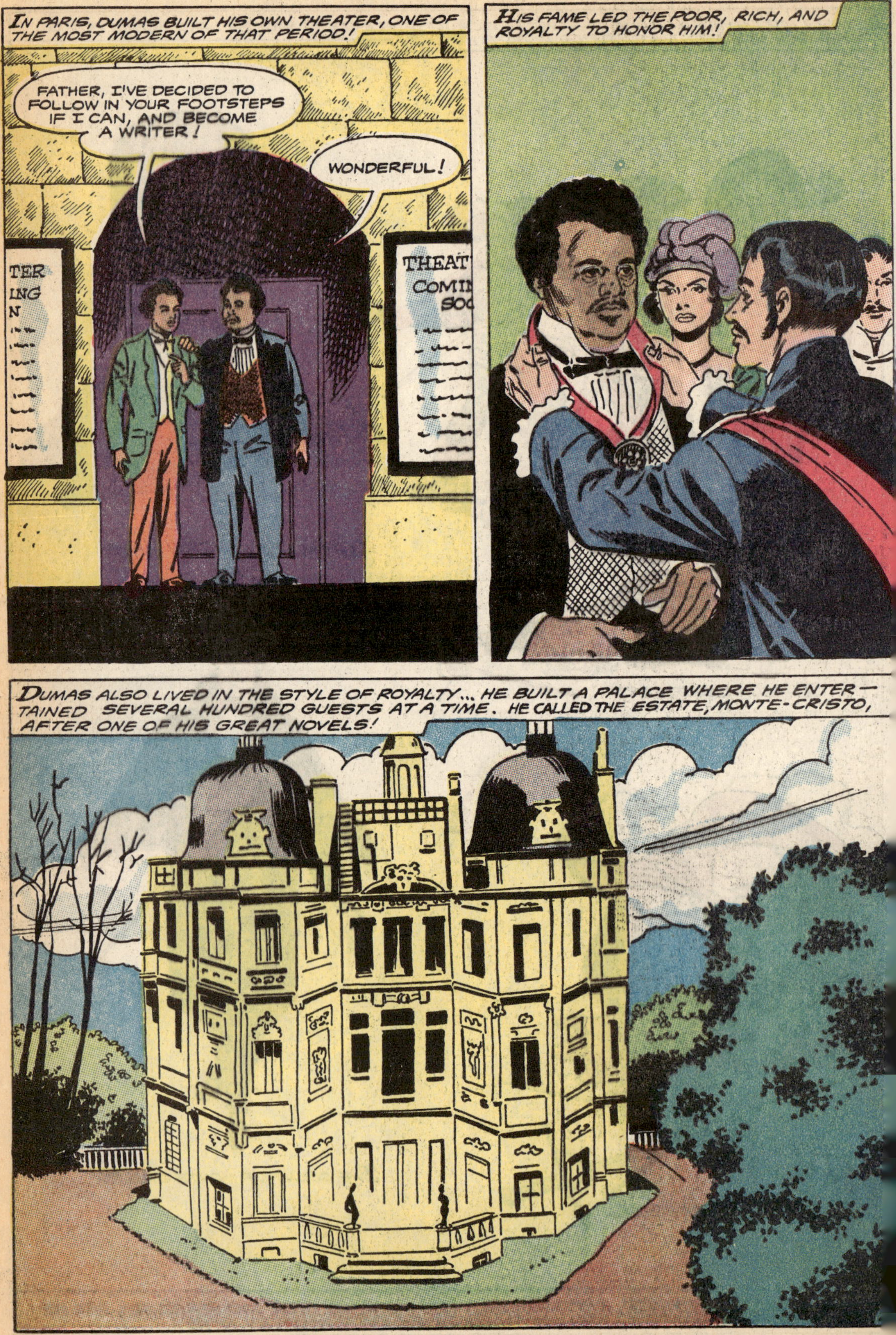

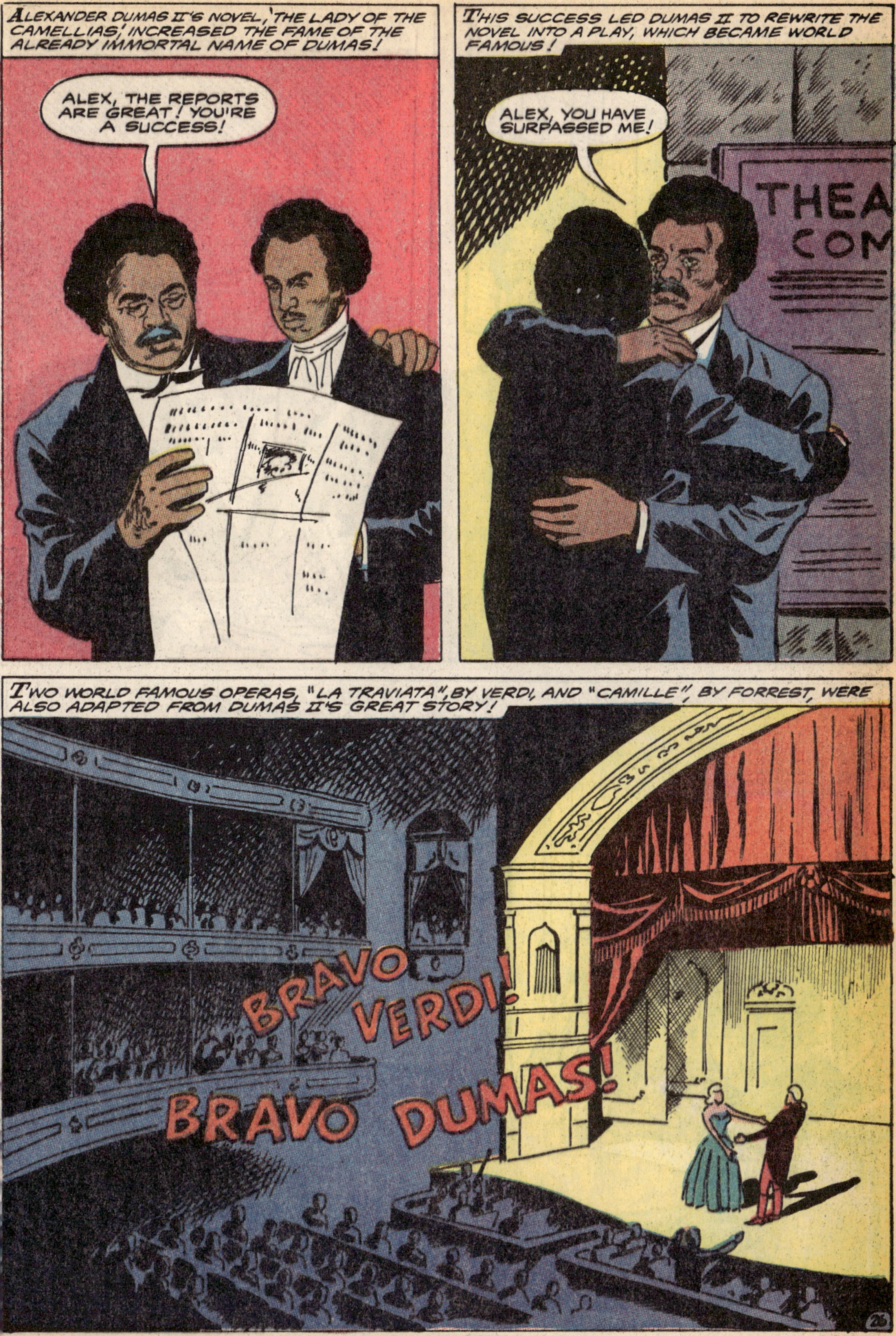

Alexander Dumas II's novel, "The Lady of the Camellias," increased the fame of the already immortal name of Dumas!

"Alex, the reports are great! You're a success!"

This success led Dumas II to rewrite the novel into a play, which became world famous!

"Alex, you have surpassed me!"

Two world famous operas, "La Traviata", by Verdi, and "Camille", by Forrest, were also adapted from Dumas II's great story!

BRAVO VERDI!
BRAVO DUMAS!

ALEXANDER DUMAS II WAS NOW AS WELL KNOWN AS HIS FATHER.

"SOME PEOPLE THINK HE'S MORE TALENTED THAN HIS FATHER."

AND FOLLOWING HIS FATHER'S FOOTSTEPS WAS NOT EASY...

BUT HE WON HONORS THAT WERE DENIED HIS FATHER. HE WAS ELECTED TO MEMBERSHIP IN THE FRENCH ACADEMY* AND LATER BECAME ITS PRESIDENT.

*HIGHEST FRENCH INTELLECTUAL HONOR

CHEVALIER DE SAINT-GEORGE
(1745-1799)

Few men ever showed such strength, quickness, grace and accuracy as did Saint-George. He was one of the greatest swordsmen that ever lived.

Joseph Boulogne Saint-George was born in 1745 on the West Indian island of Guadeloupe. He was the son of M. de Boulogne, a wealthy planter and Comptroller-General of the island, and Nanon, an African lady of great beauty. Saint-George was very young when his father brought him to France and placed him with La Boessiere, the famous fencing master.

The young man took to fencing with ease, and by the age of 15, had beaten many of the better swordsmen. When he reached the age of 21, he had challenged and beaten the best of the so-called 'master swordsmen' of Europe. Saint-George excelled at every sport: he was unequalled in running, rode the most difficult horses, was a great skater and could swim the river Seine with one arm. He was a great marksman. He also possessed a rare musical ability and it was said that his ear was so fine that he could play a tune on the air with his whip.

Saint-George was a noted composer and violinist. He composed concertos for violin, several comic operas, and a collection of symphonies. During the French Revolution, Saint-George formed the Black Legion, composed of West Indians who came to France to fight for liberty and equality.

GASTON MONNERVILLE
PRESIDENT OF THE FRENCH SENATE

As President of the French Senate, Gaston Monnerville held a position similar to the American Vice President. Had De Gaulle resigned while Monnerville was in office, he would have become the President of France.

Monnerville was born in French Guiana in 1897. His father was a minor civil servant. A brilliant student, he won a scholarship to the University of Toulouse and completed his law studies there in 1921. Shortly afterward he went to Paris to practice law. In 1928, he defended a group of countrymen from Guiana who had been accused of taking part in political riots. The man were freed and Monnerville became a hero to his people. They elected him to the French Chamber of Deputies in 1932 and again in 1936.

Monnerville was later appointed Secretary of State for the Colonies. When the war came, he joined the French Navy and later helped organize the resistance movement against the Nazis.

After the war he returned to Parliament, and in 1947 was elected President of the Council of the Republic.

When De Gaulle founded the Fifth Republic, Monnerville supported him, but they disagreed over democratic procedure and Monnerville asserted: "The Constitution is openly violated" and warned that France was headed for a dictatorship. This caused an open break with De Gaulle. However, Monnerville continued his defiance of "Strong Man" rule.

Gaston Monnerville has received many honors, including the Croix de Guerre, the Medal of Resistance, and membership in the Legion of Honor.

GOLDEN LEGACY
ILLUSTRATED HISTORY SERIES

1. Toussaint L'Overture
2. Harriet Tubman
3. Crispus Attucks
4. Benjamin Banneker
5. Matthew Henson
6. Alexander Dumas
7. Frederick Douglass Part I
8. Frederick Douglass Part II
9. Robert Smalls
10. Joseph Cinque
11. White, Wilkins & Marshall
12. Black Cowboys
13. Dr. Martin Luther King
14. Alexander Pushkin
15. Ancient African Kingdoms
16. Black Inventors

"We hope you will read, enjoy and benefit from our endeavors."

You may order GOLDEN LEGACY for your school, church, relatives, yourself-----or merely as a gift for a friend!

GOLDEN LEGACY is available in soft or hard cover editions.

Send Orders To: Fitzgerald Pub. Co., Inc.
442 Wolf Hill Road
Dix Hills, N.Y. 11746

Payment must accompany all orders in check or money order.

Softcover Edition: $24.00   Hardcover Edition: $45.00

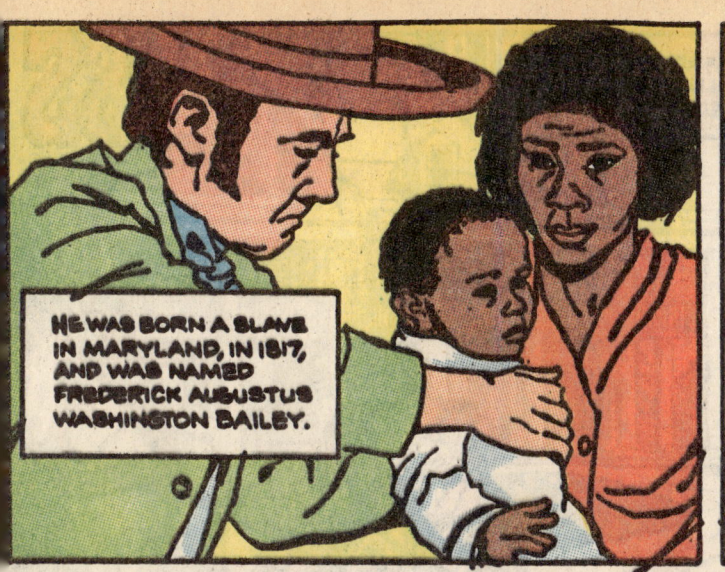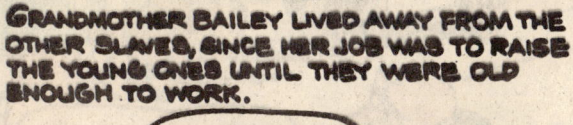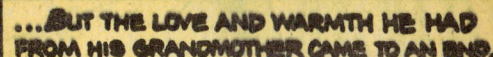

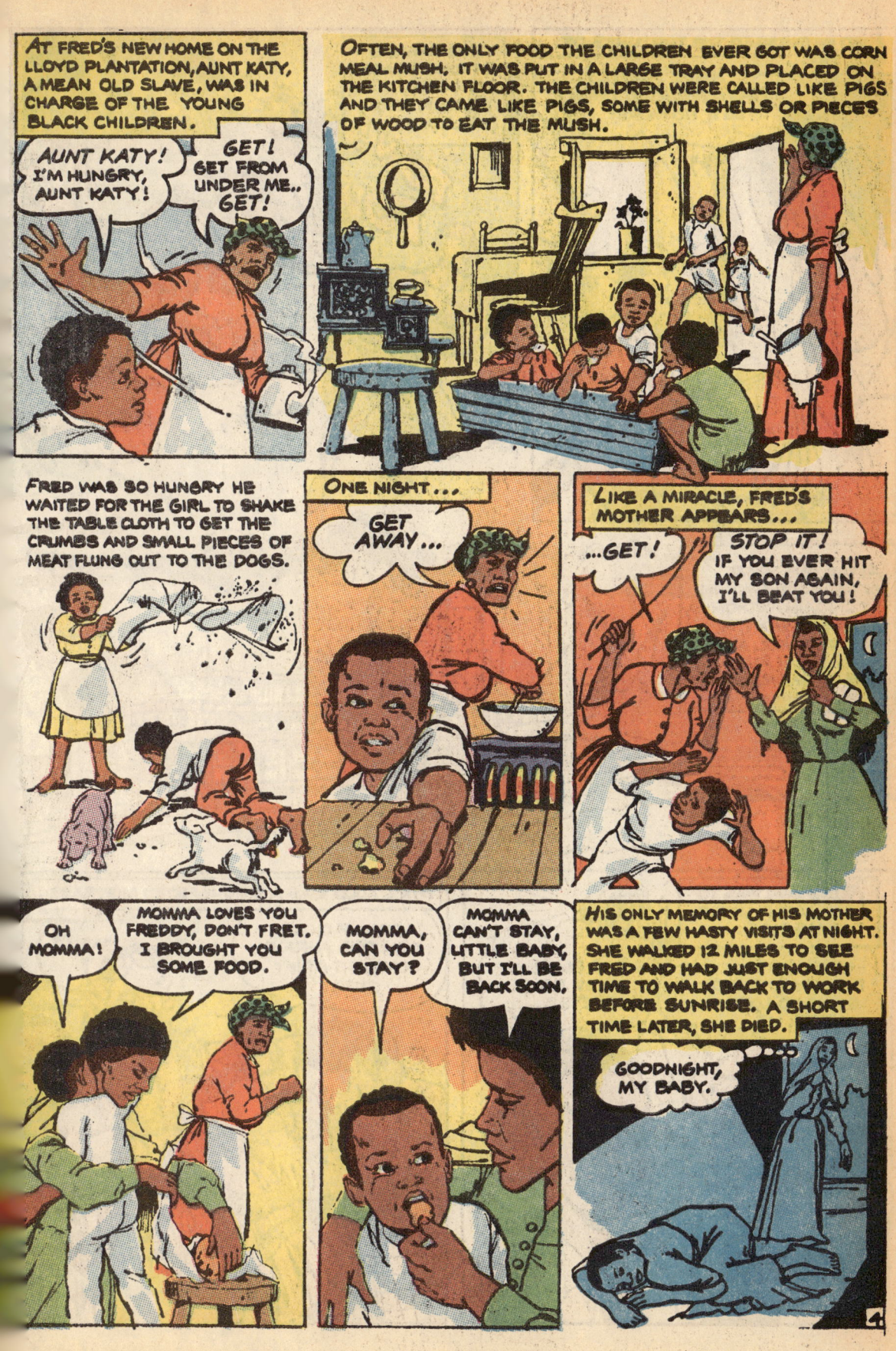

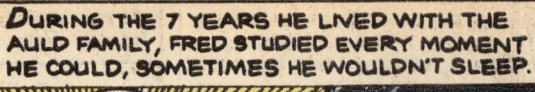

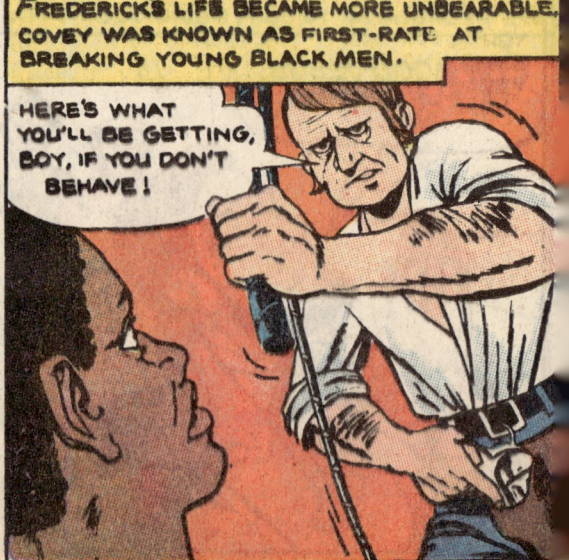

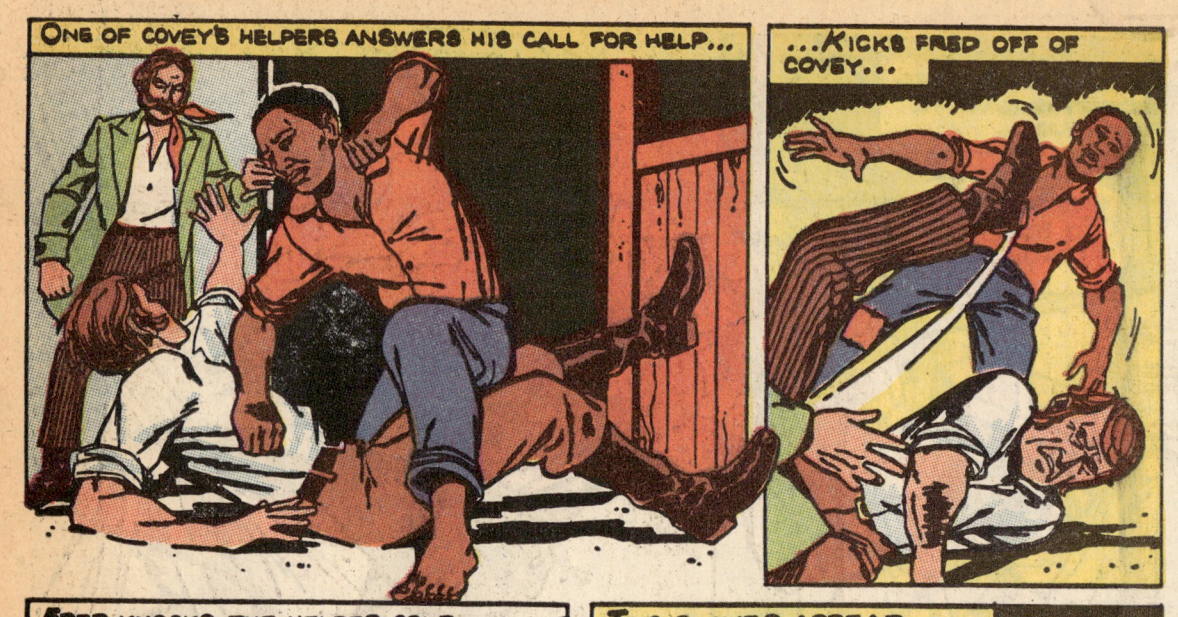

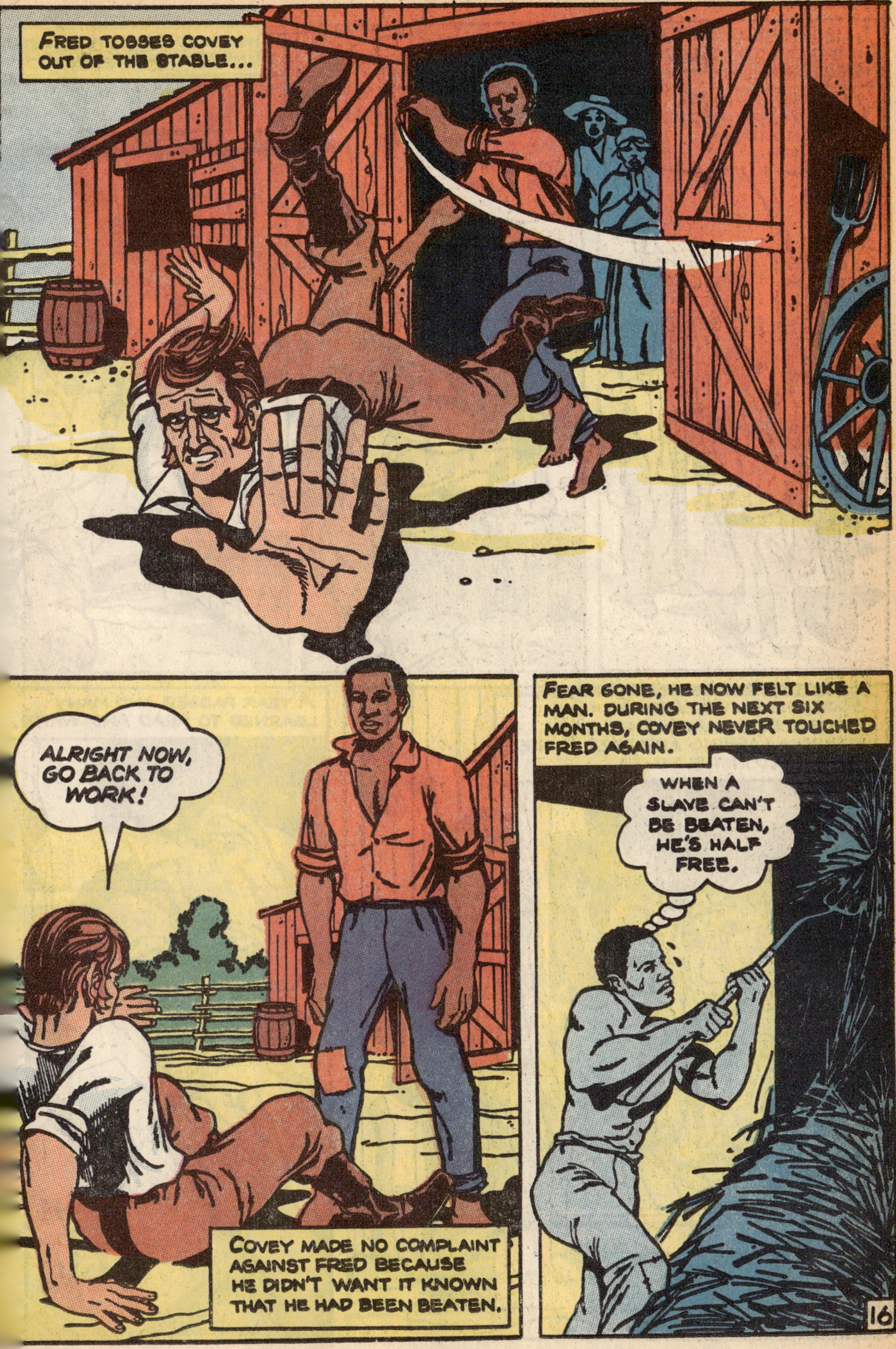

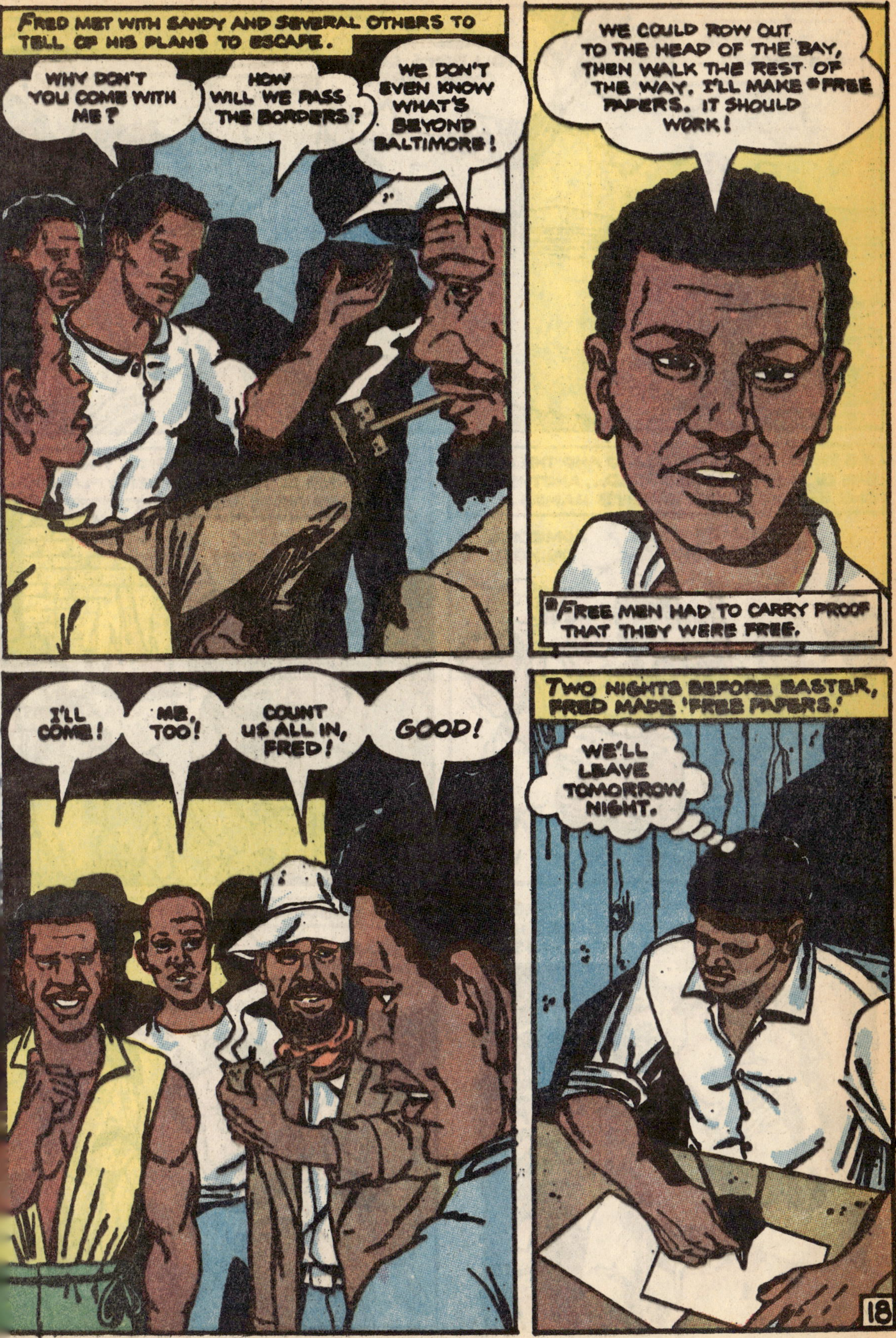

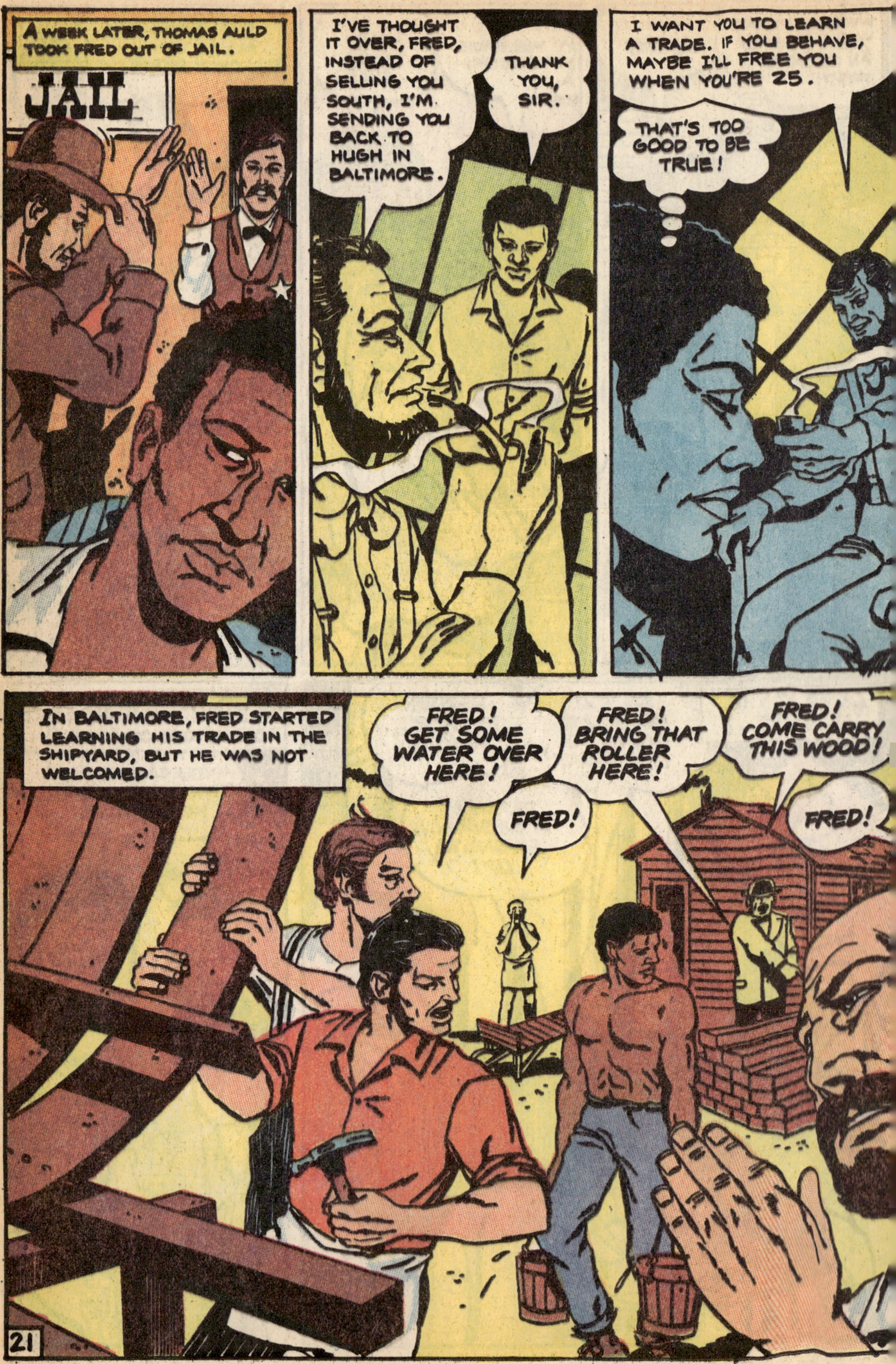

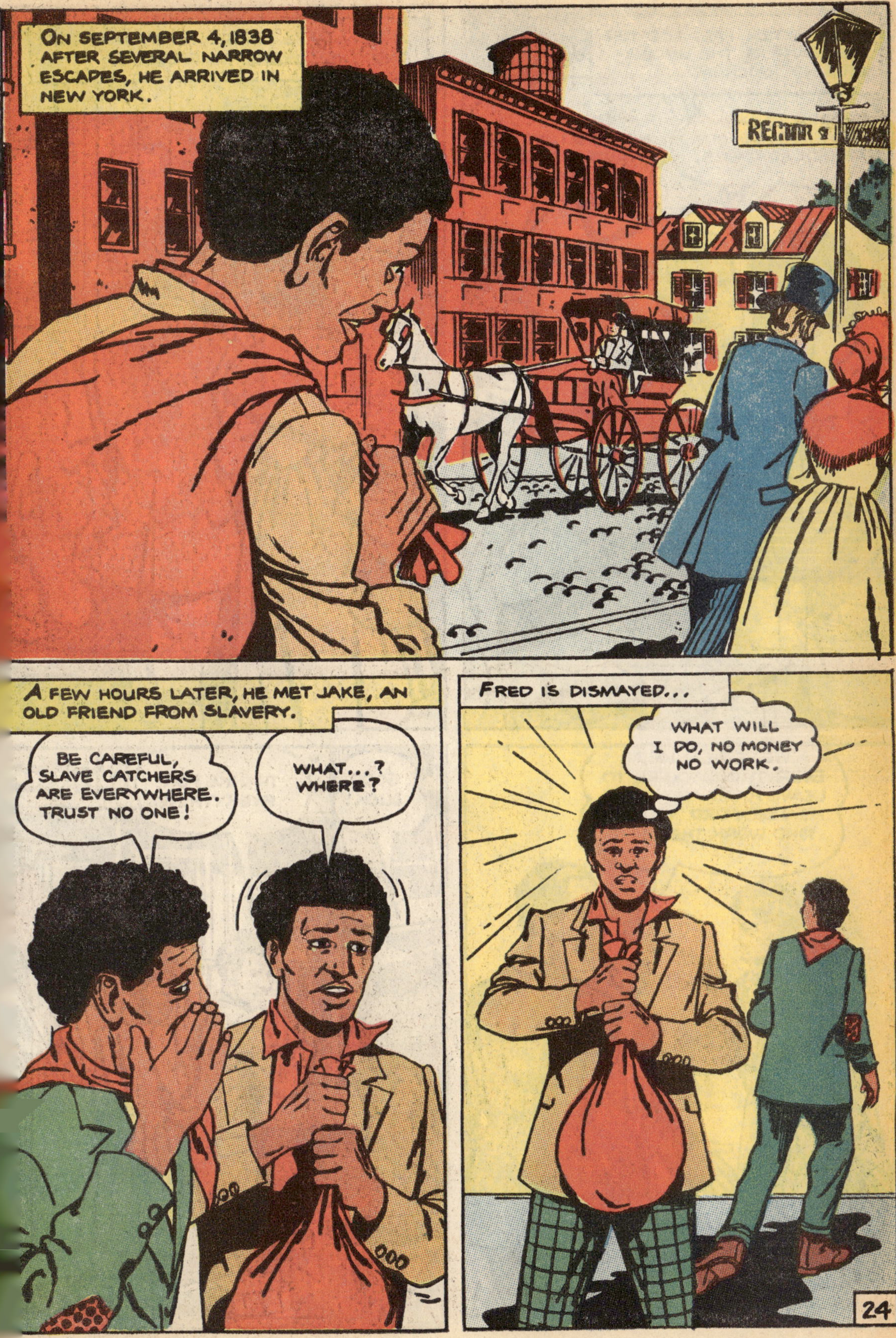

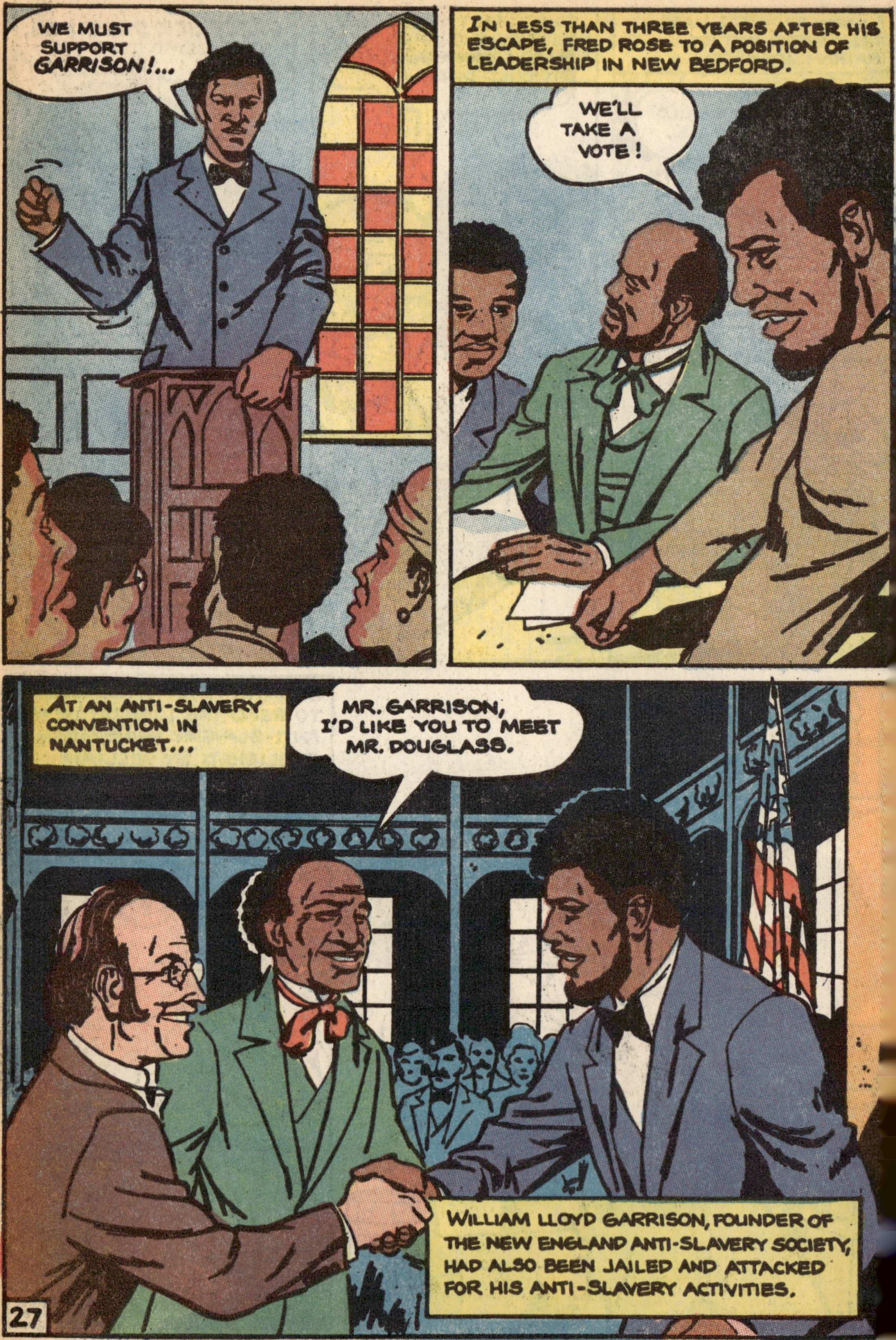

FREDERICK WAS ASKED TO SPEAK TO THE CONVENTION...

BRAVO!!

BRILLIANT!!

CLAP! CLAP!

YOU MUST BECOME A SPEAKER FOR US!

EXCELLENT SPEECH, FREDERICK!

AND SO BEGAN THE CAREER OF ONE OF *THE GREATEST SPOKESMAN FOR HUMAN RIGHTS.*

TO COME... FREDERICK DOUGLASS, PART II

JOSEPH CINQUE
(1811-1852)

Joseph Cinque and a group of other slave captives from Africa stood shivering in the slave market of Havana. It was a very warm day, but they had just been sold to Spaniards who were to transport them to the island of Principe, and the thought was enough to make their blood run cold.

The slaves were herded like cattle in the hold of the schooner Amistad and the ship set sail. Under those dreadful conditions, Joseph, son of a Mendi chief in Sierra Leone, told his fellow slaves: "You had better be killed than live many moons in misery...I could die happy, if by dying I could save so many of my brothers from bondage..."

Inspired by his words, the slaves seized the ship and ordered the Spaniards to head for the African coast. They agreed to do so, but sailed north instead. By the time Cinque discovered this treachery, the Amistad was landed on the Connecticut coast.

The Spaniards had Cinque and the others arrested for mutiny and there was a great public outcry to have them punished. A local court ordered them to be returned to the Spaniards as their "rightful property."

The Abolitionists, however, thought otherwise, and formed a committee to defend the rights of the Africans. Their case was taken up by John Quincy Adams, former President of the United States. His brilliant defense brought the case before the U.S. Supreme Court, who declared the men free to return to Africa.

Joseph Cinque's heroic action served as an important step toward ending the slave trade.

ROBERT SMALLS
(1839-1915)

As the Civil War raged in our country, one of its more daring exploits was executed by a slave seaman, named Robert Smalls. Smalls was born on a South Carolina plantation near the harbor city of Charleston in 1839. In his early twenties, as a trained seaman, he worked on the cotton boat, Planter, which the Confederates converted into a gunboat when the war erupted.

On May 13, 1862, while the ship's commander and officers slept ashore, Smalls smuggled his family and the ship's slave crew aboard. Smalls had learned to navigate by closely observing the ship's navigator at work so, before dawn, he and the slave crew sailed the Planter out to sea.

After sighting the blockade of the Union Navy, Smalls replaced the Confederate flag with a white bunk sheet. And when the Union sailors boarded the Planter, Smalls immediately surrendered the vessel. President Lincoln signed a bill, passed by Congress, awarding Robert Smalls a large sum of money for the capture of the Planter. Smalls entered the Union Navy and eventually was promoted to the rank of Captain.

Years later, Robert Smalls entered politics and was elected to Congress from South Carolina. During his several terms in Congress, he fought valiantly for the right of all men and women to vote. He died in 1915, still trying to extend equal rights to all.

GOLDEN LEGACY
ILLUSTRATED HISTORY SERIES

1. Toussaint L'Overture
2. Harriet Tubman
3. Crispus Attucks
4. Benjamin Banneker
5. Matthew Henson
6. Alexander Dumas
7. Frederick Douglass Part I
8. Frederick Douglass Part II
9. Robert Smalls
10. Joseph Cinque
11. White, Wilkins & Marshall
12. Black Cowboys
13. Dr. Martin Luther King
14. Alexander Pushkin
15. Ancient African Kingdoms
16. Black Inventors

"We hope you will read, enjoy and benefit from our endeavors."

You may order GOLDEN LEGACY for your school, church, relatives, yourself-----or merely as a gift for a friend!

GOLDEN LEGACY is available in soft or hard cover editions.

Send Orders To: Fitzgerald Pub. Co., Inc.
442 Wolf Hill Road
Dix Hills, N.Y. 11746

Payment must accompany all orders in check or money order.

Softcover Edition: $24.00   Hardcover Edition: $45.00

GOLDEN LEGACY
ILLUSTRATED HISTORY MAGAZINE

FREDERICK DOUGLASS
PART TWO

© FITZGERALD PUB. Co. Inc. 1970

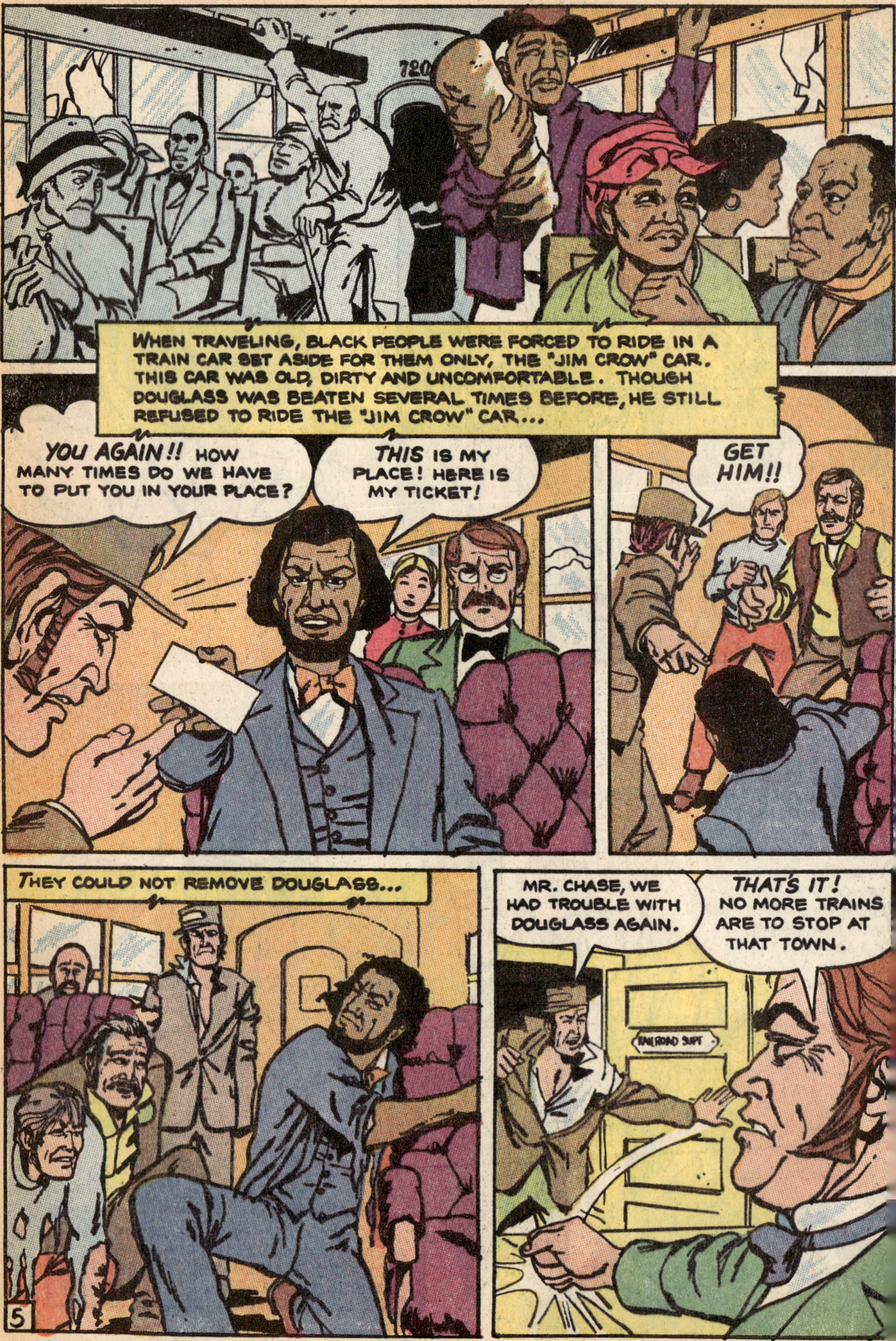

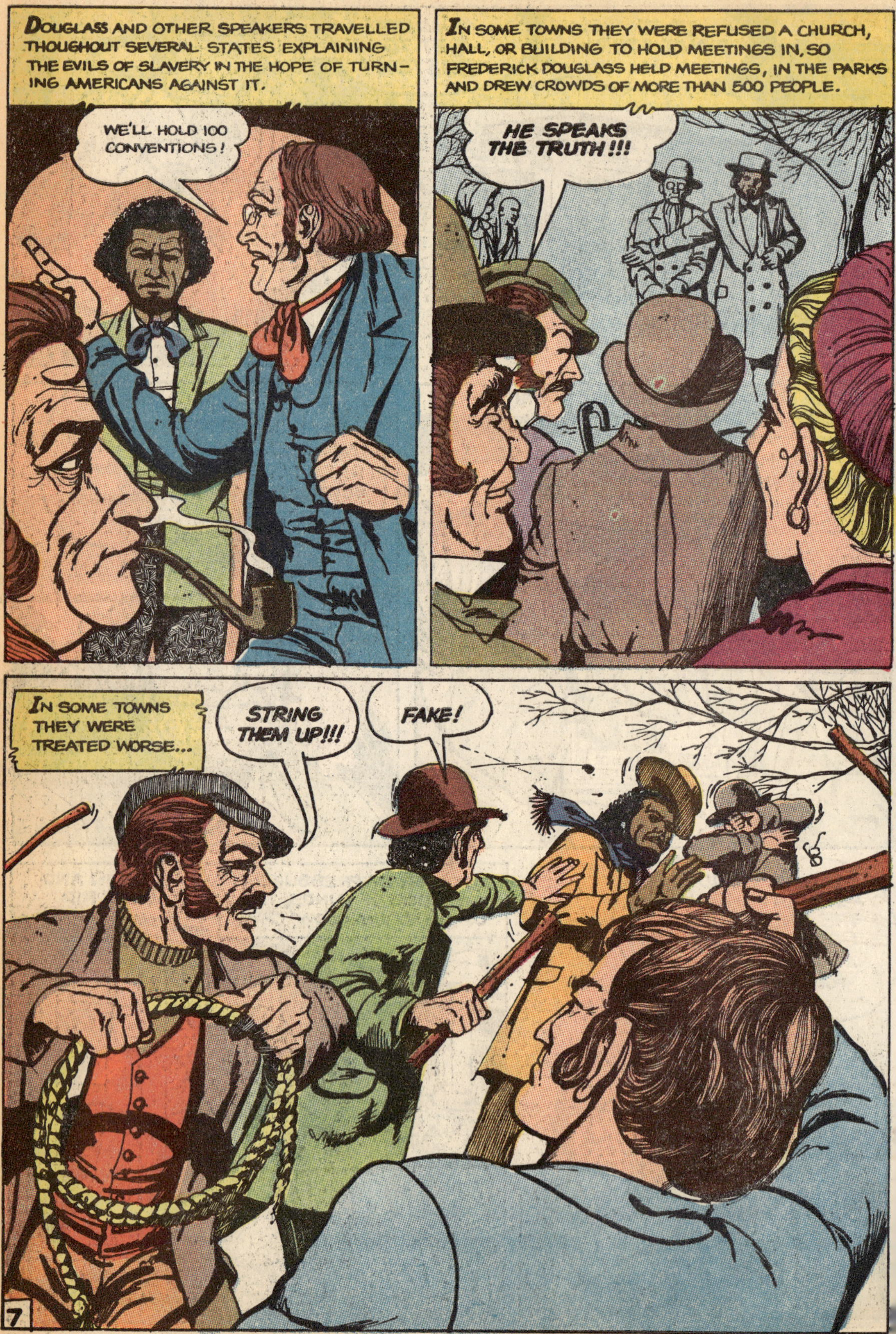

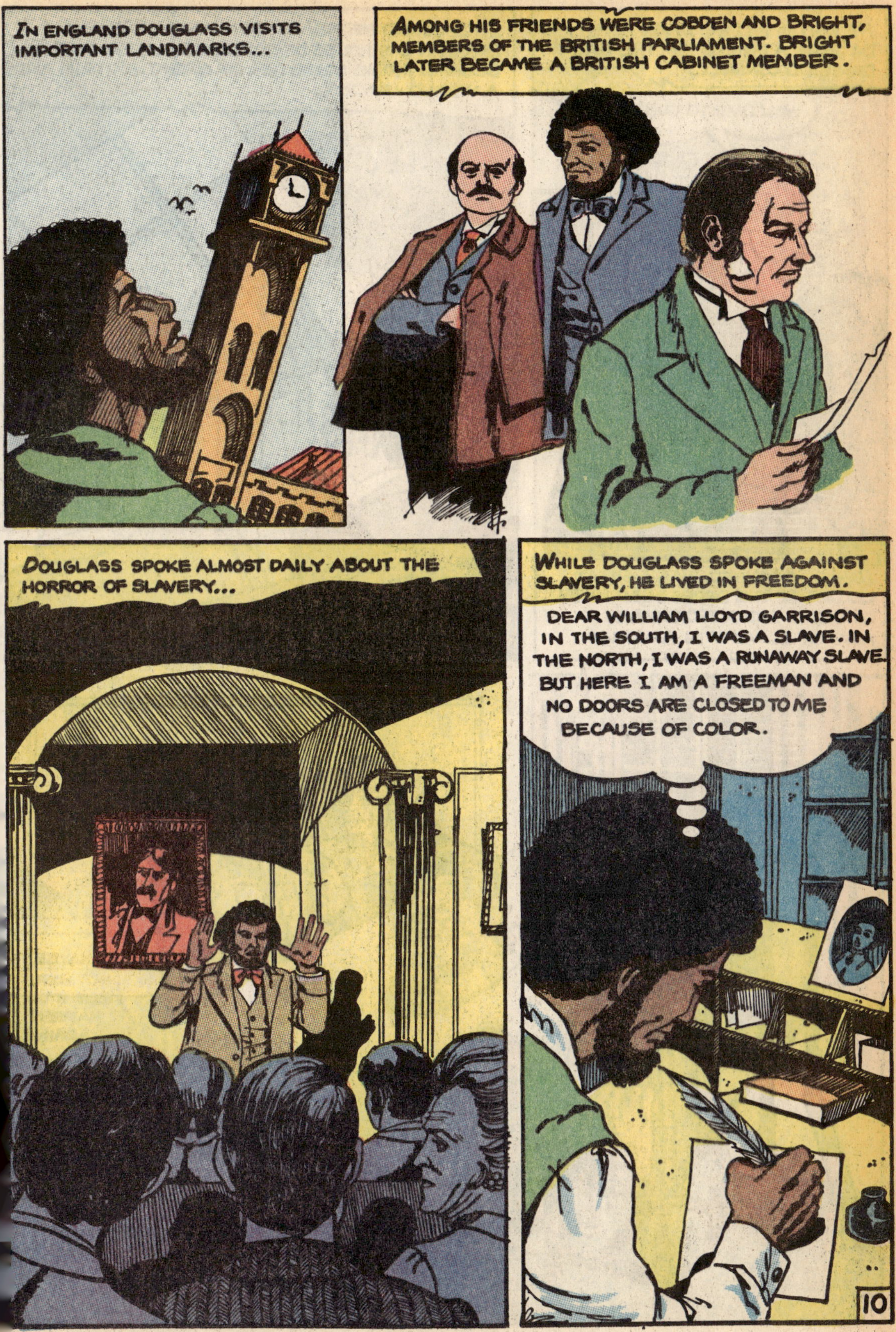

HE VISITED IRELAND WHERE HE MET AND BECAME A FRIEND OF THE GREAT DANIEL O'CONNELL.

WELCOME TO OUR HALL!

DANIEL O'CONNELL WAS A GREAT LEADER OF THE OPPRESSED IRISH CATHOLICS AND A SPOKESMAN AGAINST SLAVERY IN AMERICA.

IN ENGLAND HE HEARD BENJAMIN DISRAELI SPEAK IN THE HOUSE OF COMMONS. LATER DISRAELI BECAME PRIME MINISTER OF GREAT BRITAIN AND A WORLD LEADER.

DOUGLASS AND THE GREAT DANISH WRITER, HANS CHRISTIAN ANDERSEN WERE GUESTS OF MARY AND WILLIAM HOWITT IN LONDON.

IN NOVEMBER 1847, FREDERICK DOUGLASS MOVED HIS FAMILY TO ROCHESTER, NEW YORK WHERE HE PUBLISHED "THE NORTH STAR," AN ANTI-SLAVERY NEWSPAPER.

ALTHOUGH DOUGLASS HAD NO EXPERIENCE, HE SET HIGH STANDARDS AND HIS NEWSPAPER WAS ONE OF THE BEST OF ITS TIME.

FRED'S SHOWING THEM THAT WE CAN DO ANYTHING, IF GIVEN A FAIR CHANCE!

"THE NORTH STAR" ALSO MEANT FREEDOM. RUNAWAY SLAVES USED "THE STAR" TO GUIDE THEM NORTH. DOUGLASS' HOME SOON BECAME A "STATION" OF THE "UNDERGROUND RAILROAD," AND DURING HIS YEARS IN ROCHESTER, HE FED, HID, AND HELPED SEVERAL HUNDRED RUNAWAY SLAVES ESCAPE TO CANADA. IF CAUGHT, HE WOULD HAVE BEEN FINED AND SENT TO PRISON.

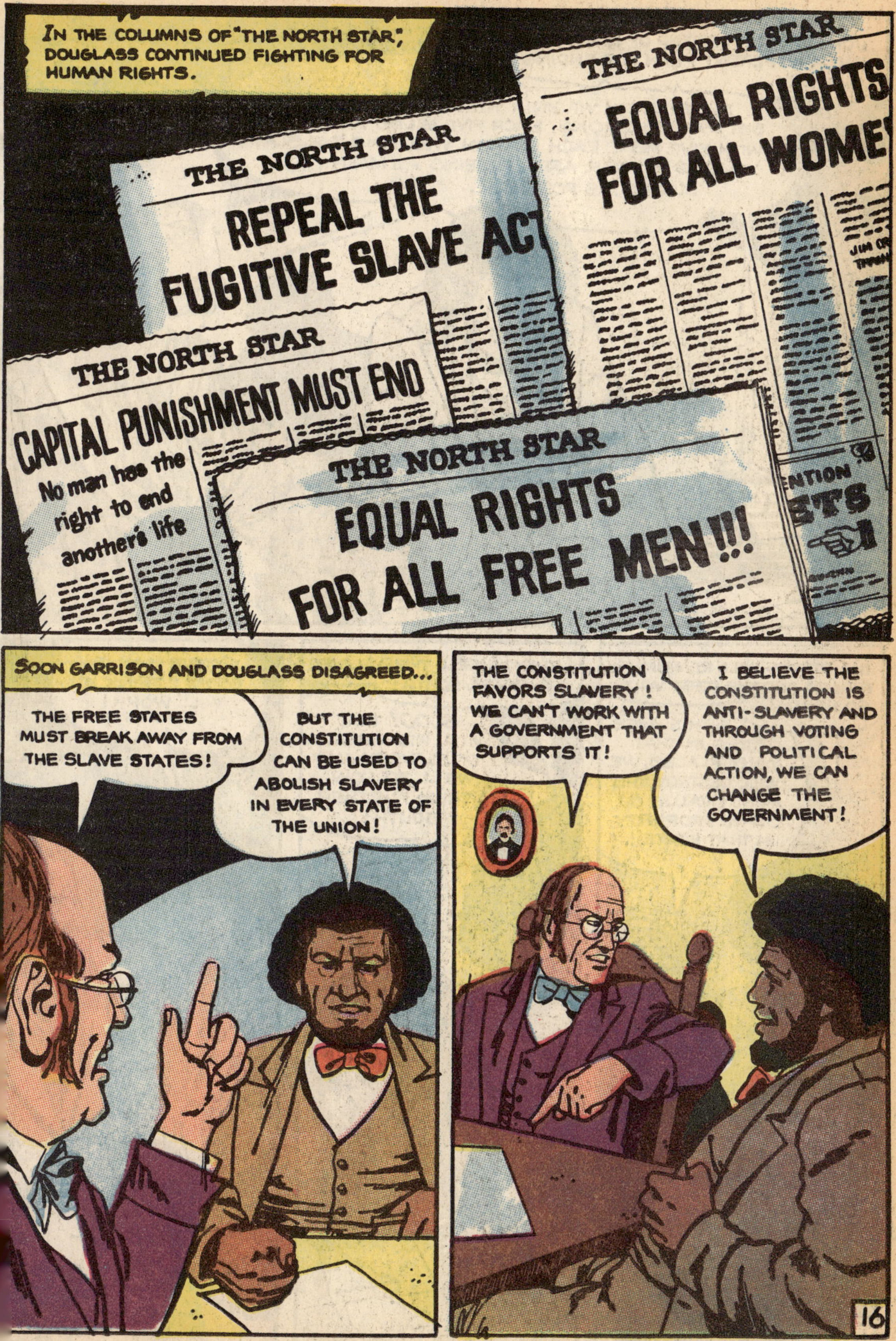

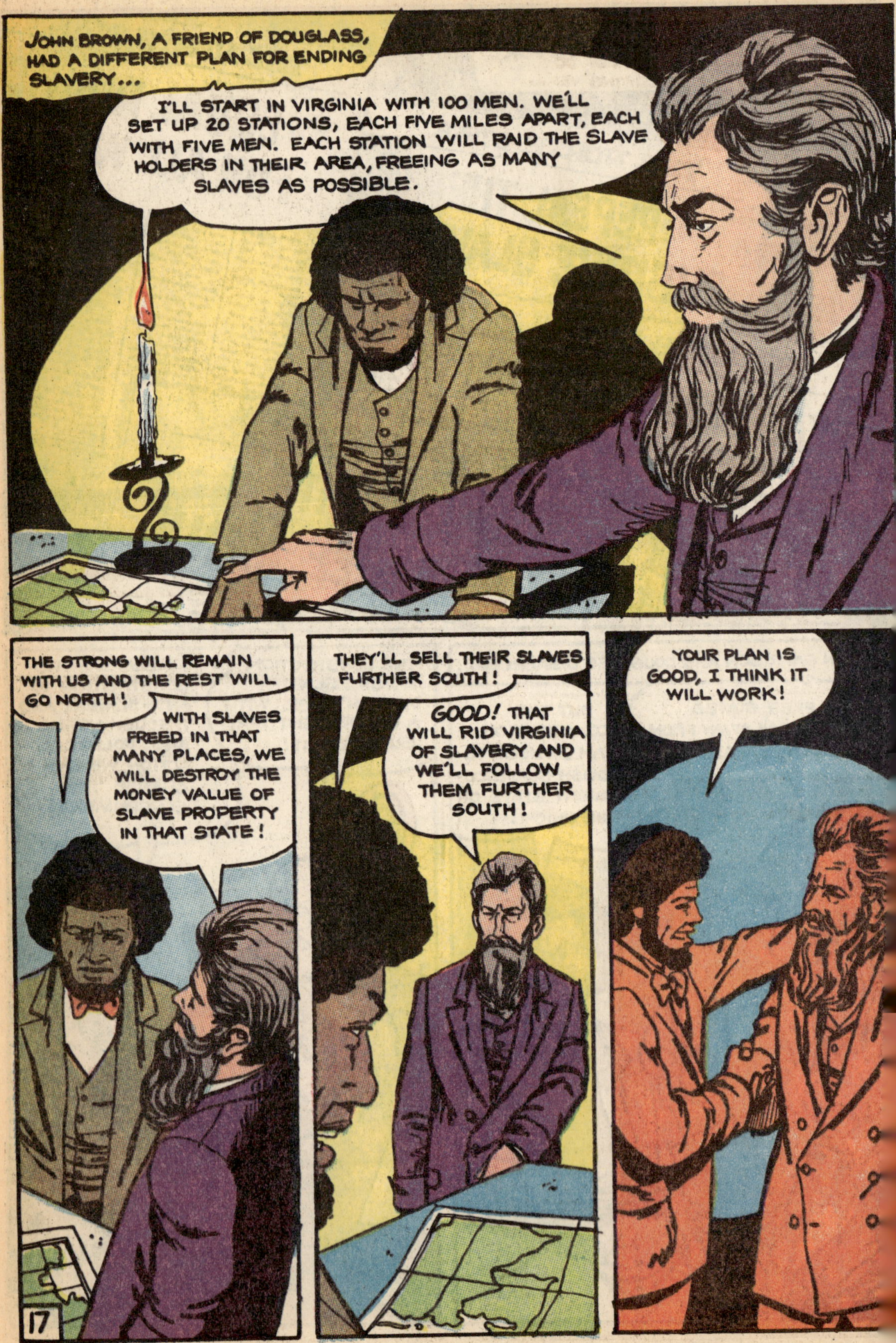

THE FREE STATES WERE AGAINST THE SPREAD OF SLAVERY BECAUSE IT WEAKENED THEM IN CONGRESS AND LIMITED THE OPPORTUNITIES OF THEIR RESIDENTS.

NOW THAT THE MISSOURI COMPROMISE HAS BEEN REPEALED, KANSAS WILL ENTER THE UNION AS A SLAVE-STATE.

NOT IF I CAN STOP IT!

ONE OF THOSE WHO "STOPPED IT" WAS THE FAMOUS JOHN BROWN WHO, WITH FIVE OF HIS SONS, FOUGHT KANSAS' PRO-SLAVERY FORCES FOR THREE YEARS.

THE SLAVE-STATES WERE SO ANGERED BY JOHN BROWN, THAT A REWARD WAS OFFERED FOR HIS CAPTURE! HE LEFT KANSAS AND WENT TO ROCHESTER, N.Y. WHERE HE STAYED AT THE HOME OF FREDERICK DOUGLASS, WORKING ON A SECRET PLAN TO FREE SLAVES.

WHEN I SEND FOR YOU AND GREEN, BRING ALL THE MONEY YOU CAN RAISE!

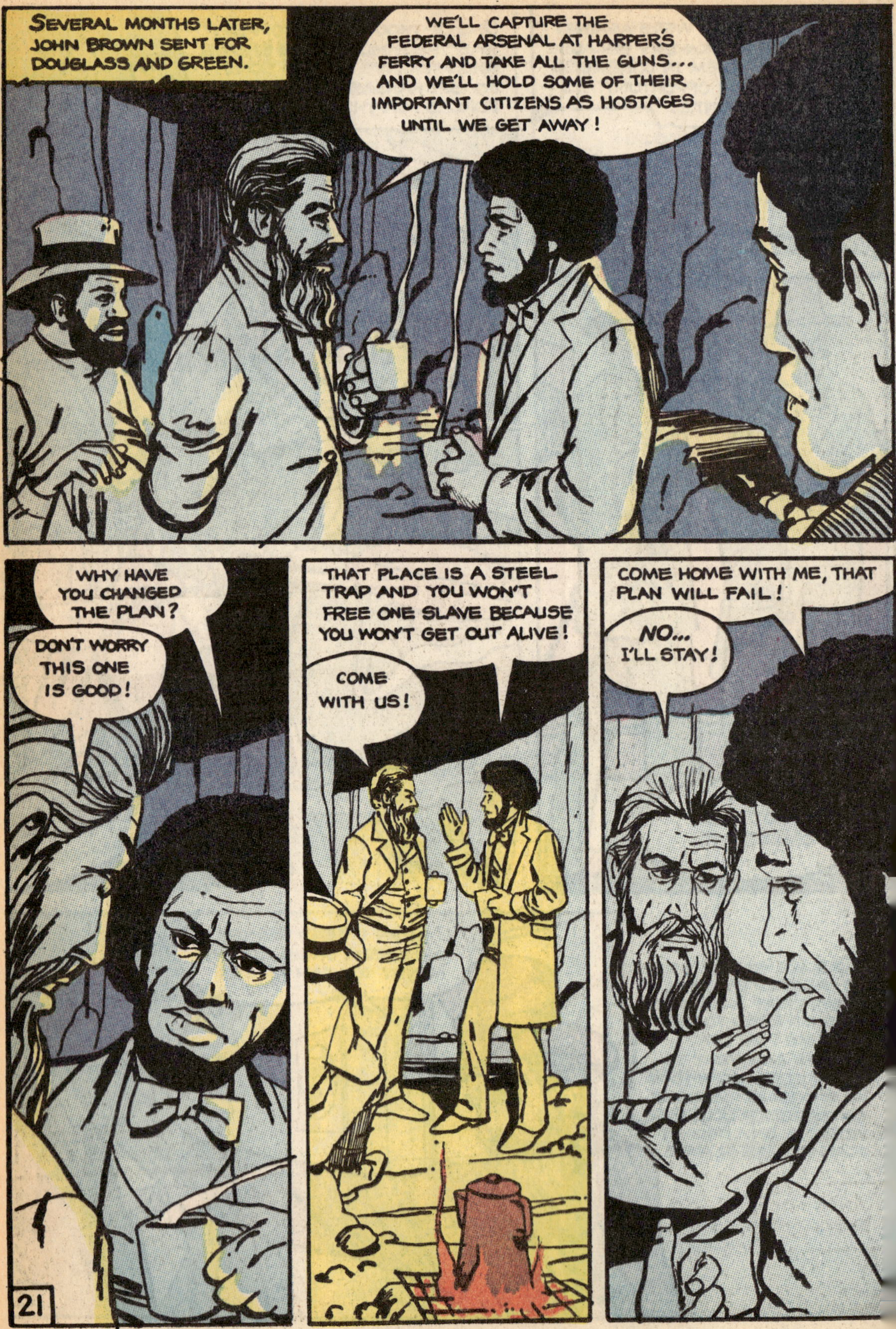

"BLACK MEN ARE WILLING TO FIGHT, IF ALLOWED TO! MAKE THIS A WAR TO END SLAVERY!"

But President Lincoln saw it as a war to preserve the Union...

"IF I COULD SAVE THE UNION WITHOUT FREEING ANY SLAVES, I WOULD DO IT. IF I COULD SAVE IT BY FREEING ALL THE SLAVES, I WOULD DO IT. AND IF I COULD SAVE IT BY FREEING SOME AND LEAVING OTHERS ALONE, I WOULD ALSO DO THAT!"

And President Lincoln soon thought he could save the Union by freeing some of the slaves. On January 1, 1863, the Emancipation Proclamation became law!

"LINCOLN HAS FREED ALL THE SLAVES IN THE CONFEDERATE STATES!"

"BUT THE WAR MUST BE WON!"

DOUGLASS BEGAN RECRUITING VOLUNTEERS, INCLUDING HIS TWO SONS. 29,000 BLACK MEN SERVED IN THE NAVY AND OVER 180,000 SERVED IN THE ARMY — FIGHTING IN MORE THAN 400 BATTLES. MANY LOST THEIR LIVES, AND MANY WERE DECORATED FOR BRAVERY.

MEN OF COLOR TO ARMS NOW OR NEVER!

AFTER TWO YEARS OF BATTLE, THE WAR WAS WON!

BUT THEN, JOY TURNS TO SORROW. PRESIDENT LINCOLN IS KILLED!

PRESIDENT LINCOLN IS ASSASSINATED

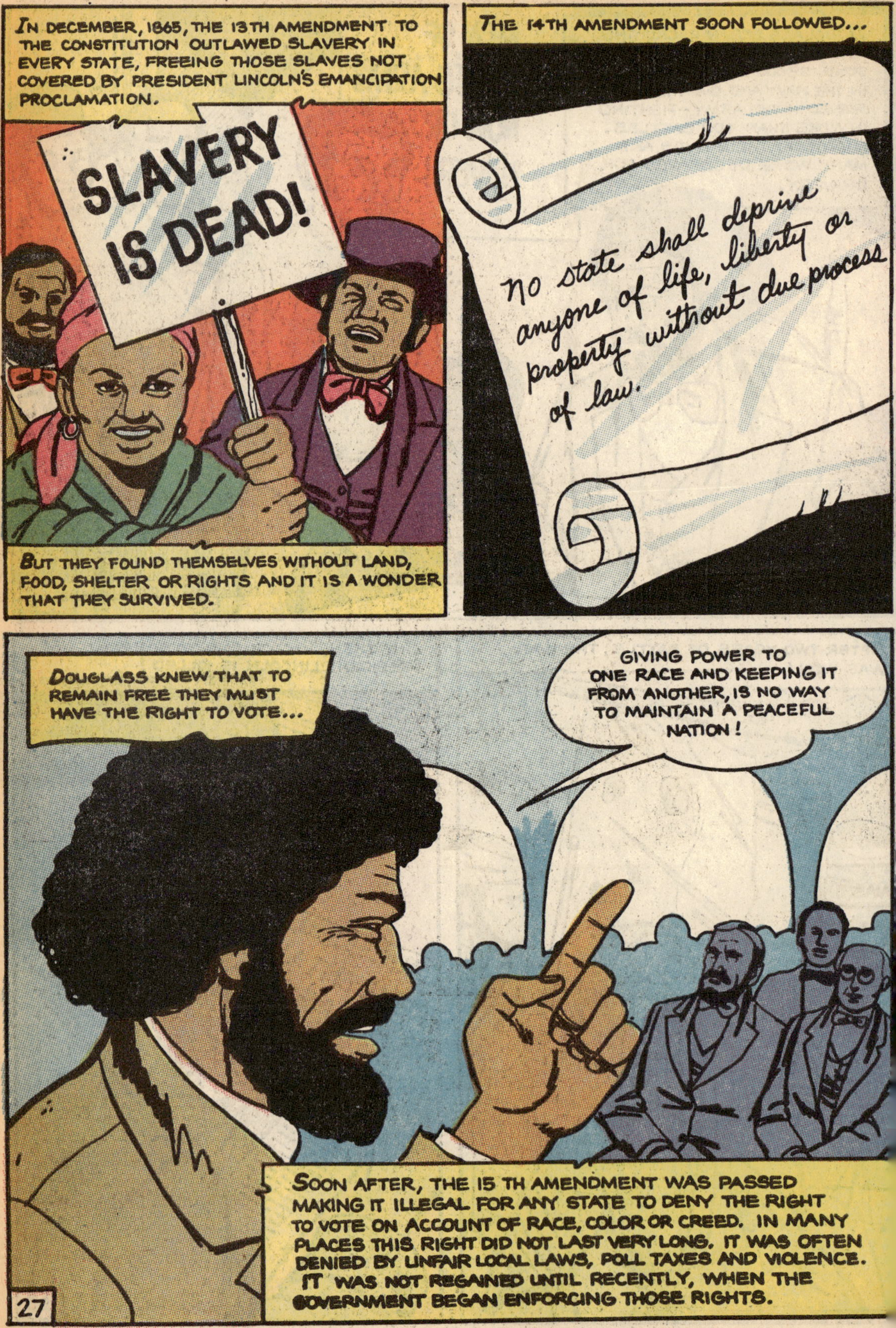

QUOTATIONS OF FREDERICK DOUGLASS

"The fact that we have endured wrongs and hardships which would have destroyed any other race, and have increased in numbers and public consideration, ought to strengthen our faith in ourselves and our future."

"Neither we, nor any other people, will ever be respected until we respect ourselves, and we will never respect ourselves until we have the means to live respectably."

"The low and the vulgar curse him, the snob and the flunky affect to despise him; the mean and the cowardly assault him, because they know that his friends are few, and with the applause of the coarse and brutal crowd. But, despite it all, the Negro remains like iron or granite, cool, strong, imperturbably and cheerful."

"The American people have this lesson to learn: That where justice is denied, where poverty is enforced, where ignorance prevails, and where any one class is made to feel that society is an organized conspiracy to oppress, rob, and degrade them, neither persons nor property will be safe."

"Hungry men will eat. Desperate men will commit crime. Outraged men will seek revenge."

"If there is no struggle, there is no progress. Those who profess to favor freedom and not agitation, are men who want crops without plowing up the ground, they want rain without thunder and lightning. They want the ocean without the awful roar of its many waters."

"This struggle may be a moral one, or it may be a physical one, or it may be both moral and physical, but it must be a struggle. Power concedes nothing without a demand. It never did and it never will."

"Men are whipped oftenest who are whipped easiest."

"If (Federal officials) can protect the rights of white men they can protect the rights of black men; if they can defend the rights of American citizens abroad, they can defend them at home; if they can use the army to protect rights of Chinamen, they can use the army to protect the rights of colored men. The only trouble is the will! the will! Here, as elsewhere, "Where there is a will there is a way."

"You degrade us and then ask why are we degraded — you shut our mouths, and then ask why we don't speak — you close your colleges and seminaries against us, and then ask why we don't know more."

" . . . . let us have peace, but let us have liberty, law and justice first."

BENJAMIN O. DAVIS, JR.
— THREE STAR GENERAL —

Lieutenant General Benjamin O. Davis, Jr., was the highest-ranking black officer ever to serve in the U.S. armed forces and was the fourth black man to graduate from the Military Academy, at West Point, N.Y.

Davis was born in Washington, D.C., on December 18, 1912. He is the son of "B.O." Davis, the first black man to attain the military rank of general in this nation's history.

During his four years at West Point, Davis, as the only black man, never had a roommate and received the "silent treatment" from his fellow classmates. However, determined to excell and prove that a black man could overcome the barriers and succeed at West Point, Davis buckled down, worked hard, and finished 35th in his graduating class. In 1936, he graduated from West Point and was commissioned a second lieutenant in the Infantry.

Davis later transferred to the Army Air Corps and commanded two different black fighter units during World War II. As a combat pilot during the war, he often found himself assigned to segregated quarters and living away from his fellow white officers. He and his wife, in those early years, were often "social lepers" in the military community. However, hard work, dignity, personal strength, and the will to succeed resulted in an impressive military record. He was awarded over forty medals and citations for distinguished service and bravery.

General Davis served in key military posts in Europe, the Far East, Washington, D.C., and as Deputy Commander of the U.S. Strike Command, he held one of the most sensitive posts in the entire military establishment.

GOLDEN LEGACY
ILLUSTRATED HISTORY SERIES

1. Toussaint L'Overture
2. Harriet Tubman
3. Crispus Attucks
4. Benjamin Banneker
5. Matthew Henson
6. Alexander Dumas
7. Frederick Douglass Part I
8. Frederick Douglass Part II
9. Robert Smalls
10. Joseph Cinque
11. White, Wilkins & Marshall
12. Black Cowboys
13. Dr. Martin Luther King
14. Alexander Pushkin
15. Ancient African Kingdoms
16. Black Inventors

"We hope you will read, enjoy and benefit from our endeavors."

You may order GOLDEN LEGACY for your school, church, relatives, yourself-----or merely as a gift for a friend!

GOLDEN LEGACY is available in soft or hard cover editions.

Send Orders To: Fitzgerald Pub. Co., Inc.
442 Wolf Hill Road
Dix Hills, N.Y. 11746

Payment must accompany all orders in check or money order.

Softcover Edition: $24.00   Hardcover Edition: $45.00

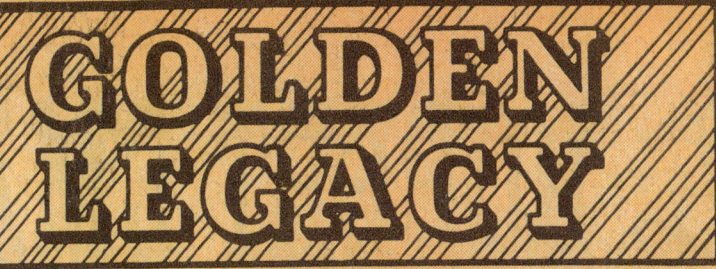

GOLDEN LEGACY
ILLUSTRATED HISTORY MAGAZINE

DON PERLIN

THE LIFE OF ROBERT SMALLS

vol. 9

© FITZGERALD PUB. Co. Inc. 1970

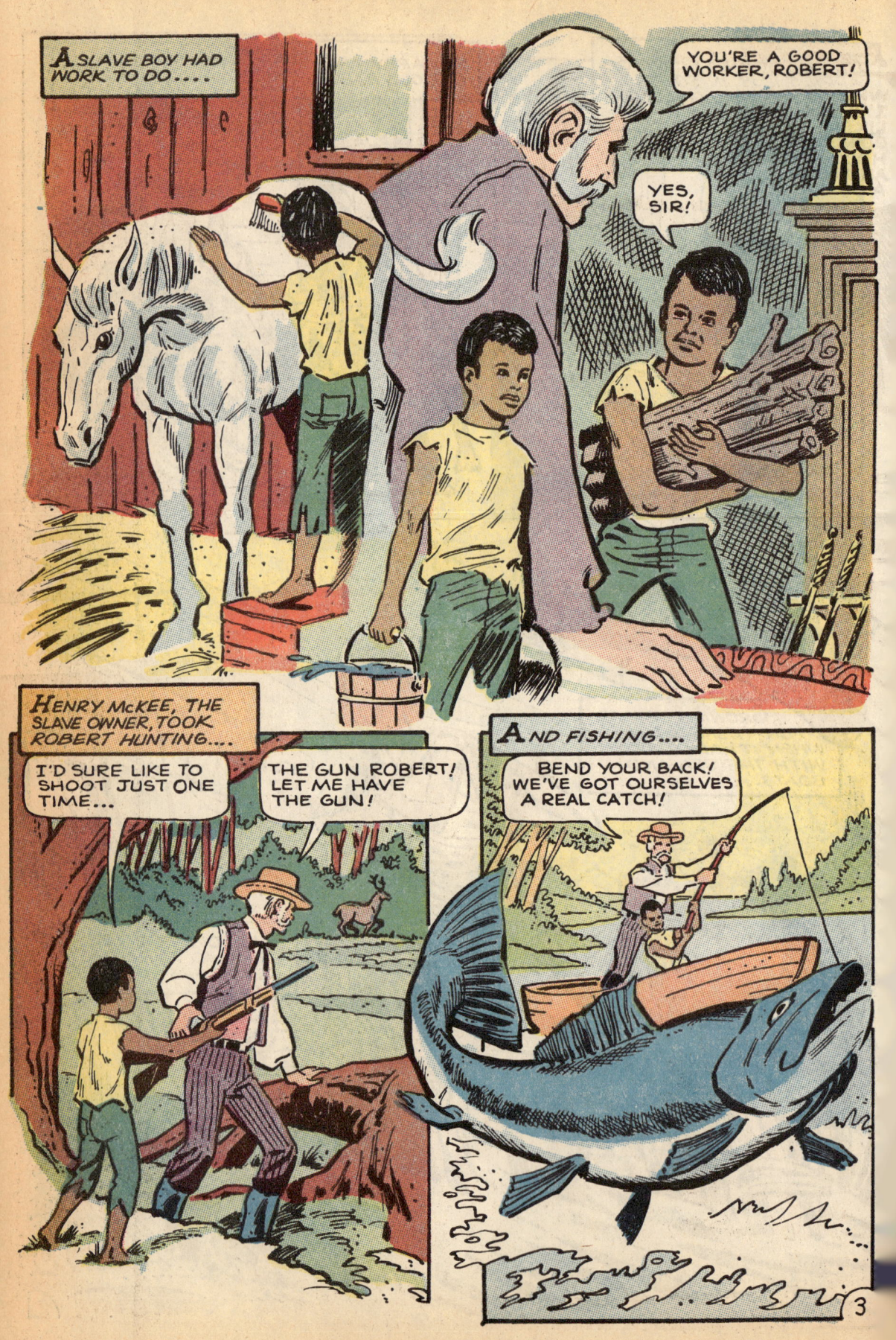

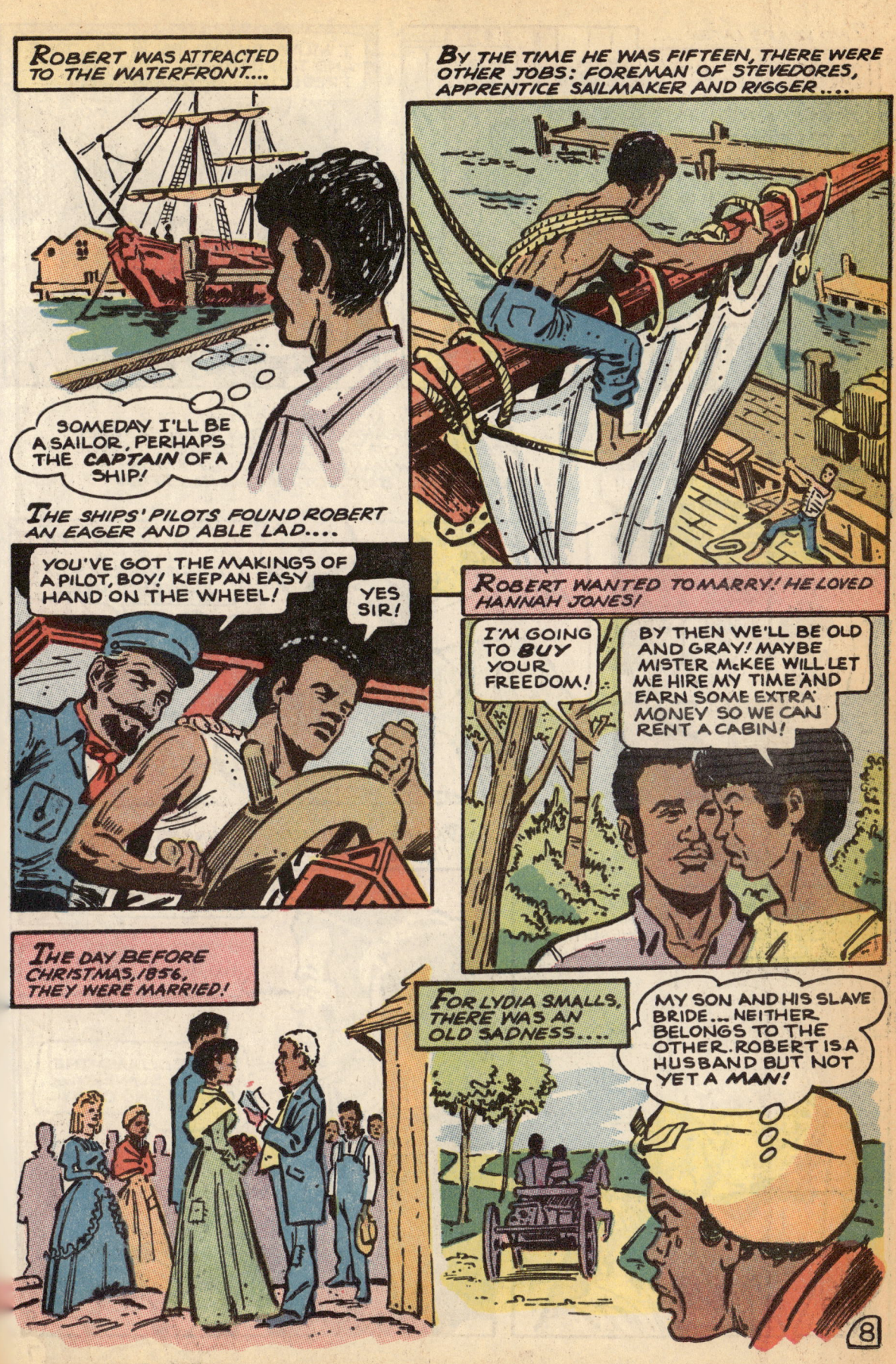

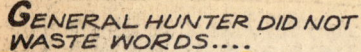

THE WAR DEPARTMENT! SECRETARY STANTON HEARD REQUESTS FROM THE PUBLIC EACH DAY! ROBERT SMALLS AND REVEREND FRENCH WAITED THEIR TURN!

KEEP THE LINE GENTLEMEN!

FINALLY....

YOU THINK SLAVES WILL FIGHT FOR THE UNION? WHY?

IF THE UNION OFFERS *FREEDOM!*

MR. LINCOLN DECLINES TO RECEIVE INDIANS OR NEGROES AS TROOPS!

COMING WAS A WASTE OF TIME!

GENTLEMEN....

MY ADVICE, GENTLEMEN IS TO TALK TO THE *PRESIDENT!* THEN SEE ME AGAIN!

16

"ARMING 5,000 NEGROES MIGHT TURN 50,000 LOYAL SOLDIERS FROM THE BORDER STATES AGAINST US, MR. SMALLS!"

"I'M DISAPPOINTED!"
"HE MUST DO WHAT IS BEST FOR THE ENTIRE COUNTRY!"

"PRESIDENT LINCOLN SAID, 'MY OBJECT IS TO SAVE THE UNION! IF FREEING SLAVES WOULD DO SO, I WILL DO THAT! IF IT IS BEST TO FREE SOME AND LEAVE OTHERS ALONE -- I WILL DO THAT TOO!'"

"THIS ORDER IS TO GENERAL HUNTER! HE IS AUTHORIZED TO ARM AND EQUIP INTO SERVICE OF THE UNITED STATES, BLACK VOLUNTEERS!"

"SIR, FOUR MILLION BLACK MEN AND WOMEN THANK YOU!"
"GENTLEMEN, I TOO WANT TO SAVE THE UNION!"

FOR SEVEN MONTHS THE PLANTER WAS IN PHILADELPHIA FOR REPAIRS. SMALLS PUT HIS TIME TO GOOD USE. HE HIRED TEACHERS AND WORKED NIGHT AND DAY TO LEARN TO READ AND WRITE!

I'M 25 YEARS OLD AND TODAY I READ MY FIRST BOOK!

HONORS OFTEN CAME TO SMALLS BUT SO DID RACIAL INSULTS! ON A STREET CAR IN PHILADELPHIA!...

NO BLACKS CAN SIT IN THESE CARS! THE LAW SAYS YOU MUST STAND ON THE OUTSIDE PLATFORM!

SMALLS WOULD NOT SUPPORT DISCRIMINATION!

THEN I WON'T RIDE UNTIL THE LAW IS CHANGED!

THE INCIDENT CAUSED A BOYCOTT OF THE STREET CARS THAT LASTED UNTIL SOME COMPANIES STOPPED DISCRIMINATING!

PHILADELPHIA INQUIRER
END DISCRIMINATION ON STREET CAR

A FEW YEARS LATER, THE LAW WAS CHANGED!

But black people continued to vote... and Robert Smalls continued to serve them!

I DEMAND THAT FEDERAL TROOPS BE SENT TO SOUTH CAROLINA TO PROTECT THE CITIZENS!

Back in South Carolina, Robert campaigned for others!

TO REMAIN *FREE* YOU MUST *VOTE!*

The Red Shirts struck harder and with more violence!

Wade Hampton was elected Governor and the Red Shirts had cause for joy!

WE'RE GOING TO CONTROL THE WHOLE STATE!

The Red Shirts and their allies wasted no time striking at their enemies! Robert Smalls was among the first....

I HAVE A WARRANT FOR YOUR *ARREST!* YOU ARE CHARGED WITH TAKING A 5,000 DOLLAR BRIBE....

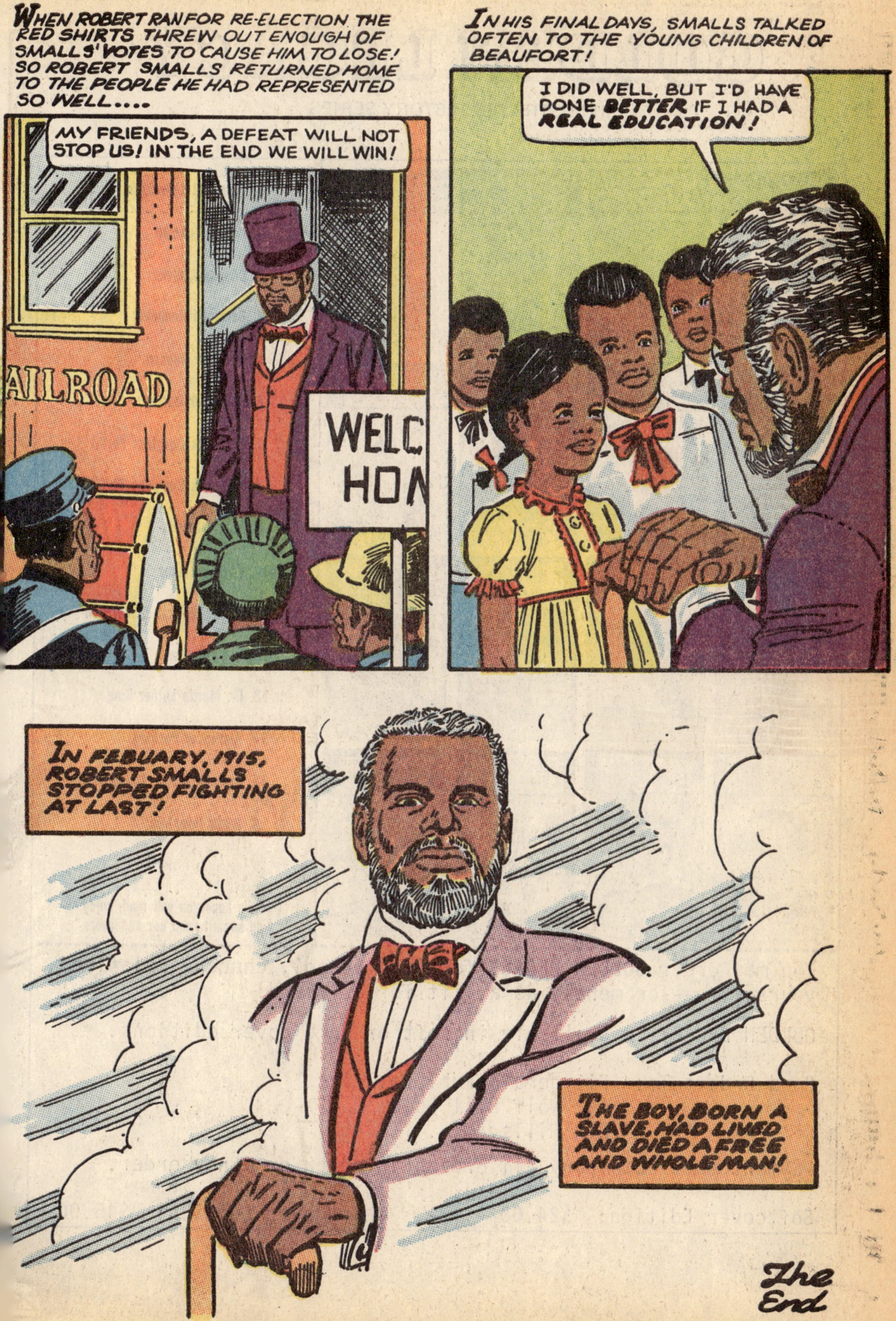

GOLDEN LEGACY
ILLUSTRATED HISTORY SERIES

1. Toussaint L'Overture
2. Harriet Tubman
3. Crispus Attucks
4. Benjamin Banneker
5. Matthew Henson
6. Alexander Dumas
7. Frederick Douglass Part I
8. Frederick Douglass Part II
9. Robert Smalls
10. Joseph Cinque
11. White, Wilkins & Marshall
12. Black Cowboys
13. Dr. Martin Luther King
14. Alexander Pushkin
15. Ancient African Kingdoms
16. Black Inventors

"We hope you will read, enjoy and benefit from our endeavors."

You may order GOLDEN LEGACY for your school, church, relatives, yourself-----or merely as a gift for a friend!

GOLDEN LEGACY is available in soft or hard cover editions.

Send Orders To: Fitzgerald Pub. Co., Inc.
442 Wolf Hill Road
Dix Hills, N.Y. 11746

Payment must accompany all orders in check or money order.

Softcover Edition: $24.00   Hardcover Edition: $45.00

GOLDEN LEGACY
ILLUSTRATED HISTORY MAGAZINE

JOSEPH CINQUÉ and THE AMISTAD MUTINY

© FITZGERALD PUB. Co. Inc. 1970

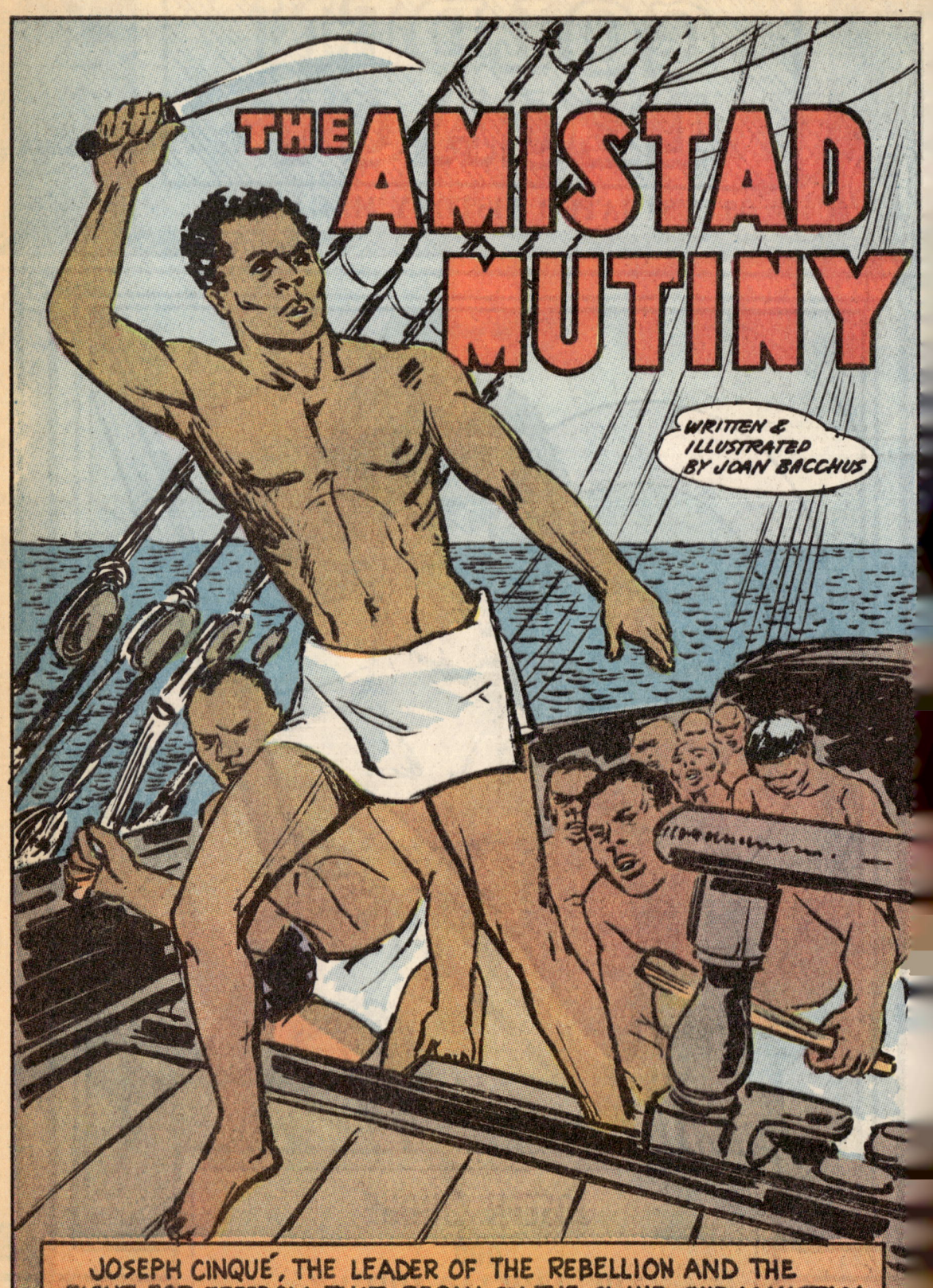

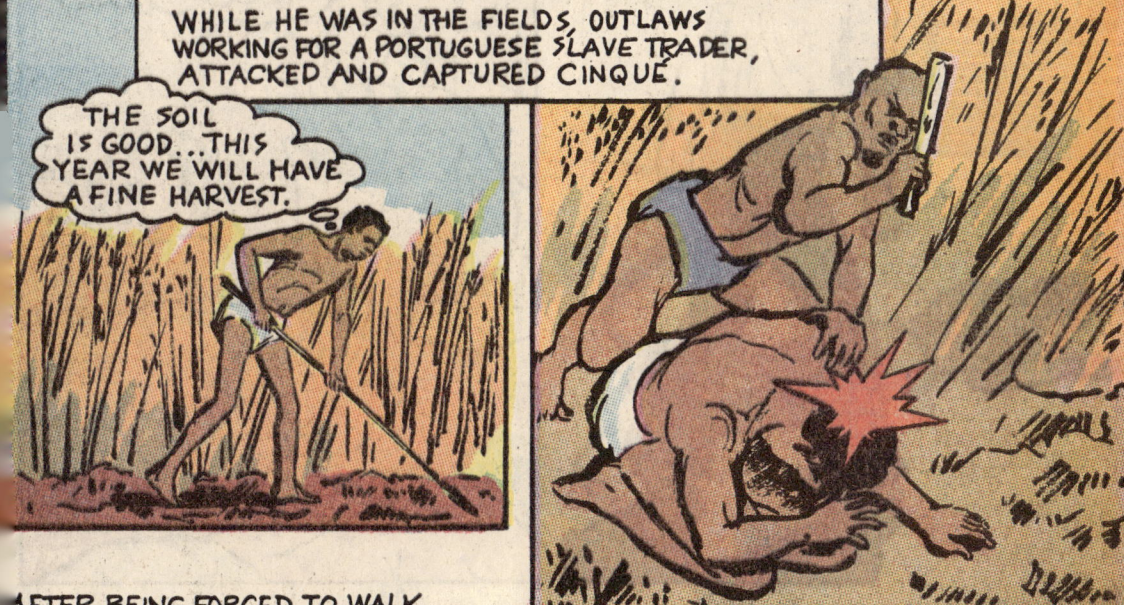

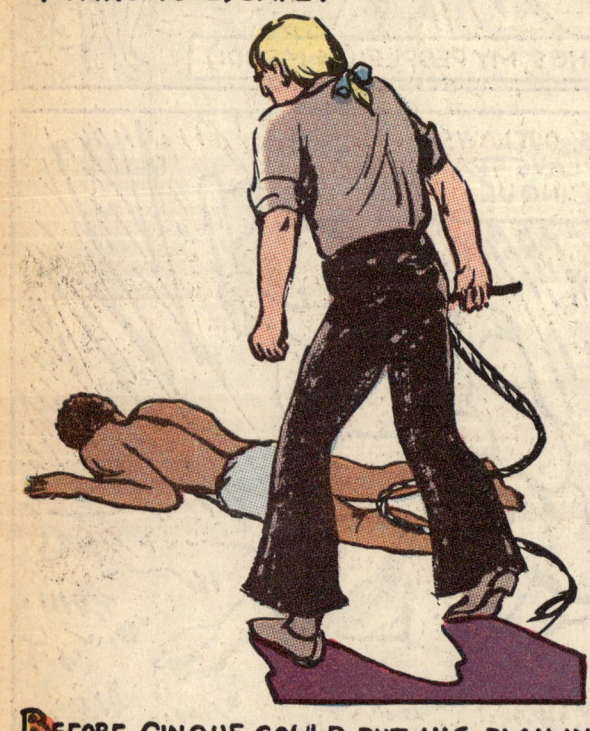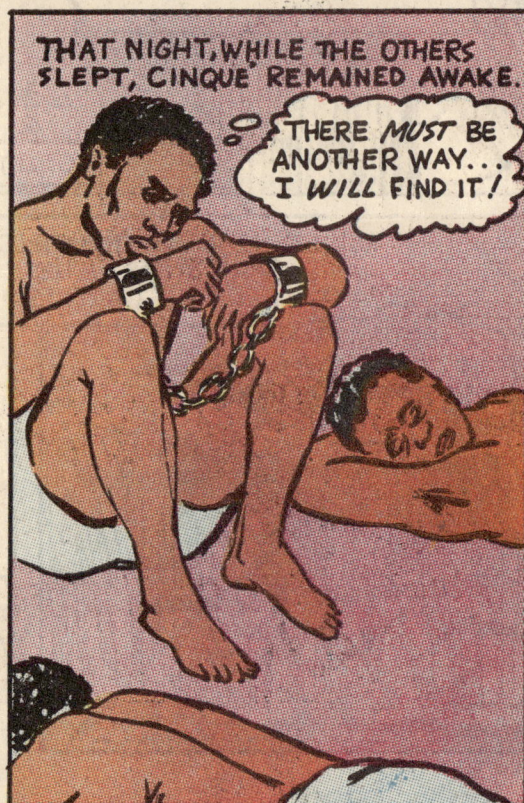

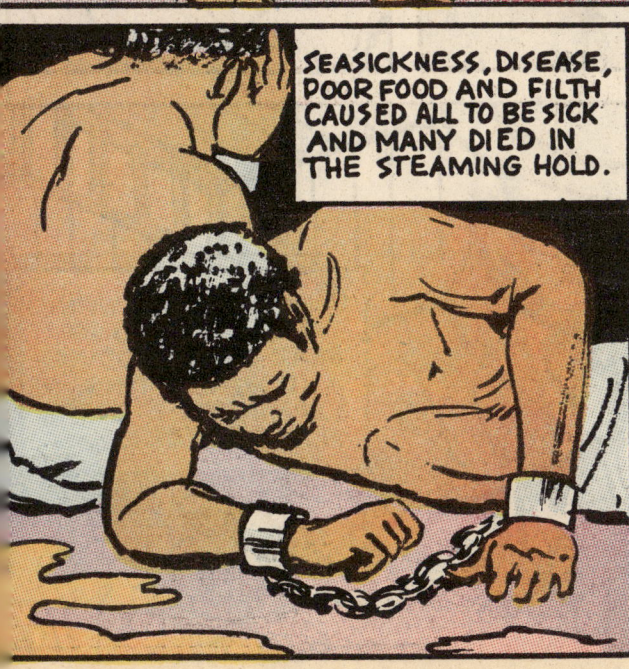

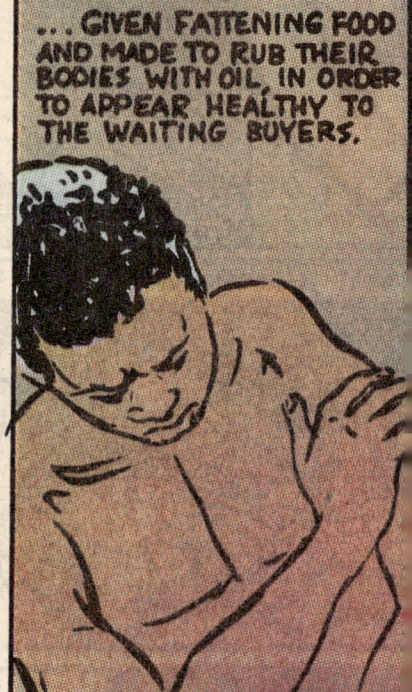

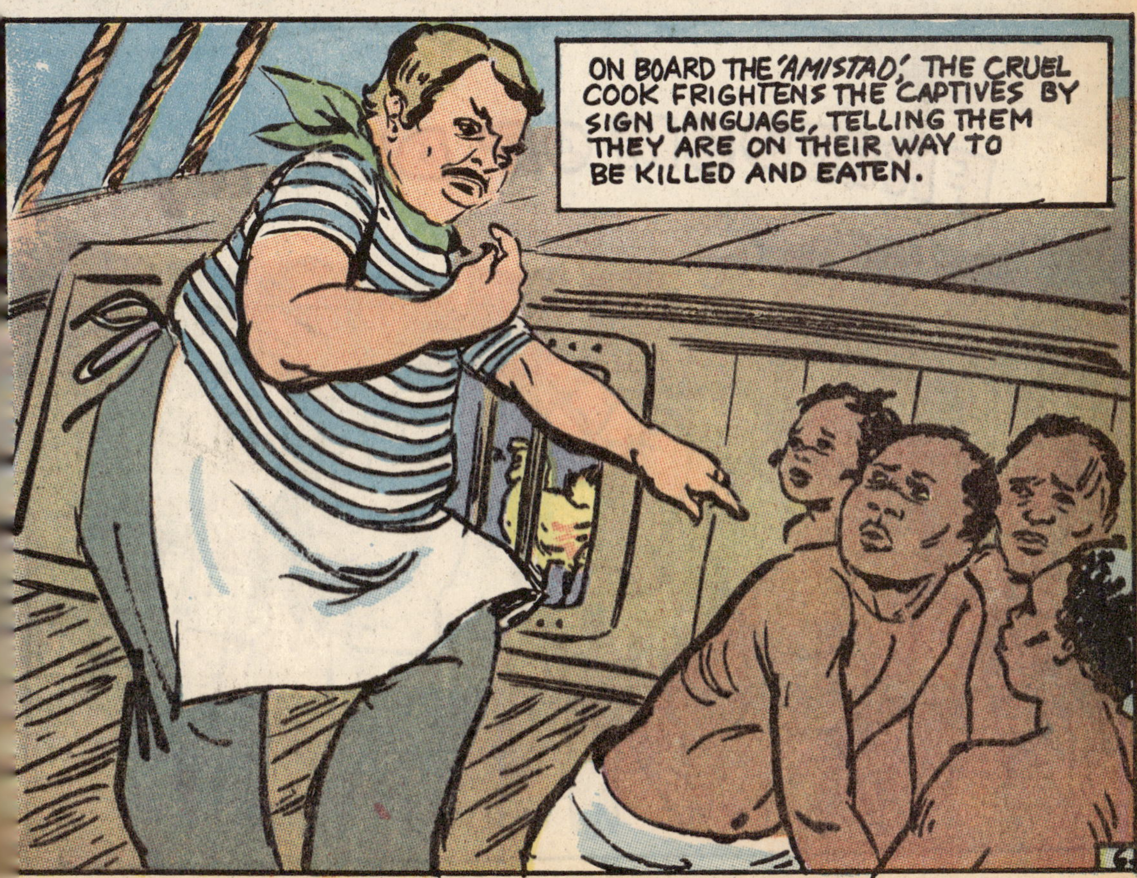

Cinqué, son of a chief, and a leader in his village, gathered the captives around him, forming a council.

"YES, YES"

"WE MUST FREE OURSELVES AND FIND A WAY TO GET BACK TO OUR HOMES AND FAMILIES!"

"CINQUÉ IS RIGHT! WHEN WE REACHED MANHOOD WE TOOK AN OATH TO PROTECT OUR PEOPLE!"

FREEDOM OR DEATH!

A FIERCE TROPICAL STORM OVERTOOK THE 'AMISTAD,' MERCILESSLY TOSSED HER ON THE WAVES. IN THE EXCITEMENT...

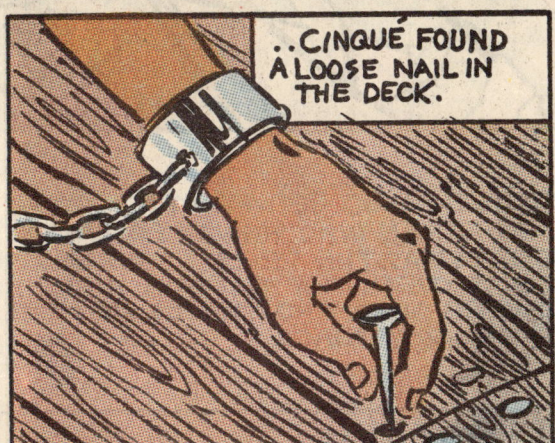

..CINQUÉ FOUND A LOOSE NAIL IN THE DECK.

QUICKLY PICKING THE LOCK ON HIS IRONS HE SOON FREED HIMSELF AND ALL THE OTHERS.

SEARCHING THE CARGO, THE MEN FOUND CUTLASSES MEANT FOR USE ON THE SUGAR PLANTATION.

ARMED NOW AND WITH THE SPIRIT OF FREEDOM RACING IN THEIR BLOOD, CINQUÉ AND THE OTHERS SILENTLY MADE THEIR WAY TO THE UPPER DECK.

In the meantime, the 'AMISTAD' met a ship at sea and was also seen from the shore. Newspapers published wild stories and rumors were even wilder.

"Say, did you see this story? Why it says here that the mystery ship is loaded with real pirates."

"I hear that they were all cannibals!"

GAZETTE — LONG LOW SCHOONER
ATLAS — PIRATE SHIP SIGHTED
COLUMBIAN CENTRAL
PEST SHIP SEEN
COMMERCIAL ADVERTISER
MYSTERIOUS SCHOONER

In reality, the men on the 'AMISTAD' were almost dead from starvation and thirst. Ten of the Africans died before the ship touched land.

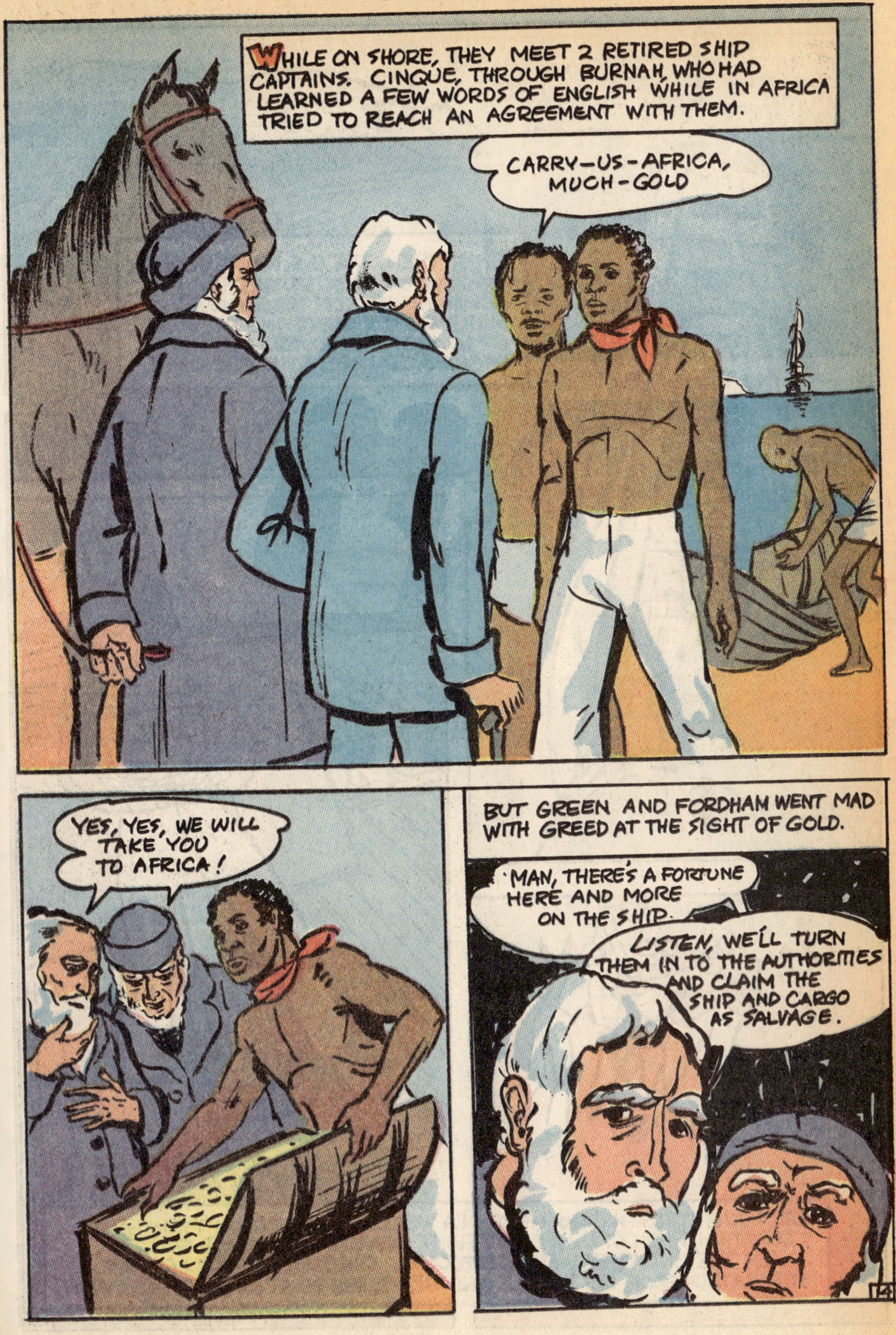

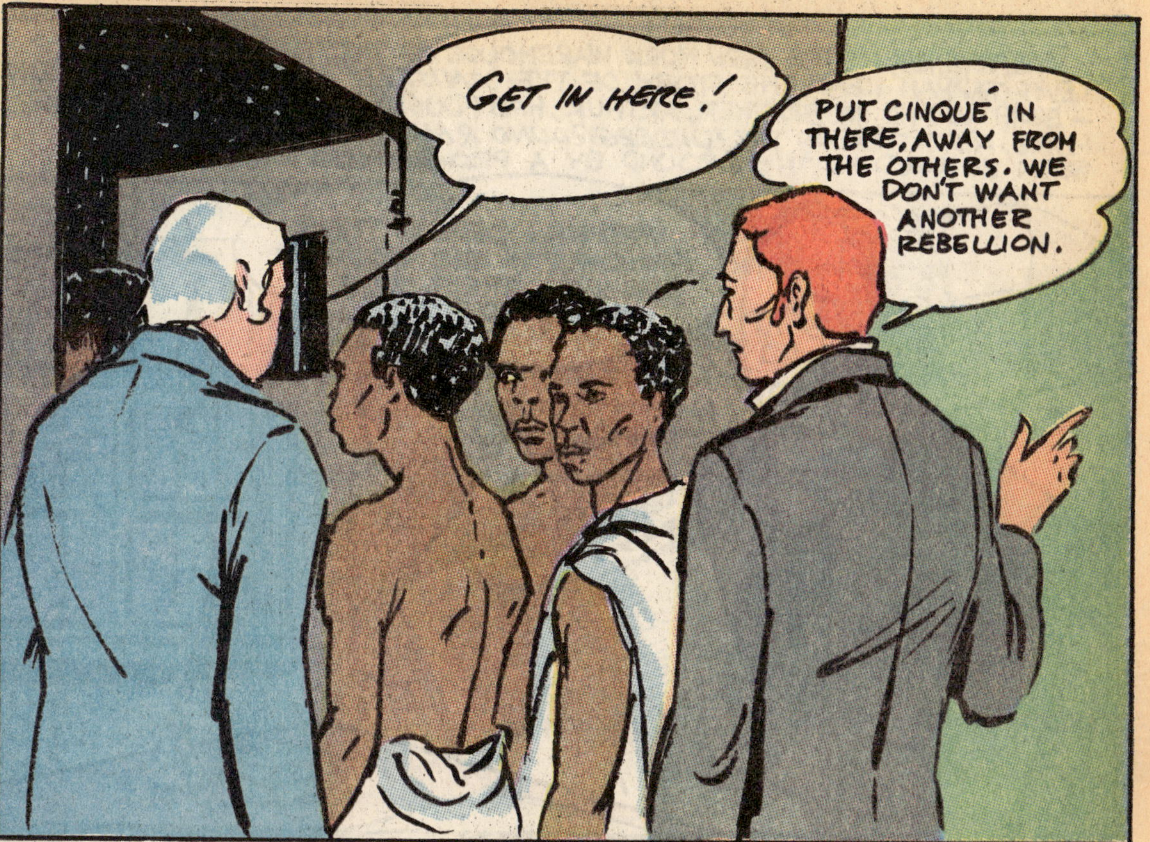

"GET IN HERE!"

"PUT CINQUÉ IN THERE, AWAY FROM THE OTHERS. WE DON'T WANT ANOTHER REBELLION."

So many people wanted to see the prisoners that Pendleton decided to charge admission to the jail.

"DON'T PUSH! I'VE PAID MY SHILLING TOO."

"THEY DON'T LOOK SO WILD TO ME."

"WILL WE EVER SEE HOME AGAIN?"

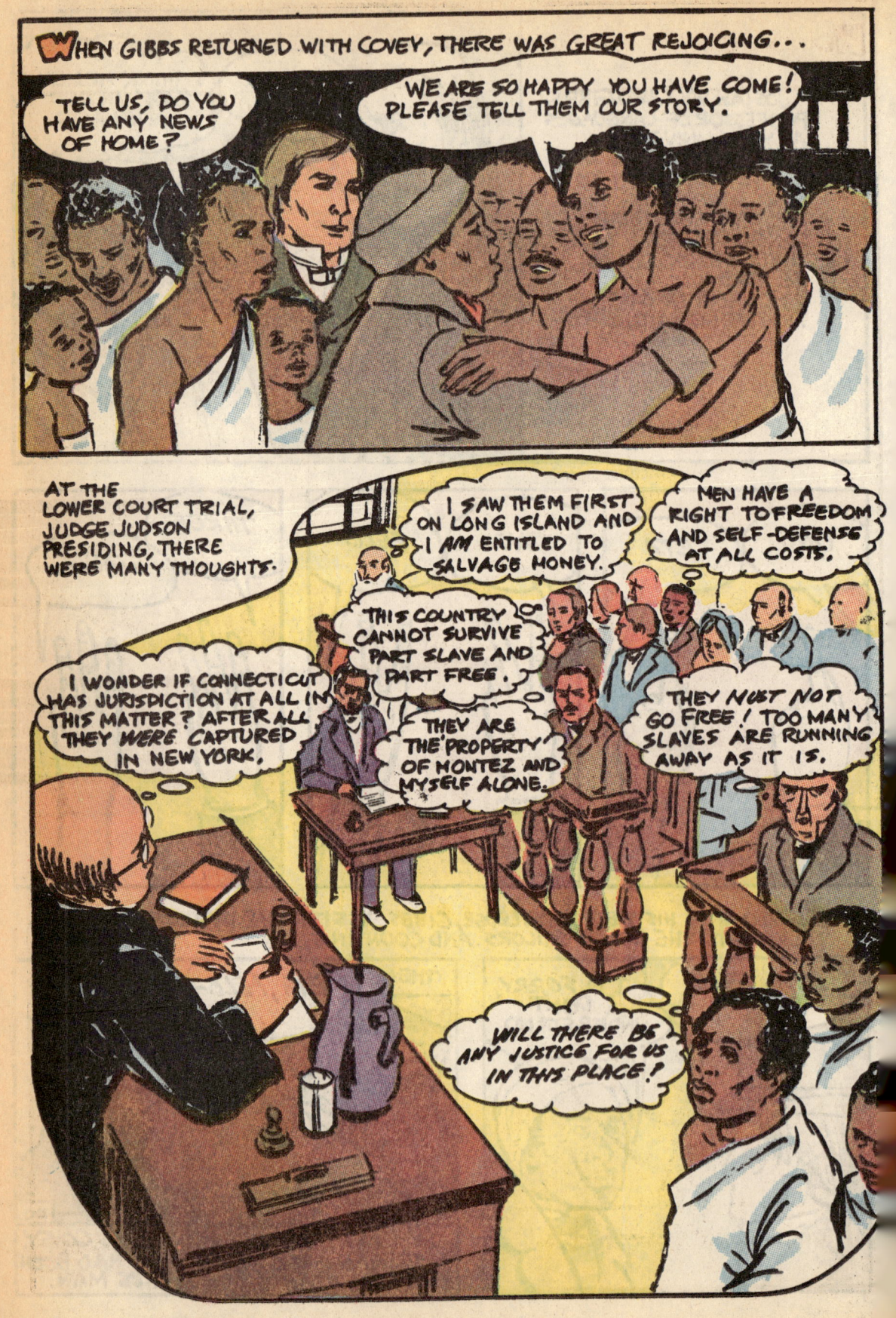

'Old Man Eloquent', John Quincy Adams, had been the 6th President of the United States and was NOW a Congressman from Massachusetts. ...He had long led the fight against slavery in Congress.

"But gentleman, it's been so long since I've argued a case in court."

"We know you can do the job because you believe in the justice of this case."

Although 73 years of age, in poor health and almost blind, Adams undertook the case.

"God give me utterance that I may prove myself in every respect equal to the task"

In behalf of the 'Amistad' Africans, John Quincy Adams spoke 8½ hours before the Supreme Court of the United States!

27

THE SUPREME COURT DECLARED THAT THE 'AMISTAD' AFRICANS SHOULD NOT BE PLACED IN CUSTODY OF THE PRESIDENT *BUT MUST BE FREED IMMEDIATELY!*

"HE WHO WOULD BE FREE MUST STRIKE THE FIRST BLOW"

"THERE IS NO PROGRESS WITHOUT STRUGGLE"
— Frederick Douglass.

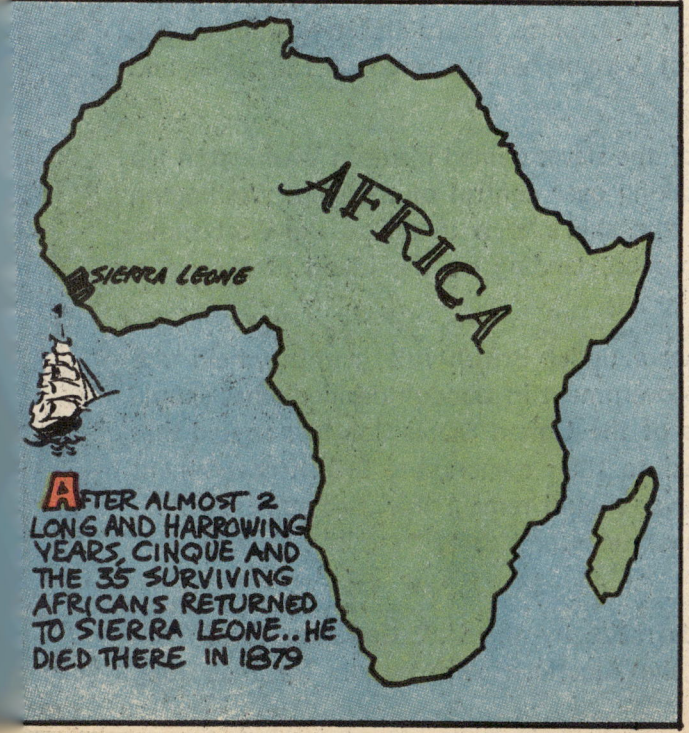

AFTER ALMOST 2 LONG AND HARROWING YEARS, CINQUE AND THE 35 SURVIVING AFRICANS RETURNED TO SIERRA LEONE.. HE DIED THERE IN 1879

THIS WAS NOT THE END OF THE AMISTAD STORY. THE ORIGINAL COMMITTEE, FORMED TO AID THE AFRICANS, GREW INTO THE AMERICAN MISSIONARY ASSOCIATION WHICH FOUNDED 500 SCHOOLS IN THE SOUTH AFTER THE CIVIL WAR... THESE INCLUDE DILLARD AND FISK UNIVERSITIES, HOUSTON-TILLOTSON, LE MOYNE, TALLADEGA AND TOUGALOO COLLEGES.

THE STORY ALSO CONTINUES IN THE FORM OF THE AMISTAD RESEARCH CENTER AND RACE RELATIONS DEPARTMENT AT FISK UNIVERSITY.

IT ALL BEGAN WITH ONE MAN'S FIGHT FOR *FREEDOM*.

MUTINY ON THE CREOLE

In 1841, another mutiny took place aboard the slave ship, Creole. The Creole left the shores of Virginia with a cargo of 130 slaves and headed for New Orleans.

While out at sea, one of the slaves named Madison Washington led a revolt that succeeded in taking over control of the ship. Washington and the other slaves forced the ship's crew to sail to the West Indies where slavery had been abolished, landing on the island of Nassau in the Bahamas.

The Bahama Islands were under British rule, and they held the slaves in Nassau while their government in London decided what should be done. While the members of the United States Congress argued that the slaves should be returned to their owners, the British government decided that the escaped slaves should remain free. Secretary of State Daniel Webster, opposed their release, and some American slave owners called for war.

Because of the demands made by the U.S. Congress, the British government eventually paid the American slave owners for their loss.

PRIME MINISTER LYNDEN O. PINDLING

When the new constitution of the Commonwealth of the Bahama Islands took effect on May 10, 1969, Lynden O. Pindling became their first Prime Minister.

Lynden O. Pindling was born on March 22, 1930. As a youngster, Pindling was a good student and a high school track star. At 18, he left the Bahamas to attend the University of London where he received a Law degree in 1952.

Shortly after his return, he joined the Progressive Liberal Party and was elected to the House of Assembly. By 1962, he had become the chairman of his party and after self-government came in 1964, he led his party's move to win control of the government. In the general election of 1967, the Progressive Liberal Party won control of the government and Pindling became the Premier.

Now as Prime Minister, Lynden O. Pindling seeks to develop tourism and encourages outside investors to participate in the islands' economic expansion. In addition, he has provided the country's highest budget for education.

GOLDEN LEGACY
ILLUSTRATED HISTORY SERIES

1. Toussaint L'Overture
2. Harriet Tubman
3. Crispus Attucks
4. Benjamin Banneker
5. Matthew Henson
6. Alexander Dumas
7. Frederick Douglass Part I
8. Frederick Douglass Part II
9. Robert Smalls
10. Joseph Cinque
11. White, Wilkins & Marshall
12. Black Cowboys
13. Dr. Martin Luther King
14. Alexander Pushkin
15. Ancient African Kingdoms
16. Black Inventors

"We hope you will read, enjoy and benefit from our endeavors."

You may order GOLDEN LEGACY for your school, church, relatives, yourself-----or merely as a gift for a friend!

GOLDEN LEGACY is available in soft or hard cover editions.

Send Orders To: Fitzgerald Pub. Co., Inc.
442 Wolf Hill Road
Dix Hills, N.Y. 11746

Payment must accompany all orders in check or money order.

Softcover Edition: $24.00   Hardcover Edition: $45.00

HE COULD HAVE LIVED AN EASIER LIFE AS A WHITE MAN, BUT INSTEAD, HE CHOSE TO LIVE PROUDLY AS A BLACK MAN AND MADE THIS WORLD A BETTER PLACE FOR ALL.

WALTER F. WHITE

WALTER F. WHITE WAS BORN, JULY 1, 1893, TO A VERY RELIGIOUS FAMILY. THEY LIVED IN A COMFORTABLE HOUSE AND EVERY MORNING THEY PRAYED TOGETHER.....

DEAR LORD, LET OUR PEOPLE LIVE IN PEACE AND FREEDOM.

...THEN DINED TOGETHER.

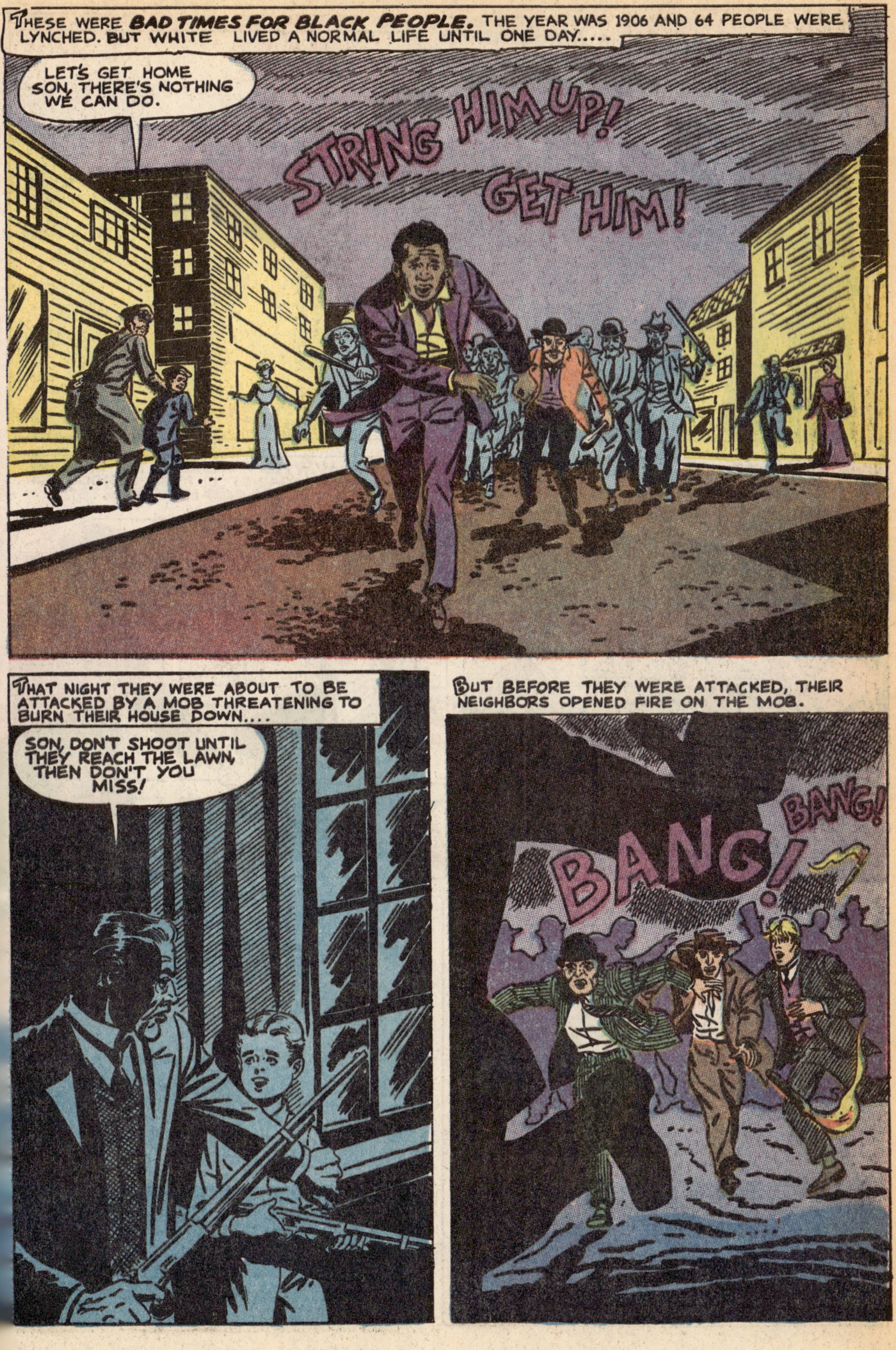

ATLANTA WAS A GOOD TOWN FOR A STUDENT. IT HAD SEVERAL COLLEGES AND **WALTER** GRADUATED FROM **ATLANTA UNIVERSITY**.

SHORTLY AFTER, THE POLITICIANS WANTED TO SAVE MONEY....

"LET'S CUT THE BUDGET OF THOSE BLACK SCHOOLS!"

"YEAH, THEY DON'T PAY TAXES."

WALTER WHITE WAS ONE OF THE LEADERS OF THE FIGHT AGAINST CUTTING SCHOOL FUNDS AND THE **NAACP** HEADQUARTERS IN **N.Y.C.** SENT HELP....

"GLAD YOU COULD COME DOWN TO GIVE US A HAND."

"WHY YOU PEOPLE PAY A LOT OF TAXES!"

.....AND THEY WON THEIR CASE TOO!

A LOCAL BRANCH OF THE **NAACP** WAS SET UP IN ATLANTA, **WALTER WHITE** WAS ONE OF ITS LEADERS.

"WE'VE GOT TO PUT A STOP TO LYNCHING!"

WALTER WORKED LONG AND HARD AND WAS REWARDED WITH A TRANSFER TO THE HEADQUARTERS.

THE FAMOUS WRITER JAMES WELDON JOHNSON WAS THE EXECUTIVE SECRETARY OF THE NAACP.

HMM, I CAN SEE YOU'RE JUST THE MAN WE'RE LOOKING FOR.

WALTER WHITE INVESTIGATED RIOTS AND LYNCHINGS. BECAUSE OF HIS APPEARANCE HE WASN'T NOTICED AND THE EVIDENCE HE GATHERED SOMETIMES FREED INNOCENT PEOPLE AND HELPED CONVICT GUILTY ONES!

THE WORK WAS DANGEROUS AND ONCE AFTER A LYNCHING....

THEY KNOW WHO YOU ARE, GET OUT OF TOWN, OR YOU'RE NEXT!

THANKS, MAN.

....HE CLIMBED ONTO A TRAIN JUST AS IT WAS LEAVING!

YOU'RE LEAVING TOO SOON. THEY PLAN TO LYNCH ANOTHER ONE WHO'S BEEN SPYING ON US.

A MAN OF GREAT COURAGE, WHITE INVESTIGATED 41 LYNCHINGS AND 8 RIOTS.

WALTER WHITE'S WORK WAS OUTSTANDING FOR MANY YEARS AND HIS EFFORTS WERE REWARDED WHEN, IN 1931, HE WAS ELECTED EXECUTIVE SECRETARY OF THE NAACP.

"CONGRATULATIONS, MR. WHITE."

WHEN TWO BLACK DEFENSE WORKERS WERE HIRED, WHITE WORKERS WALKED OFF THE JOB...

IF BLACK AND WHITE CAN'T WORK TOGETHER, HOW WILL THEY EVER LIVE TOGETHER?

AND WALTER WHITE'S EFFORTS WERE LARGELY RESPONSIBLE FOR PRESIDENT ROOSEVELTS' EXECUTIVE ORDER ON FAIR EMPLOYMENT PRACTICES IN DEFENSE PLANTS. THIS ORDER HELPED, THOUSANDS OF BLACK PEOPLE TO FIND WORK DURING WORLD WAR II.

ADVANCES WERE MADE DURING THIS PERIOD, BUT NOT ENOUGH... *BLACK* SOLDIERS ON LEAVE WERE OFTEN UNABLE TO GET TRANSPORTATION HOME, OR BACK TO CAMP.

"THOSE CARS ARE HALF *EMPTY!*"

"BUT THE COLORED CAR IS FULL, SORRY."

BLACK PEOPLE WERE DENIED DINING CAR AND RESTURANT SERVICES THAT WERE AVAILABLE TO WAR PRISONERS.

AS THE HEAD OF THE *NAACP* WHITE WORKED VERY HARD TO INCREASE UNDERSTANDING BETWEEN THE RACES AND TO HAVE THE FEDERAL GOVERNMENT PROTECT AND ENFORCE *CIVIL RIGHTS.*

"LAWS AND COURT DECISIONS BY THEMSELVES WON'T CURE EVIL, BUT THEY WILL CREATE ACCEPTANCE OF THE BASIC RIGHT OF EVERYONE TO LIVE, LEARN, WORK, PLAY AND PRAY IN FREEDOM!"

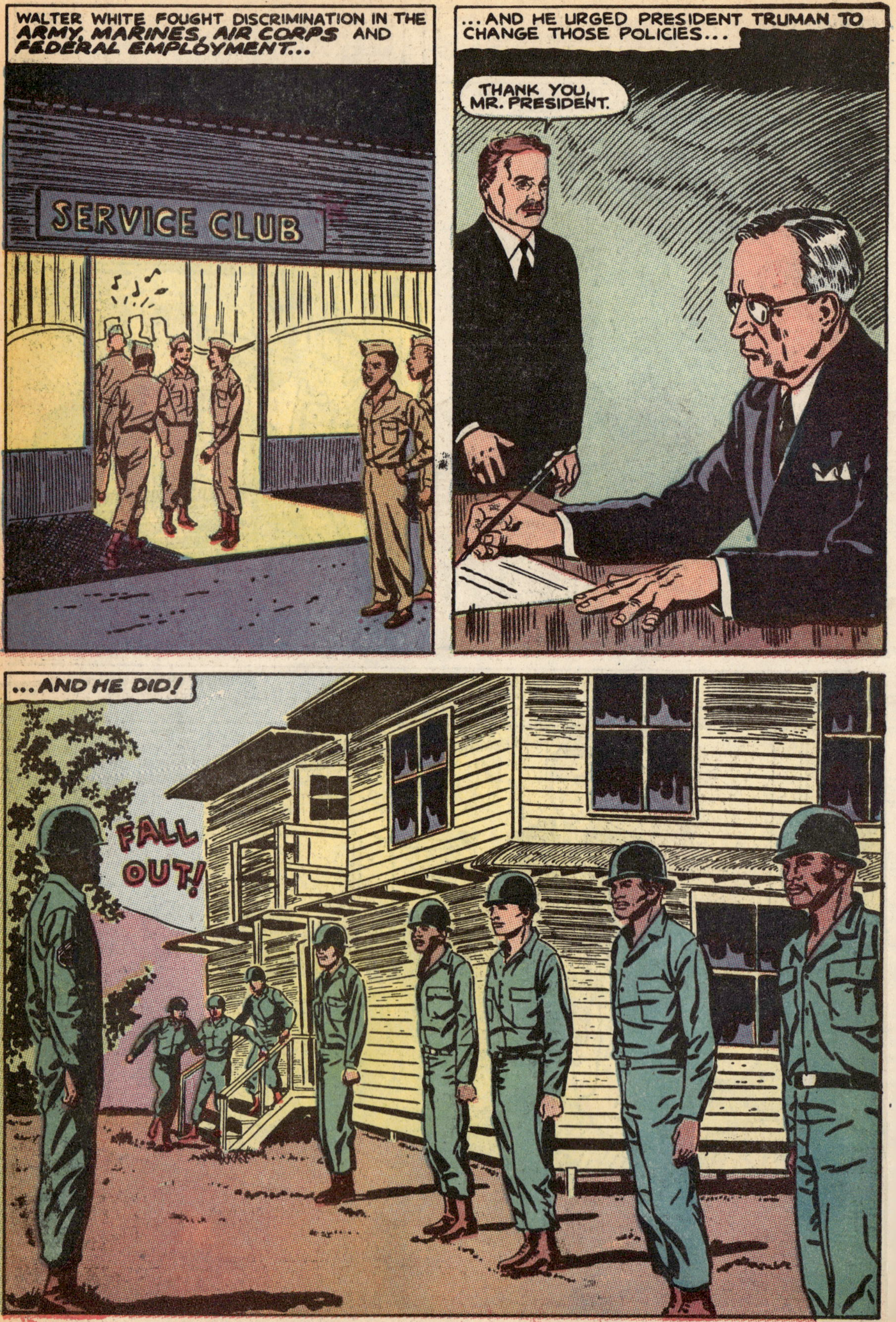

BLACK VOTERS' HOMES WERE BOMBED! AT THIS POINT, WALTER WHITE DIRECTED MORE OF THE NAACP'S ACTIVITIES TOWARD THE PROTECTION OF VOTING RIGHTS.

"IF THIS VIOLENCE CONTINUES, WE WON'T HAVE ANY PEOPLE LEFT TO REGISTER. LET'S GET TO WORK ON IT!"

IT WAS A LONG HARD FIGHT, BUT THEY WERE MAKING PROGRESS!

"UNDER THE LAW OF OUR LAND, ALL CITIZENS ARE ENTITLED TO VOTE! IT'S TIME THIS STATE JOINED THE UNION!"

IN SPITE OF A BUSY SCHEDULE, WALTER WHITE FOUND TIME TO WRITE SIX BOOKS AND TWO WEEKLY NEWSPAPER COLUMNS...

AND ALSO SERVED AS A CONSULTANT TO THE U.S. DELEGATION WHEN THE UNITED NATIONS WAS ORGANIZED IN 1945 AND AGAIN AT THE GENERAL ASSEMBLY IN 1948...

WHITE WORKED WITH ROY WILKINS TO CORRECT THE INJUSTICES OF SEGREGATED SCHOOLS....

"ROY, LET'S TRY TO HAVE LAWS PASSED WHILE MARSHALL STARTS COURT ACTION!"

SO *THURGOOD MARSHALL* LED THE *NAACP'S* LEGAL STAFF IN A SERIES OF COURT ACTIONS DESIGNED TO END SEGREGATION IN SCHOOLS.

SEVERAL YEARS LATER, ON MAY 17, 1954, AFTER MANY COURT VICTORIES AND THE HELP OF MANY EXPERTS, THEY MADE A GREAT BREAKTHROUGH WHEN THE U.S. SUPREME COURT DECIDED...

"IN THE FIELD OF PUBLIC EDUCATION... SEPARATE EDUCATIONAL FACILITIES ARE... IN THEMSELVES... UNEQUAL"

CHIEF JUSTICE EARL WARREN

ALTHOUGH ILL, WHITE TRAVELLED THROUGHOUT THE COUNTRY GIVING SPEECHES AND WORKING FOR EQUAL JUSTICE.

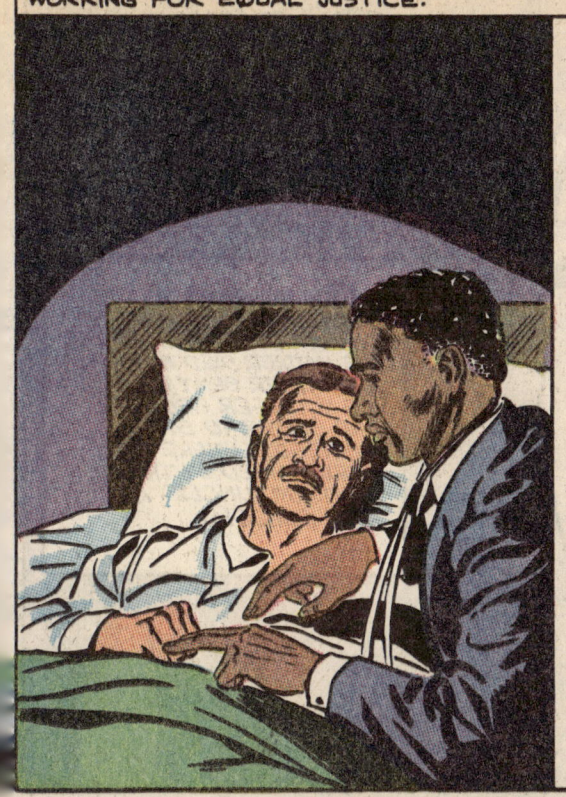

ON MARCH 21, 1955, AT THE AGE OF 61, WALTER WHITE DIED. HIS LIFE WAS FULL, HIS TASK WAS GREAT, AND HIS ACCOMPLISHMENTS WERE BEYOND MEASURE!

THE END

THERE HAS PASSED FROM THE SCENE A VIGOROUS CHAMPION OF JUSTICE AND EQUALITY FOR ALL OUR CITIZENS... PRESIDENT DWIGHT D. EISENHOWER - MARCH, 1955

ROY WILKINS

ROY WILKINS WAS BORN IN ST. LOUIS, MISSOURI ON AUGUST 30, 1901. AFTER HIS MOTHER DIED IN 1906, HIS FATHER SENT HIM AND HIS YOUNGER BROTHER AND SISTER TO ST. PAUL, MINNESOTA WHERE THEY WERE RAISED BY THEIR AUNT AND UNCLE. AFTER HIGH SCHOOL...

HE ATTENDED THE UNIVERSITY OF MINNESOTA AND BECAME AN EDITOR ON THE SCHOOL NEWSPAPER.

HE EARNED MONEY FOR HIS EDUCATION BY WORKING AS A CADDY, DISHWASHER, PORTER, AND WAITER.

ALTHOUGH HE HAD FACED ONLY MILD FORMS OF INJUSTICE HE WON THE SCHOOL'S SPEAKING CONTEST FOR HIS STRONG SPEECH AGAINST LYNCHING...

...AND FOUND THE TIME TO SERVE AS AN OFFICER OF THE ST. PAUL BRANCH OF THE **NAACP**!

ROY WILKINS' GOOD WORK DID NOT GO UN-NOTICED AND, IN 1931, HE JOINED THE NAACP HEADQUARTERS STAFF IN NEW YORK AS ASSISTANT SECRETARY....

OUR REPORT ON DISCRIMINATION AT THE FEDERAL FLOOD CONTROL PROJECT HAS BEEN IGNORED. WE NEED MORE INFORMATION. I'D LIKE YOU TO GET IT.

THE BLACK WORKERS WERE PAID ONLY 10¢ AN HOUR AND THE WORK CAMPS AND LIVING CONDITIONS WERE TERRIBLE... WILKINS LIVED IN CAMPS AND WORKED AS A LABORER WHILE GATHERING INFORMATION....

...IF HE HAD BEEN CAUGHT, HE PROBABLY WOULD HAVE BEEN LYNCHED!

A BOOKLET WAS PREPARED, INFORMING CONGRESS AND THE PUBLIC OF THE WAGES AND CONDITIONS... AN INVESTIGATION WAS HELD.

WE MUST SET STANDARDS FOR CONDITIONS AND WAGES!

AND THEY DID!!

IN 1932, THE ATTORNEY GENERAL CALLED A CONFERENCE ON CRIME BUT REFUSED TO INCLUDE LYNCHING SO ROY WILKINS PICKETED.... AND WAS ARRESTED.

END LYNCHING

BUT THEY CONTINUED TO REGISTER AND VOTE IN GREATER NUMBERS IN SPITE OF THE VIOLENCE!

VOTER REGISTRATION

AND IN 1954, THEY WON A GREAT VICTORY WHEN THE U.S. SUPREME COURT DECISION OVERTURNED PUBLIC SCHOOL SEGREGATION.

GENTLEMEN, THIS IS THE DAWN OF A NEW DAY!!

THE FOLLOWING YEAR, AFTER THE DEATH OF WALTER WHITE, **WILKINS** WAS ELECTED EXECUTIVE SECRETARY OF THE NAACP!

WE'VE GOT TO GET THE PRESIDENT, THE CONGRESS, THE COURTS, AND THE PEOPLE MORE INVOLVED IN OUR STRUGGLE FOR EQUAL RIGHTS.

For over 80 years, each effort to pass civil rights bills was defeated. As chairman of the *Leadership Conference on Civil Rights, ROY WILKINS......

"I KNOW THIS BILL IS VERY WEAK, BUT IT IS A BEGINNING. TELL YOUR CONGRESSMEN TO PASS IT AND BETTER BILLS WILL FOLLOW!"

*COMPOSED OF EIGHTY NATIONAL CIVIC, LABOR AND RELIGIOUS ORGANIZATIONS.

Wilkins was right! After the passage of the 1957 Civil Rights Bill, stronger bills and executive orders followed and Roy Wilkins played a major role in each!

CIVIL RIGHTS ACT OF 1960
VOTING RIGHTS ACT OF 1964
OPEN HOUSING ACT OF 1968

During those years, there were sit-ins of every type, boycotts, freedom rides, and marches... and Wilkins through the NAACP, supported these efforts with either legal services, bail bonds, financial aid, or leadership.

"MR. WILKINS, THE NAACP HAS BEEN CALLED ON TO DEFEND 1600 STUDENTS ARRESTED IN SIT-INS."

"NEGRO YOUTH IS FINISHED WITH RACIAL SEGREGATION!"

AND WILKINS, TOO, WAS AGAIN ARRESTED FOR PICKETING.

Roy Wilkins has fought segregation throughout his career and speaks out against anyone, black or white, who favors separation.

"I wish more people really knew how difficult it's been to get this far and if we favor racial separation on any level, we'll find ourselves right back where we started!"

Under his skillful leadership, the NAACP has doubled its membership, its staff, and now has more than 1700 branch offices and youth groups.

"We must work to rid the country of poverty and slums. We must also try to improve employment, health services and the quality of education!!"

Roy Wilkins is the author of many articles which have appeared in all of the major magazines and also writes two newspaper columns. He has received many awards for his service in the cause of human rights, including the Medal of Freedom, which is this country's highest civil honor!

"Roy Wilkins, you are a unique American whose contributions transcend the boundaries of both time and territory!"

THURGOOD MARSHALL

Thurgood Marshall, former director of the NAACP's Legal Defense and Education Fund and one of America's most successful lawyers, was the first black man to serve as a justice on the U.S. Circuit Court of Appeals, as the Solicitor-General, and as a justice of the United States' Supreme Court.

Illustrated by Don Perlin

OUR RIGHTS AND OUR LIBERTIES

THURGOOD MARSHALL WAS BORN IN BALTIMORE MARYLAND ON JULY 2, 1908. HE WAS A CAREFREE AND FUN LOVING YOUNGSTER BUT ALSO A BRILLIANT STUDENT. AFTER GRADUATION FROM LINCOLN UNIVERSITY, HE ENROLLED IN HOWARD UNIVERSITY'S LAW SCHOOL.

ONE OF HIS INSTRUCTORS CHARLES HOUSTON, WHO ALSO WAS AN ATTORNEY FOR THE NAACP SOON BECAME IMPRESSED BY THIS YOUNG MAN'S TALENTS. AFTER GRADUATING AT THE TOP OF HIS CLASS....

"THINK ABOUT WORKING WITH US AT THE *NAACP*, WE COULD USE *YOU*."

AFTER A FEW YEARS OF LAW PRACTICE, MARSHALL JOINED HOUSTON AT THE NAACP, WHERE, TOGETHER, THEY PLANNED A SERIES OF LEGAL ACTIONS WHICH LATER LED TO THE SUPREME COURTS RULING ON THE "SEPARATE BUT EQUAL" DECISION WHICH, SINCE 1896, HAD BEEN A BARRIER TO BLACK PEOPLE'S CHANCE FOR AN EDUCATION.

THE PAY WAS SHORT AND THE HOURS LONG, BUT MARSHALL ARGUED ALL TYPES OF CASES THAT INVOLVED BASIC RIGHTS AND COLOR DISCRIMINATION. HE HAD CONVICTIONS REVERSED WHEN CONFESSIONS WERE OBTAINED ILLEGALLY...

"THE RACK AND TORTURE CHAMBER MAY NOT BE SUBSTITUTED FOR THE WITNESS STAND!"

HE DEFENDED VICTIMS OF RACE RIOTS AND HIS LIFE WAS OFTEN IN DANGER, BUT HE CONTINUED....

SOON MARSHALL BECAME THE SPECIAL COUNSEL IN CHARGE OF ALL NAACP CASES.

"I WANT YOU TO SERVE AS DIRECTOR OF THE LEGAL DEFENSE AND EDUCATION FUND."

"IT HAS ALWAYS BEEN MY BELIEF THAT YOU CAN NEVER BE *TOO* PREPARED FOR A CASE SO..."

MONTHS WERE SPENT ON RESEARCH, PLANNING, REHEARSALS AND....

They were always ready for any "surprises" their opponents might have...

"MARSHALL'S DONE IT AGAIN, THANK THE LORD!"

In many states black teachers were paid much less than white male teachers, in some states their pay was less than half. Marshall and his staff traveled around the country, winning cases that provided equal salaries for black teachers. In winning these victories he won equal pay for white female teachers who were also discriminated against.

"MR. MARSHALL HELPED ALL OF US."

Black students were not allowed to attend many state colleges and universities because other "separate but equal" colleges were provided.... but Marshall proved them to be UNEQUAL.

Once admitted, some black students found they were segregated in the classrooms, libraries and cafeterias.... so Marshall went back to the Supreme Court.... and WON!

JAMES WELDON JOHNSON
1871-1938

FORMER SECRETARY OF THE N.A.A.C.P.

James Weldon Johnson is best known for writing the lyrics of "Lift Every Voice and Sing", sometimes called the "Negro National Anthem." But he was also famous for his work as a poet, writer, diplomat and former Secretary of the N.A.A.C.P.

Johnson was born on June 17, 1871 in Jacksonville, Florida, and educated at Atlanta and Columbia Universities. He served the public as a lawyer, school principal and U.S. Consul to Venezuela.

Over the years, he and his brother, J. Rosamond Johnson, who was a famous music composer, together wrote many popular songs and shows. Johnson also wrote several books of Poetry which are still very popular today and have been performed on the stage and television

In 1916, Johnson was appointed Field Secretary and Organizer of the N.A.A.C.P. and his work led to the organization of many branches in the South and West. For a short while, James Weldon Johnson was called to serve as Acting Secretary of the N.A.A.C.P., but later in 1920, he became the Secretary.

Under his wise and steady leadership, the N.A.A.C.P.'s branches increased from 67 to 372 by the time of his resignation.

W. E. B. DUBOIS
1868-1963

Educator, author, scholar editor and militant civil rights leader.

William E. B. DuBois was born in Massachusetts on February 23, 1868 and graduated from both Fisk and Harvard Universities. He also attended the University of Berlin and returned to Harvard for his Ph.D.

Dr. DuBois became a professor of Latin and Greek at the University of Pennsylvania and Wilberforce College and professor of Economics and History at Atlanta University. He also was the author of many scholarly books and social science studies on the living conditions of black Americans.

In 1905, Dr. DuBois was one of the founders of the Niagara Movement, which demanded an immediate end to racial segregation and discrimination, and in 1909, he was one of the founders of the N.A.A.C.P. He also founded and edited the N.A.A.C.P.'s magazine, "Crisis."

Throughout his life, he protested the injustices suffered daily by black Americans, but his activities went beyond America to Africa. He foresaw the end of colonialism and knew that one day Africa would have free black states. With the future in mind, he took part in six Pan-African Congresses held between 1900 and 1945.

When he died in 1963, at the age of 95, Dr. W.E.B. Dubois was a citizen of the new African republic of Ghana. In his last years, he was at work on an encyclopedia of African art, history and culture.

GOLDEN LEGACY
ILLUSTRATED HISTORY SERIES

1. Toussaint L'Overture
2. Harriet Tubman
3. Crispus Attucks
4. Benjamin Banneker
5. Matthew Henson
6. Alexander Dumas
7. Frederick Douglass Part I
8. Frederick Douglass Part II
9. Robert Smalls
10. Joseph Cinque
11. White, Wilkins & Marshall
12. Black Cowboys
13. Dr. Martin Luther King
14. Alexander Pushkin
15. Ancient African Kingdoms
16. Black Inventors

"We hope you will read, enjoy and benefit from our endeavors."

You may order GOLDEN LEGACY for your school, church, relatives, yourself-----or merely as a gift for a friend!

GOLDEN LEGACY is available in soft or hard cover editions.

Send Orders To: Fitzgerald Pub. Co., Inc.
442 Wolf Hill Road
Dix Hills, N.Y. 11746

Payment must accompany all orders in check or money order.

Softcover Edition: $24.00   Hardcover Edition: $45.00

GOLDEN LEGACY
ILLUSTRATED HISTORY MAGAZINE

BLACK COWBOYS

ol. 12

© FITZGERALD PUB. Co. Inc. 1972

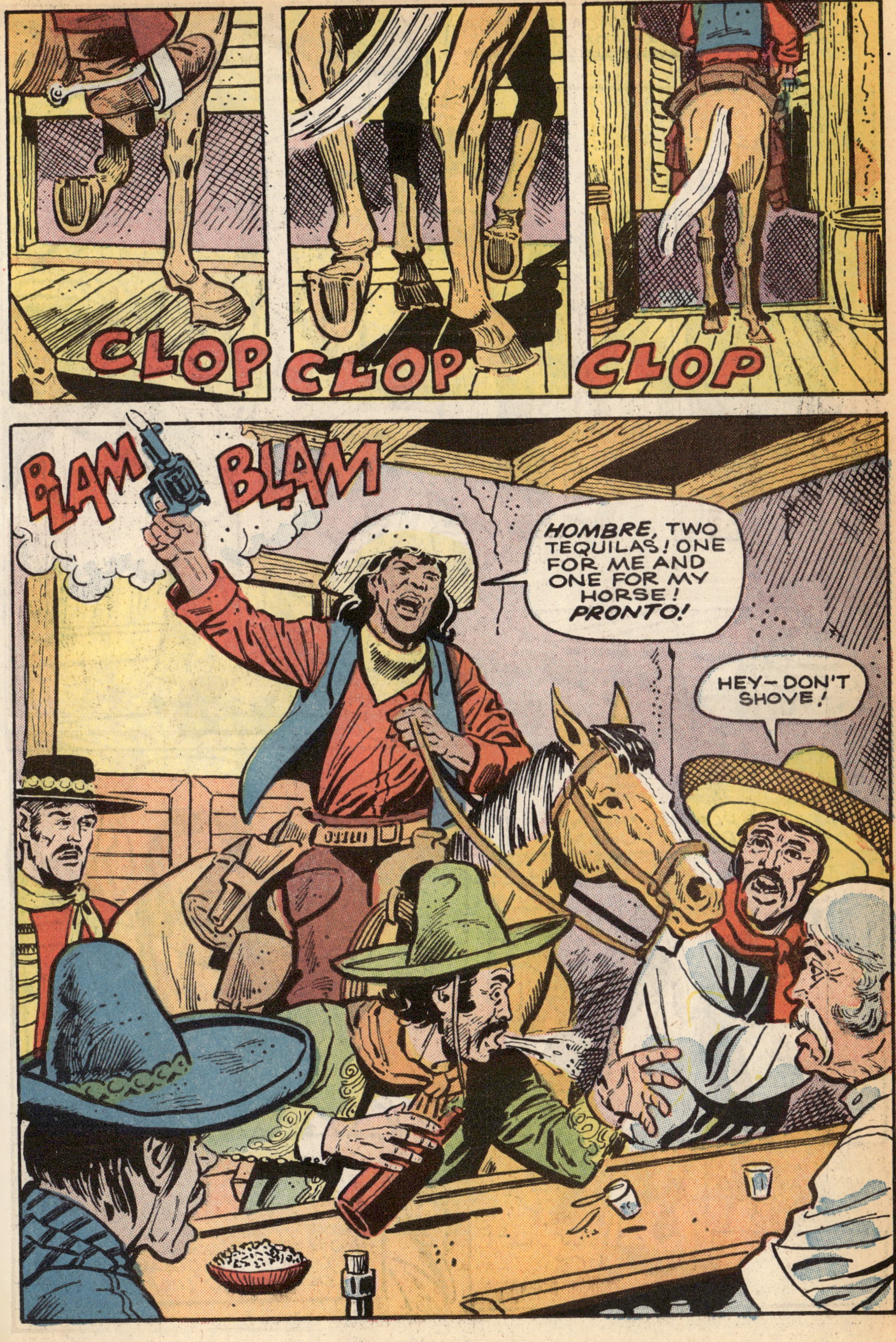

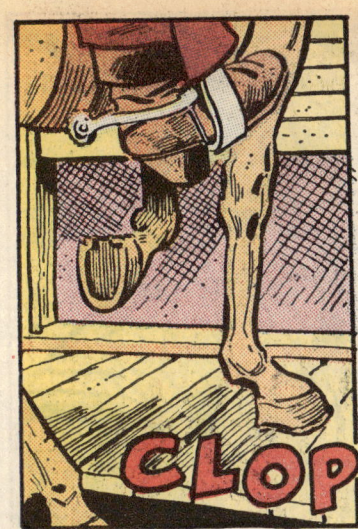  

THE MEXICANS OVERCAME THEIR SURPRISE AND WENT FOR THEIR GUNS! NAT THOUGHT HE'D BETTER LEAVE!

NAT LOVE PLAYED THE WAY HE LIVED, HARD AND ROUGH! SUCH MEN WERE NEEDED TO CONQUER THE WEST.

AT THE END OF HIS TRAIL DRIVING DAYS HE WROTE A BOOK CALLED, "THE LIFE AND ADVENTURES OF NAT LOVE; BETTER KNOWN IN THE CATTLE COUNTRY AS DEADWOOD DICK."

End

CHEROKEE BILL WAS TAKEN TO FORT SMITH, ARKANSAS, WHERE HE WAS TRIED, CONVICTED AND SENTENCED TO DEATH BY JUDGE PARKER, THE WEST'S MOST FAMOUS HANGING JUDGE! WHILE AWAITING EXECUTION HE TRIED TO ESCAPE....

....AFTER SHOOTING THE HEAD JAILER, CHEROKEE WAS DISARMED!

CHEROKEE BILL WAS AGAIN BROUGHT BEFORE JUDGE PARKER....

IT IS TOO BAD YOU CAN ONLY BE HUNG ONCE!

WHEN ASKED IF HE HAD ANY LAST WORDS, HE SAID, "I'M HERE TO DIE, NOT MAKE A SPEECH."
THUS ON MARCH 17, 1896, AT THE AGE OF TWENTY, CRAWFORD GOLDSBY, ALIAS CHEROKEE BILL MET HIS FATE.

HE PUT ALL OF HIS SKILL TO USE IN PREVENTING THE FRIGHTENED STEER FROM INJURING THE SPECTATORS! THEN WILL ROGERS CAME TO HELP.

TOGETHER THEY GOT THE STEER BACK INTO THE ARENA! THE DELIGHTED AUDIENCE GAVE THEM A STANDING OVATION!

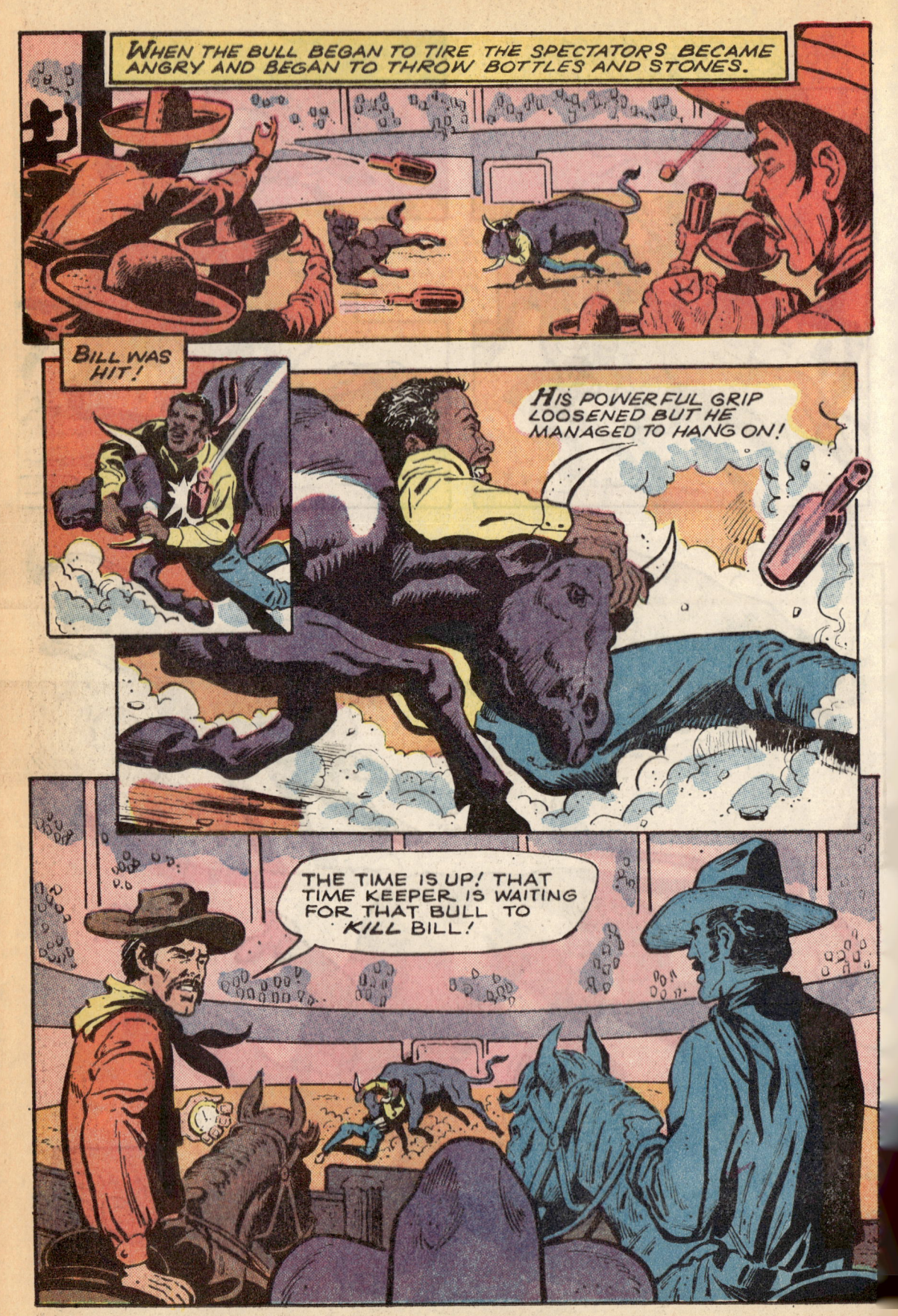

YAHOO YIPPEE

THE 101 BOYS WENT INTO ACTION!

"COME ON BILL, GET OFF THAT CRITTER!"

AMID JEERS AND CATCALLS BILL PAID HIS RESPECTS TO THE PRESIDENT AND LED HIS WOUNDED HORSE OUT OF THE ARENA....

THE CROWD THAT HAD COME TO SEE THE DEATH OF THE COWBOY WHO DARED WRESTLE A FIGHTING BULL BAREHANDED, FELT CHEATED AND THEY RIOTED!

Willis Peoples

WILLIS PEOPLES WAS ONE OF THE WEST'S FEW BLACK RANCHERS. THIS IS THE STORY OF HOW HE SOLVED A PROBLEM THAT WOULD HAVE RUINED MANY OF THE CATTLEMEN IN THE CIMARRON VALLEY!

THE RANCHERS' HERDS WERE BEING DESTROYED BY A LARGE KILLER WOLF!

THE RANCHERS NAMED HIM "TWO TOES" BECAUSE HE HAD LOST PART OF ONE PAW IN A TRAP.

THE AMOUNT OF CATTLE THE RANCHERS LOST TRIPLED WHEN "TWO TOES" WAS JOINED BY A FEROCIOUS SHE-WOLF... THE CATTLEMEN OFFERED A REWARD...

...BUT ALL ATTEMPTS FAILED. THE REWARD WAS INCREASED AND PROFESSIONAL HUNTERS WERE BROUGHT IN! BUT THEY WERE ALSO UNSUCCESSFUL.

I LOST NINE COWS LAST NIGHT!

ANYONE GOT ANY IDEAS? WE CAN'T SURVIVE THIS MUCH LONGER!

RIFLE IN HAND, WILLIS PEOPLES ADVANCED CAUTIOUSLY UNTIL....

THE CIMARRON VALLEY HERDS WERE NOW SAFE FROM "TWO TOES"....

SO WILLIS PEOPLES COLLECTED HIS REWARD AND RETURNED TO HIS RANCH.

THE STORY OF WILLIS PEOPLES IS THE STORY OF THE WEST; STRONG MEN CARVING A NEW CIVILIZATION FROM A WILDERNESS!

End

JAMES P. BECKWOURTH

BECKWOURTH WAS ONE OF A GROUP OF PIONEER TRADERS AND TRAPPERS, KNOWN AS "MOUNTAIN MEN." HE ALSO OWNED AND OPERATED A RANCH AND A GENERAL STORE.

BECKWOURTH DISCOVERED A PASS THROUGH THE SIERRA NEVADA MOUNTAINS, TO CALIFORNIA. THIS PASS IS KNOWN TODAY AS "BECKWOURTH PASS."

HE DIED AT THE AGE OF 69, WHILE ON A PEACE MISSION TO THE CROW INDIANS.

JESSE STAHL

JESSE STAHL WAS A RODEO STAR AT SAME TIME AS BILL PICKETT. JESSE WON ENOUGH BULLDOGGING AND BULL RIDING CONTESTS TO BE CALLED THE WORLD'S BEST BRONCO RIDER!

BOB LEMMONS

BOB LEMMONS WAS A "MUSTANGER." HE CAUGHT HERDS OF WILD HORSES FOR RESALE.

LEMMONS WAS UNUSUAL IN THAT HE HAD HIS OWN METHOD AND WORKED ALONE. HE SPENT WEEKS WITH A HERD UNTIL THEY ACCEPTED HIM AS ONE OF THEM. HE THEN BECAME THEIR LEADER AND LED THEM INTO THE CORRAL.

BARNEY FORD

FORD OWNED AND OPERATED THE "INTER-OCEAN HOTEL," IN DENVER, COLO. THIS WAS THE MOST ELEGANT AND FAMOUS HOTEL BETWEEN ST. LOUIS AND SAN FRANCISCO. IT WAS HOST TO MILLIONAIRES, STATESMEN AND PRESIDENTS. THE REPUTATION OF FORD'S HOTEL WAS SO GREAT THAT HE WAS ASKED TO BUILD ANOTHER ONE IN CHEYENNE, WYOMING!

FORD WAS ALSO VERY ACTIVE IN THE POLITICS OF COLORADO, AND HELPED IT ATTAIN STATEHOOD.

GOLDEN LEGACY
ILLUSTRATED HISTORY SERIES

1. Toussaint L'Overture
2. Harriet Tubman
3. Crispus Attucks
4. Benjamin Banneker
5. Matthew Henson
6. Alexander Dumas
7. Frederick Douglass Part I
8. Frederick Douglass Part II
9. Robert Smalls
10. Joseph Cinque
11. White, Wilkins & Marshall
12. Black Cowboys
13. Dr. Martin Luther King
14. Alexander Pushkin
15. Ancient African Kingdoms
16. Black Inventors

"We hope you will read, enjoy and benefit from our endeavors."

You may order GOLDEN LEGACY for your school, church, relatives, yourself----or merely as a gift for a friend!

GOLDEN LEGACY is available in soft or hard cover editions.

Send Orders To: Fitzgerald Pub. Co., Inc.
442 Wolf Hill Road
Dix Hills, N.Y. 11746

Payment must accompany all orders in check or money order.

Softcover Edition: $24.00   Hardcover Edition: $45.00

GOLDEN LEGACY
ILLUSTRATED HISTORY MAGAZINE

THE LIFE OF
MARTIN LUTHER KING JR.

© FITZGERALD PUB. Co. Inc. 1972

Dr. Martin Luther King Jr.

Few men in world history have brought as much pride and progress to so many, as did Martin Luther King, Jr. The seeds of greatness were planted in him early by his father, the Rev. Martin Luther King Sr.

As one of ten children, M.L. King, Sr. worked very hard on a run-down farm. The entire family's work as sharecroppers hardly provided them enough to live on and King, Sr. could go to school only three months a year, until he was fifteen.

AFTER GRADUATION FROM CROZER, REV. KING WENT TO BOSTON UNIVERSITY. WHILE THERE, HE MET AND COURTED CORETTA SCOTT...

THEY WERE MARRIED BY REV. KING SR. ON JUNE 18, 1953, IN THE GARDEN OF THE BRIDE'S FAMILY IN MARION, ALABAMA.

DR. KING COULD HAVE HAD A CHURCH IN THE NORTH, BUT HE CHOSE TO RETURN TO THE SOUTH, CLOSER TO THE PROBLEMS OF HIS PEOPLE.

THE YOUNG MINISTER BEGAN PREACHING SUCH THINGS AS PRIDE AND LOVE OF ALL MANKIND...

"HOLD YOUR HEADS UP HIGH AND LOVE EVEN THOSE WHO OPPRESS US."

BUT EVEN THEN DR. KING DID NOT SHOW ANGER...

"TAKE YOUR WEAPONS HOME! HE WHO LIVES BY THE SWORD SHALL PERISH BY THE SWORD! MEET HATE WITH LOVE...."

THE BUS BOYCOTT CONTINUED! DR. KING AND OTHER LEADERS WERE ARRESTED ON FALSE CHARGES, AND SENTENCED TO MORE THAN A YEAR AT HARD LABOR! THEY WERE RELEASED WHILE APPEALING THE CONVICTION AND THEY CONTINUED THE BOYCOTT...

MONTGOMERY'S BUS SEGREGATION LAWS WERE RULED ILLEGAL AND THE SUPREME COURT UPHELD THAT RULING... AFTER BOYCOTTING FOR 381 DAYS, DR. KING AND HIS FOLLOWERS WON A GREAT VICTORY OVER INJUSTICE!

BUT VIOLENCE CAME WITH VICTORY...BLACK CHURCHES AND HOMES WERE ATTACKED AND BOMBED!

DR. KING'S LEADERSHIP HAD SPREAD THROUGHOUT THE SOUTH AND HE WAS ELECTED PRESIDENT OF THE NEWLY FORMED SOUTHERN CHRISTIAN LEADERSHIP CONFERENCE.

BLACK AND WHITE COLLEGE STUDENTS FROM THE NORTH AND SOUTH JOINED TOGETHER IN A SERIES OF "SIT-INS" AT LUNCH COUNTERS AND OTHER BUSINESSES THAT WOULD NOT SERVE BLACKS...

WHITE ONLY

THEY'D BETTER *MOVE* OUT OF HERE *NOW!*

...AND WERE OFTEN ATTACKED, INJURED AND JAILED, BUT CONTINUED THEIR NON-VIOLENT "SIT-INS" AT LUNCH COUNTERS, THEATERS, PARKS, BEACHES AND WHITE CHURCHES.

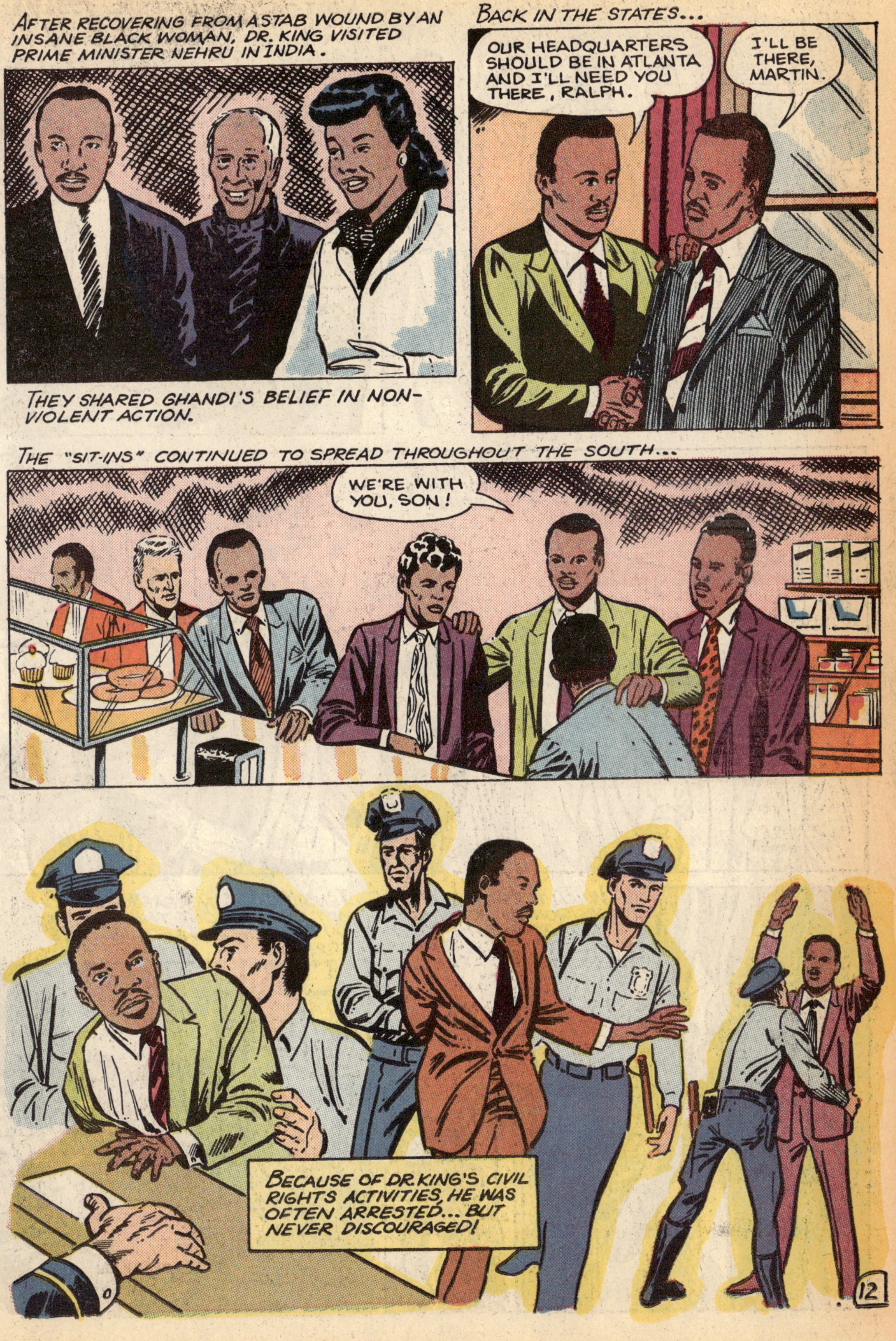

...AND AFTER EACH RELEASE FROM JAIL, DR. KING RETURNED TO LEAD THE STRUGGLE FOR RIGHTS AND JUSTICE.

MOST OF THE SOUTH BEGAN TO MAKE SMALL CHANGES, BUT SOME CITIES CONTINUED TO ENFORCE STRICT SEGREGATION.

"BIRMINGHAM IS NEXT!"

BIRMINGHAM WAS UNWILLING TO CHANGE AND ITS DIRECTOR OF PUBLIC SAFETY, BULL CONNOR, WAS WELL KNOWN FOR "KEEPING BLACKS IN THEIR PLACE"!

FREEDOM NOW!

EQUAL RIGHTS

WHEN THEY WON A COURT DECISION PERMITTING THEM TO USE THE TOWN PARKS, BIRMINGHAM CLOSED THE PARKS...

TENSION WAS INCREASING... GROUPS MET THROUGHOUT THE CITY TO RAISE BAIL MONEY FOR FUTURE ARRESTS.

Birmingham outlawed civil rights demonstrations, but Dr. King refused to obey unjust laws, even if it meant going to jail.

DEEP IN MY HEART I DO BELIEVE...

Dr. King and Rev. Abernathy were arrested and no one was allowed to see or talk to them.

After two days Mrs. King became worried and called the White House. President Kennedy investigated and called...

HE'S SAFE, I'VE SENT THE F.B.I. IN!

THANK YOU MISTER PRESIDENT!

Dr. King writes ministers who criticized him for breaking the law...

AN UNJUST LAW IS A CODE THAT A MAJORITY COMPELS A MINORITY GROUP TO OBEY, BUT DOES NOT MAKE BINDING ON ITSELF... WE SHOULD NEVER FORGET THAT EVERYTHING HITLER DID IN GERMANY WAS 'LEGAL' AND EVERYTHING THE HUNGARIAN FREEDOM FIGHTERS DID IN HUNGARY WAS 'ILLEGAL'...

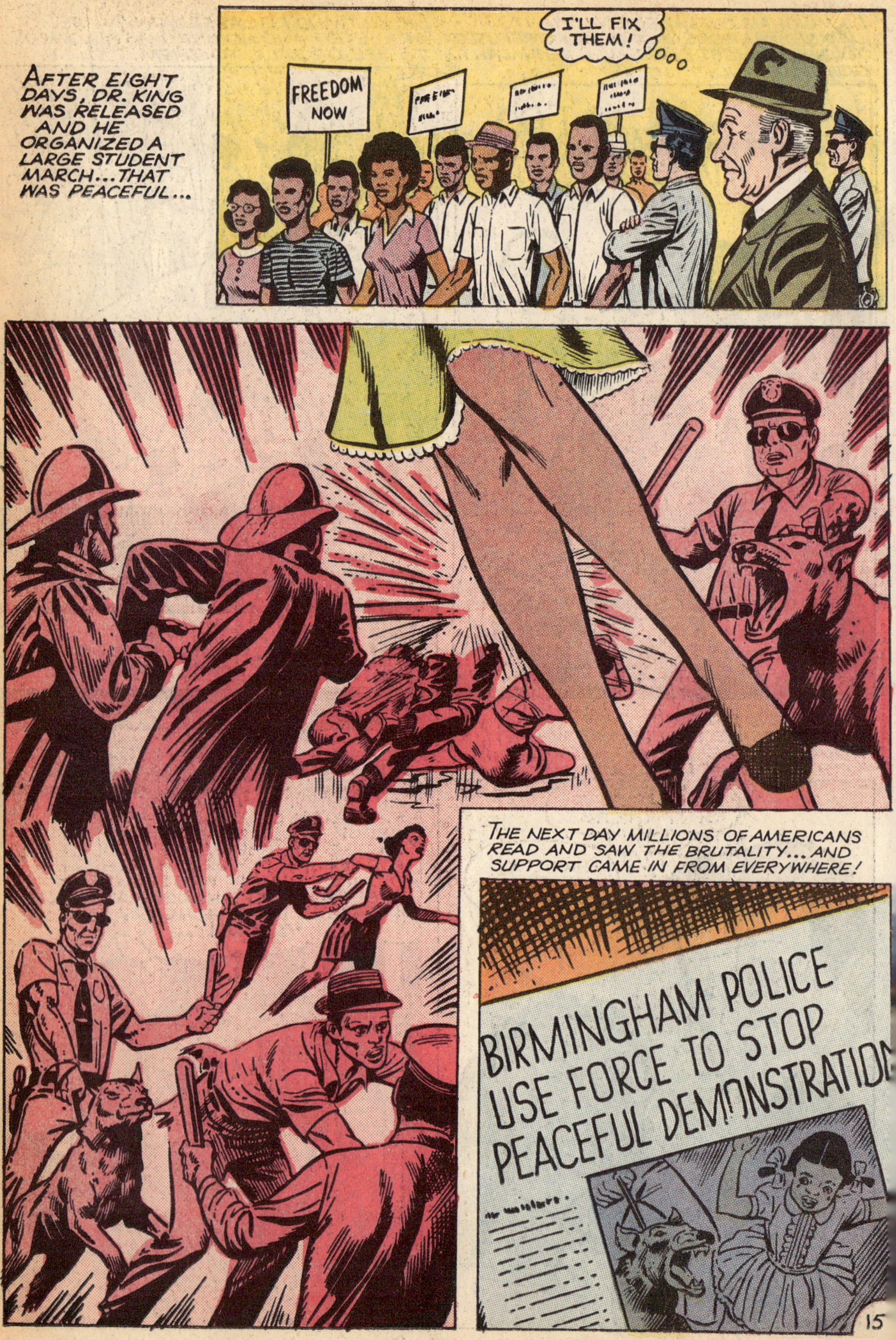

BUT ON SEPT. 15, 1963, THE VIOLENCE AND HATRED CONTINUED....

THE NATION WAS SHAKEN WHEN A BIRMINGHAM CHURCH WAS BOMBED—FOUR SUNDAY SCHOOL GIRLS WERE KILLED...AND MANY INJURED!

SOON AFTER, THE WORLD SHOOK WHEN PRESIDENT KENNEDY WAS MURDERED!

WE WERE ALL INVOLVED IN THE DEATH OF JOHN F. KENNEDY. WE *TOLERATED* HATE... WE *TOLERATED* VIOLENCE IN ALL WALKS OF LIFE... AND *TOLERATED* THE IDEA THAT A MAN'S LIFE WAS SACRED ONLY IF WE AGREED WITH HIS VIEWS.

True civil rights meant voting rights. Dr. King chose St. Augustine, Florida, for a peaceful protest for the right of black people to register as voters.

The police did not stop the marchers, nor did they stop their attackers... but Dr. King was arrested.

After his release he was honored by Yale University.

The Civil Rights Act of 1964 was a giant step forward in assisting black citizens to vote and use public accomodations and facilities.

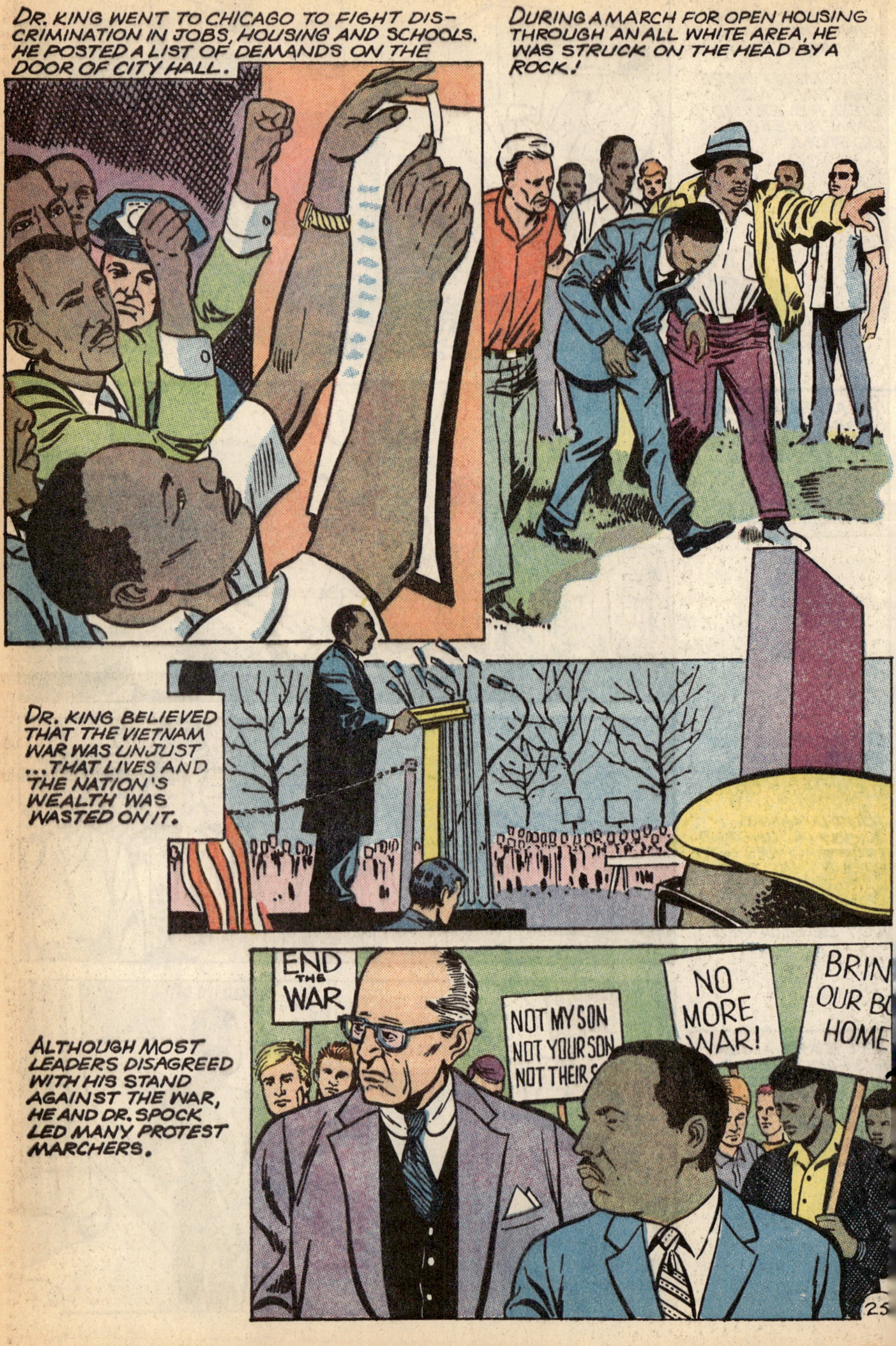

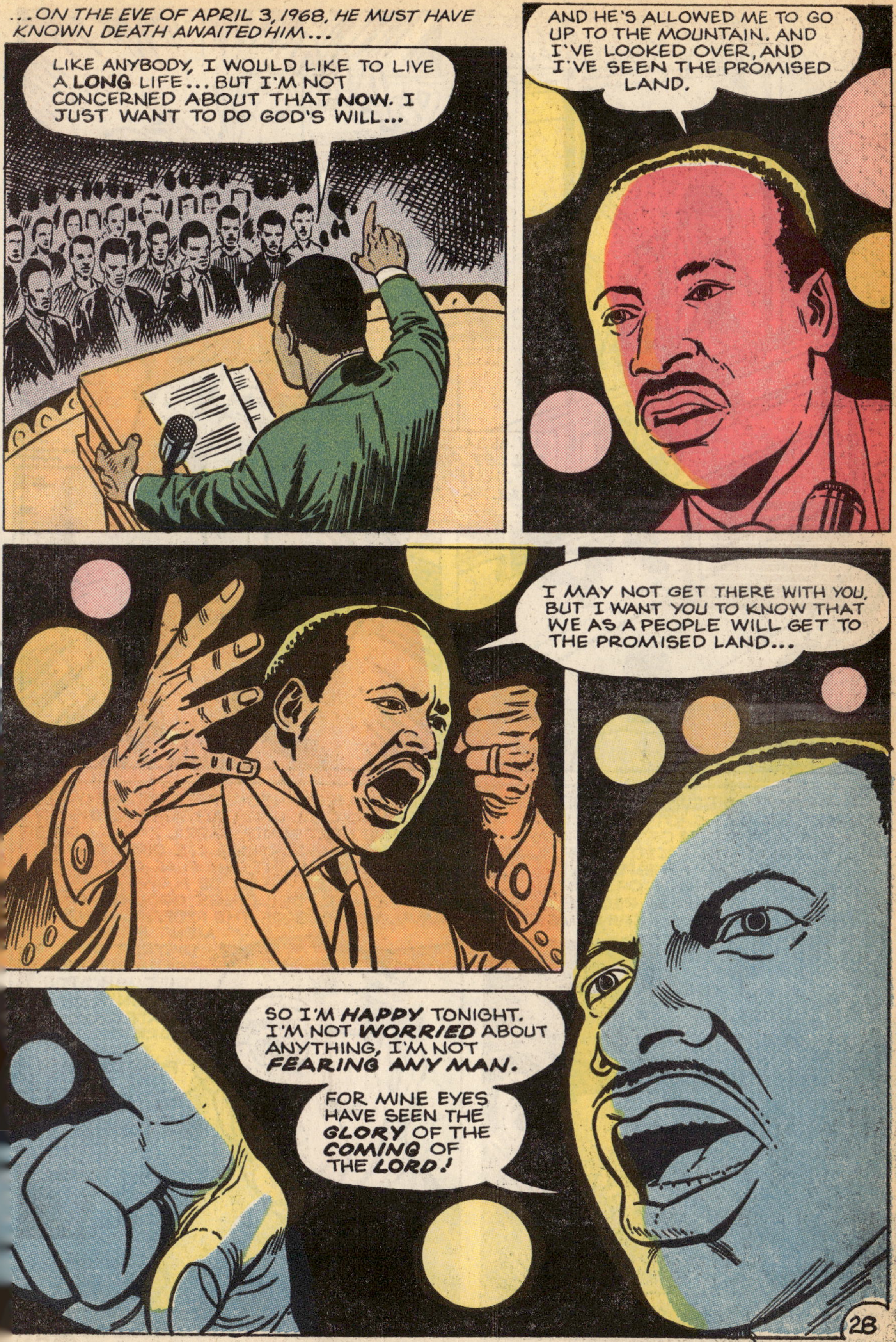

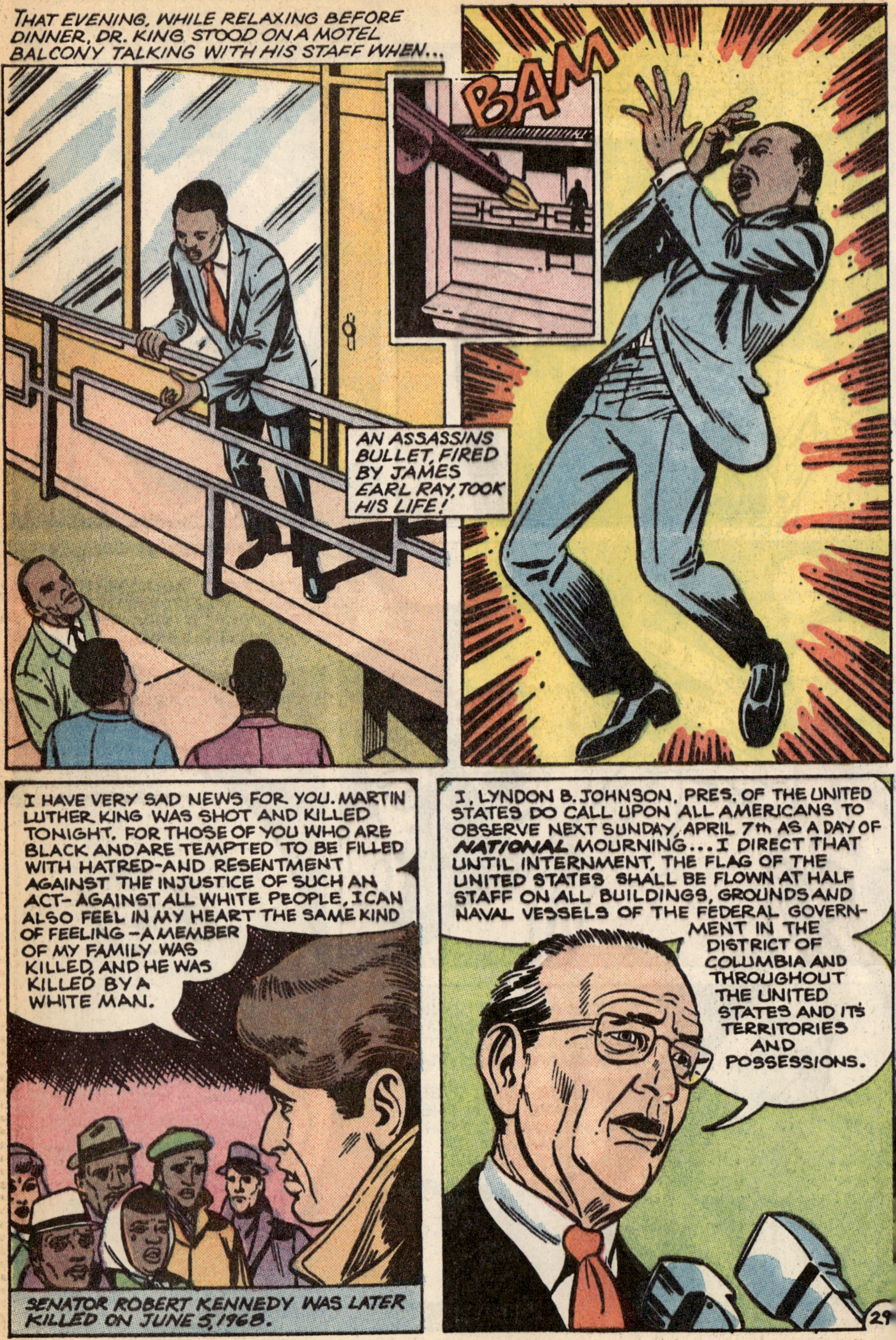

GOLDEN LEGACY
ILLUSTRATED HISTORY SERIES

1. Toussaint L'Overture
2. Harriet Tubman
3. Crispus Attucks
4. Benjamin Banneker
5. Matthew Henson
6. Alexander Dumas
7. Frederick Douglass Part I
8. Frederick Douglass Part II
9. Robert Smalls
10. Joseph Cinque
11. White, Wilkins & Marshall
12. Black Cowboys
13. Dr. Martin Luther King
14. Alexander Pushkin
15. Ancient African Kingdoms
16. Black Inventors

"We hope you will read, enjoy and benefit from our endeavors."

You may order GOLDEN LEGACY for your school, church, relatives, yourself-----or merely as a gift for a friend!

GOLDEN LEGACY is available in soft or hard cover editions.

Send Orders To: Fitzgerald Pub. Co., Inc.
442 Wolf Hill Road
Dix Hills, N.Y. 11746

Payment must accompany all orders in check or money order.

Softcover Edition: $24.00   Hardcover Edition: $45.00

GOLDEN LEGACY
ILLUSTRATED HISTORY MAGAZINE

THE LIFE OF ALEXANDER PUSHKIN

Vol. 14

© FITZGERALD PUB. Co. Inc. 1972

RUSSIA'S GREATEST AND MOST BELOVED POET! RUSSIANS READ AND ENJOY HIS POETRY AS MUCH TODAY, AS THEY DID WHEN HE WAS A LIVING HERO! SOME OF THE GREATEST OF RUSSIAN WRITERS CALLED THEMSELVES "HIS PUPILS". AMONG THEM WERE DOSTOEVSKI ✻ AND TURGENEV ✻

PUSHKIN ✻ POOSH-KIN   TURGENEV ✻ TOOR-GAIN-YEF   DOSTOEVSKI ✻ DAS-TA-YEF-SKI

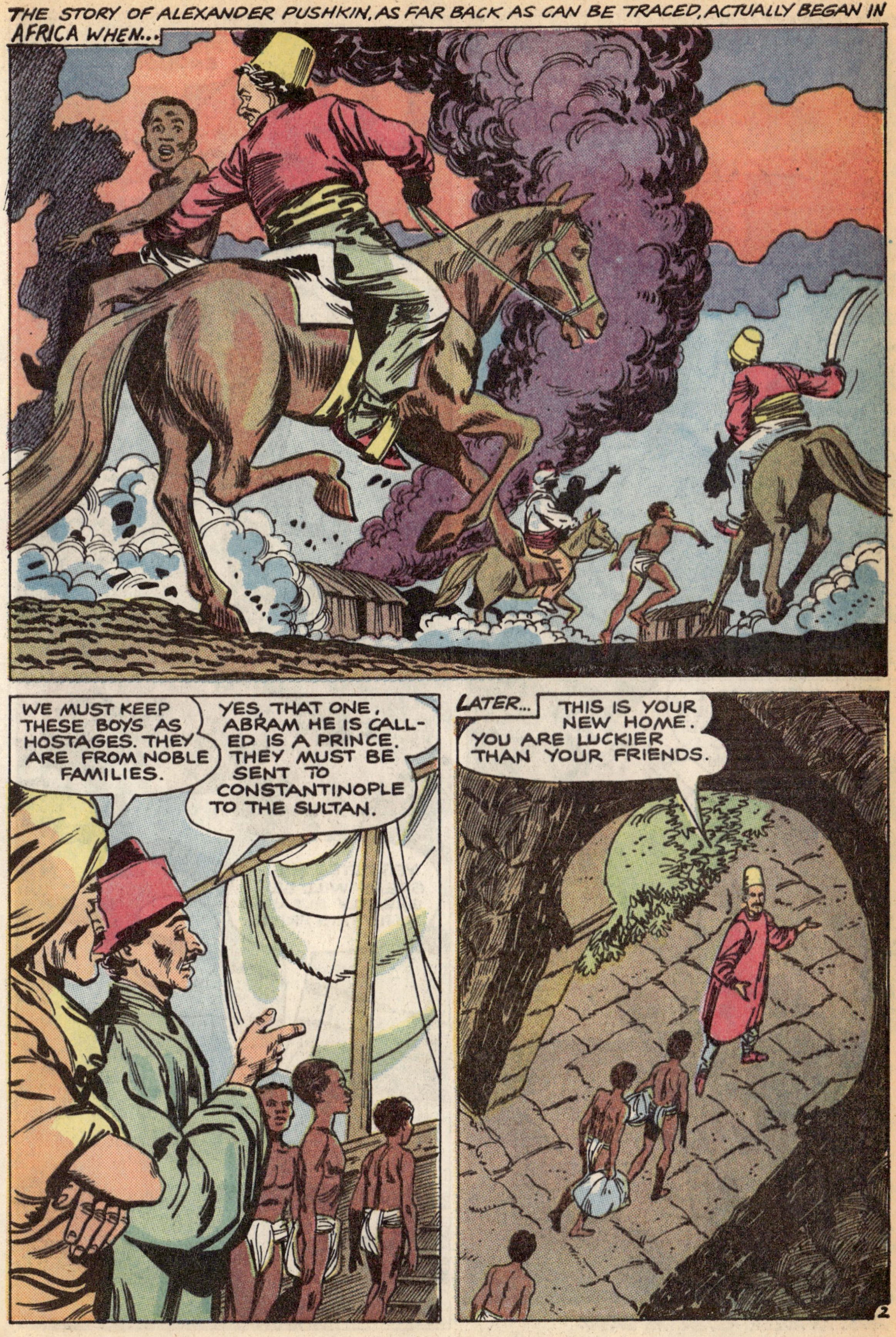

ONE YEAR PASSED. THEN... GATHER YOUR BELONGINGS QUIETLY AND COME WITH ME.

...BUT, WHERE ARE WE GOING?

SHHHH, YOU'LL FIND OUT SOON ENOUGH.

THIS IS THE LAD I WISH, HERE IS YOUR GOLD. WE MUST BE ON OUR WAY TO THE TSAR*.

*RUSSIAN RULER-PETER THE GREAT.

YES, PETER THE GREAT WILL BE GREATLY PLEASED WITH THIS PRIZE.

AND MUCH LATER...
FOR YOU WE WILL ADOPT THE FAMILY NAME OF HANNIBAL SINCE BOTH OF YOU ARE FROM AFRICA.

AND YOU MUST CONTINUE YOUR STUDIES. YOU WILL GO TO PARIS TO STUDY ENGINEERING AND MATH.

ABRAM LEARNED WELL. AFTER GRADUATING FROM SCHOOL HE SERVED IN A WAR IN SPAIN AND UPON HIS RETURN TO RUSSIA...

YOU, ABRAM, WILL BE AN ENGINEER IN MY ARMY AND TEACH MATH TO MY SON.

BUT AFTER PETER THE GREAT'S DEATH.

PETER HAS GIVEN HIM TOO MANY HONORS. WE WILL FIX THAT. MAKE OUT ORDERS FOR SOME SMALL JOB FOR HIM IN SIBERIA* AND SEE TO IT THAT HE STAYS THERE.

*FREEZING COLD PART OF RUSSIA.

ANYONE COULD HAVE SEEN TO THIS SMALL JOB. WHY WAS I PICKED FOR THIS?

ABRAM WAS GIVEN SMALLER AND SMALLER JOBS AND PUSHED FURTHER INTO SIBERIA UNTIL...

WHAT DO YOU MEAN I'M UNDER ARREST? WHAT ARE THE CHARGES?

THE CHARGES WILL BE MADE KNOWN TO YOU WHEN WE REACH MOSCOW.

MEANWHILE THE RULER WAS REPLACED BY EMPRESS ANNA IVANOVA AND... AND THIS ABRAM DID.

THE ONLY CRIME YOU WERE GUILTY OF WAS THAT OF BEING LOVED BY PETER THE GREAT. UNDER MY RULE YOU WILL CONTINUE TO BUILD BRIDGES AND FORTRESSES AS THE GREAT ENGINEER YOU ARE.

TO ADD TO YOUR WELL DESERVED COLLECTION OF MEDALS AND AWARDS WE PROMOTE YOU TO ENGINEER GENERAL.

AND HE WAS OFTEN HONORED...

PUSHKIN'S GRANDFATHER OSIP ABRAMOVICH BECAME A MAJOR IN THE ARTILLERY.

PUSHKIN'S MOTHER, DESCRIBED AS A BEAUTIFUL CREOLE, WAS THE ONLY SURVIVING CHILD OF OSIP. THIS COMPLETED THE AFRICAN HERITAGE OF WHICH PUSHKIN WAS SO PROUD AND CONTINUED TO RECALL AND TO REFER TO IN HIS WORKS.

PUSHKIN'S FATHER'S SIDE OF THE FAMILY COULD CLAIM SIX-HUNDRED YEARS OF NOBILITY, THEIR NAME WAS INCLUDED IN THE PEDIGREE BOOK OF IVAN THE TERRIBLE, THE FIRST TSAR OF RUSSIA.

THEY SERVED ON THE COUNCIL...

AS COURT OFFICIALS...

GOVERNORS OF PROVINCES...

AND AMBASSADORS...

PUSHKIN WAS EQUALLY PROUD OF HIS NOBLE RUSSIAN BACKGROUND.

PUSHKIN'S FATHER SERGEI LVOVICH* WAS A RETIRED ARMY OFFICER WHO SPENT MOST OF HIS TIME WITH POETRY AND PLAYS. HE LOVED HIGH SOCIETY.

PUSHKIN'S MOTHER NEDEZHDA OSIPOVNA* ALSO WAS A PART OF HIGH SOCIETY.

ALEXANDER PUSHKIN WAS BORN ON MAY 26, 1799 AND DURING HIS EARLY CHILDHOOD...

"ALEX READS BOOKS ALL NIGHT."

"I THINK HE WANTS TO BE A WRITER."

THE PUSHKIN LIBRARY WAS A FAVORITE MEETING PLACE FOR RUSSIA'S LEADING WRITERS.

PUSHKIN'S LOVE FOR POETRY WAS NO ACCIDENT AND HE BEGAN WRITING AT AN EARLY AGE.

HIS GENIUS, HOWEVER, WAS UNNOTICED BY HIS PARENTS AND HE WAS SHIPPED OFF TO A NEW SCHOOL * OPENED BY THE EMPEROR.

*THE LYCEUM

THE SCHOOL WAS AN EDUCATIONAL PARADISE AND PUSHKIN WAS ADMITTED AFTER PASSING THE TEST.

AT THE SAME TIME PUSHKIN WORKED FEVERISHLY ON HIS POEMS.

IN HIS BARE LITTLE ROOM

WHILE HE WAS SICK.

AT HIS MOTHER'S VILLAGE RECOVERING FROM AN ILLNESS.

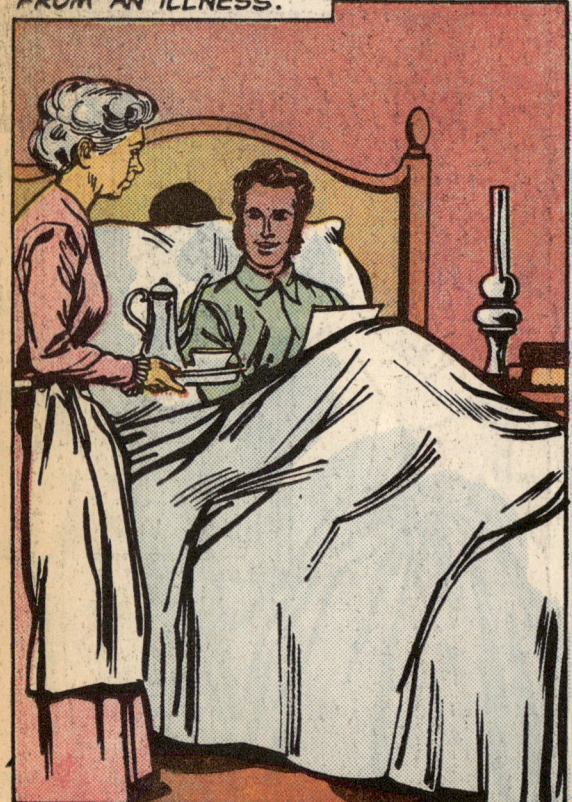

AND IN 1820 HE FINISHED THE POEM* THAT WAS TO LET RUSSIA KNOW THAT HER GREATEST POET AND ARRIVED.

AH, AT LAST MY FIRST MASTERPIECE IS FINISHED.

* RUSLAN AND LIUDMILA.

DUELS WERE QUITE COMMON IN PUSHKIN'S DAY AND HE WAS INVOLVED IN MANY.

PUSHKIN WAS AN EXPERT SHOT BUT NOT SERIOUS ENOUGH ABOUT HIS DUELS.

SHOOT, SHOOT.

THIS IS SILLY, LET'S GO DRINK TEA.

THOUGH PUSHKIN FOUGHT MANY DUELS, MOST OF THEM WERE AFFAIRS OF HONOR AND WERE BLOODLESS.

PUSHKIN MADE MANY FRIENDS AMONG THE YOUNG, RICH OFFICERS IN PETERSBURG'S HIGH SOCIETY.

THESE MEN LOVED HIM AND HE OFTEN RECITED HIS POEMS FOR THEM.

PUSHKIN WAS BECOMING A HERO TO THE PEOPLE OF RUSSIA.

"PUSHKIN IS THE GREATEST POET IN ALL OF RUSSIA."

AT THAT TIME A REVOLUTION WAS BREWING BECAUSE RUSSIA WAS RULED BY OLD AND RICH FAMILIES WHO STILL HELD SERFS*

*SLAVES

THE RICH FAMILIES HAD GREAT INFLUENCE ON THE TSAR ALEXANDER I.

IT WOULD BE NO GOOD TO FREE THE SERFS, THEY ARE NOT WORTHY.

BESIDES, YOU'LL GIVE YOUR POWER TO THE PEOPLE. IF THIS BECOMES THAT TYPE OF GOVERNMENT THEN YOU WILL LOSE ALL OF YOUR POWER.

THERE WILL BE NO MORE TALK OF POLITICAL CHANGE. THE TSAR HAS PLACED ME IN CHARGE OF HANDLING THESE AFFAIRS.

THE TSAR WAS ANGERED BY PUSHKIN'S FREEDOM POEMS AND DEMANDED PUNISHMENT.

"PUSHKIN MUST BE SEVERLY PUNISHED. EVEN SIBERIA IS TOO GOOD FOR AN OFFENSE AS SERIOUS AS THIS."

PUSHKIN'S WORRY TURNED INTO FEAR.

"YOU HAVE INFLUENCE WITH THE TSAR. I DON'T WANT TO GO TO SIBERIA."

AND...

"PUSHKIN IS YOUNG AND BOLD. HE MEANT NO HARM."

"HIS TALENT WILL BRING GLORY TO RUSSIA ONE DAY."

"PUSHKIN IS RUSSIA'S GREATEST WRITER. TO EXILE HIM WOULD AFFECT ALL OF RUSSIA."

"I WILL NOT EXILE HIM, BUT HE MUST PAY IN SOME WAY. IF HE PROMISES NOT TO WRITE ANYTHING AGAINST THE GOVERNMENT HE WILL BE SENT TO SOUTH RUSSIA FOR ONLY A SHORT TIME."

"Good-bye my friend, write many beautiful poems while you are away and take care."

"Take care my friends, I will see you soon."

During his banishment Pushkin began to realize how important a writer he was.

"My work is among the best in Russia. It is enjoyed and appreciated by many, yet I have little money. I must learn to make a living at my writing."

Pushkin was the first Russian to earn money for his poetry.

"We were able to get 5 rubles* a line for your poem. You have shown that a poet can live by his work."

*Russian coin equal to $1.10. The poem mentioned was 600 lines. Pushkin later earned as much as 10 rubles a line.

"Everyone in Moscow has read your work and think that you are the greatest poet in the world."

THE REVOLUTION WAS QUICKLY PUT DOWN AND ITS LEADERS WERE LATER ARRESTED AND HUNG.

...OR EXILED.

BECAUSE HE HAD WRITTEN MANY POEMS THAT INSPIRED THESE MEN AND BECAUSE THEY WERE KNOWN FRIENDS OF HIS, PUSHKIN BEGAN TO FEAR FOR HIS SAFETY AGAIN.

ON SEPTEMBER 3RD, 1826.

"PUSHKIN, PUSHKIN, THE TZAR WISHES TO SEE YOU AT ONCE. YOU MUST RETURN TO MOSCOW."

PUSHKIN HURRIEDLY PREPARED AND BEGAN HIS JOURNEY.

HE COVERED THE 500 MILES TO MOSCOW IN THE UNBELIEVABLE TIME OF FOUR DAYS.

AS SOON AS HE REACHED MOSCOW...

ALEXANDER PUSHKIN HAS ARRIVED, SIRE.

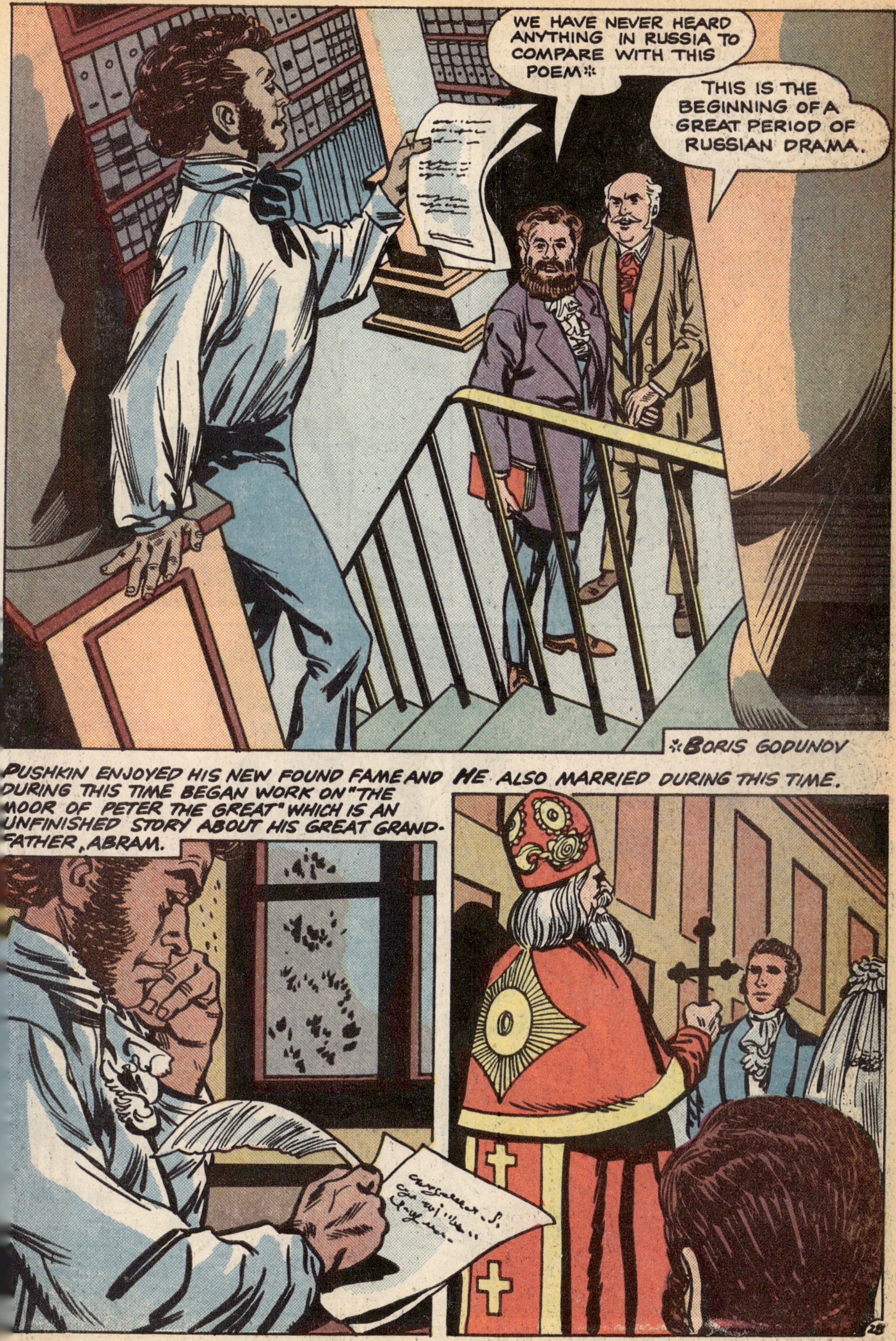

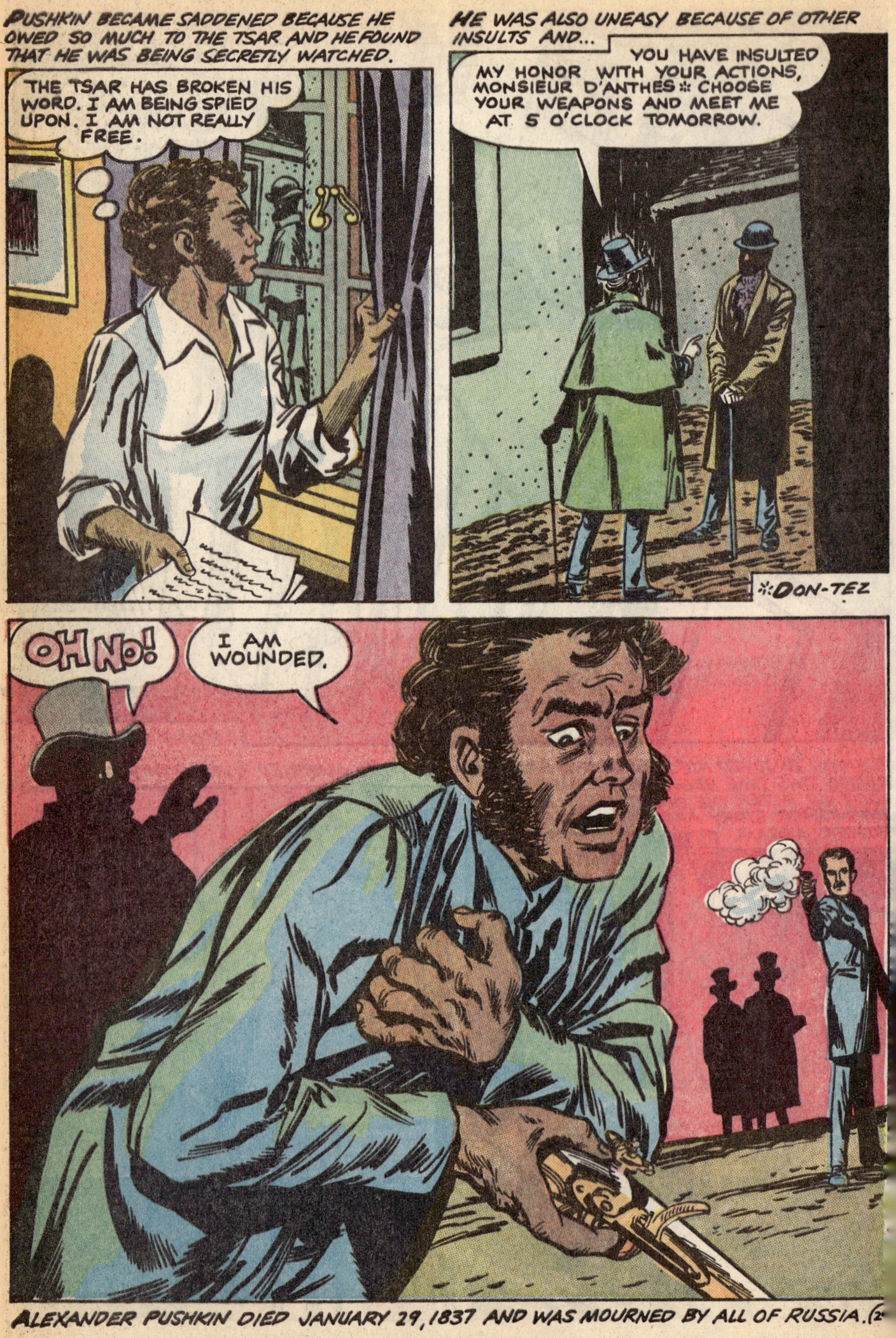

PUSHKIN POSSESSED A BRILLIANT MIND AND WAS ENDOWED WITH A POETIC TALENT WHICH RUSSIA HAS NOT KNOWN SINCE. TO HIS MEMORY THERE IS A STATUE OF PUSHKIN IN MOSCOW.

THE PUSHKIN THEATRE IN ST. PETERSBURG.

AND PUSHKIN, A CITY NEAR LENINGRAD.

PUSHKIN'S WORK IS NOT WIDELY KNOWN IN AMERICA BECAUSE IT IS DIFFICULT TO TRANSLATE AND RETAIN ALL OF ITS BEAUTY. IT WILL TAKE ANOTHER PUSHKIN TO DO THIS FOR US.

GOLDEN LEGACY
ILLUSTRATED HISTORY SERIES

1. Toussaint L'Overture
2. Harriet Tubman
3. Crispus Attucks
4. Benjamin Banneker
5. Matthew Henson
6. Alexander Dumas
7. Frederick Douglass Part I
8. Frederick Douglass Part II
9. Robert Smalls
10. Joseph Cinque
11. White, Wilkins & Marshall
12. Black Cowboys
13. Dr. Martin Luther King
14. Alexander Pushkin
15. Ancient African Kingdoms
16. Black Inventors

"We hope you will read, enjoy and benefit from our endeavors."

You may order GOLDEN LEGACY for your school, church, relatives, yourself------or merely as a gift for a friend!

GOLDEN LEGACY is available in soft or hard cover editions.

Send Orders To: Fitzgerald Pub. Co., Inc.
                 442 Wolf Hill Road
                 Dix Hills, N.Y. 11746

Payment must accompany all orders in check or money order.

Softcover Edition: $24.00   Hardcover Edition: $45.00

GOLDEN LEGACY
ILLUSTRATED HISTORY MAGAZINE

ANCIENT AFRICAN KINGDOMS

Vol. 15

© FITZGERALD PUB. Co. Inc. 1972

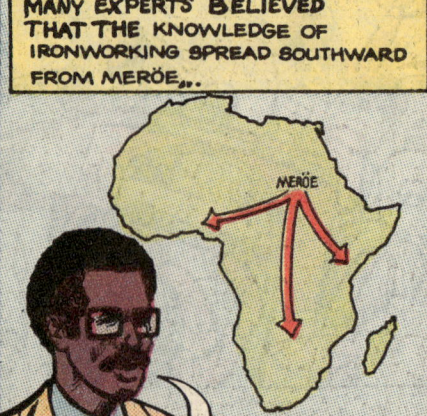

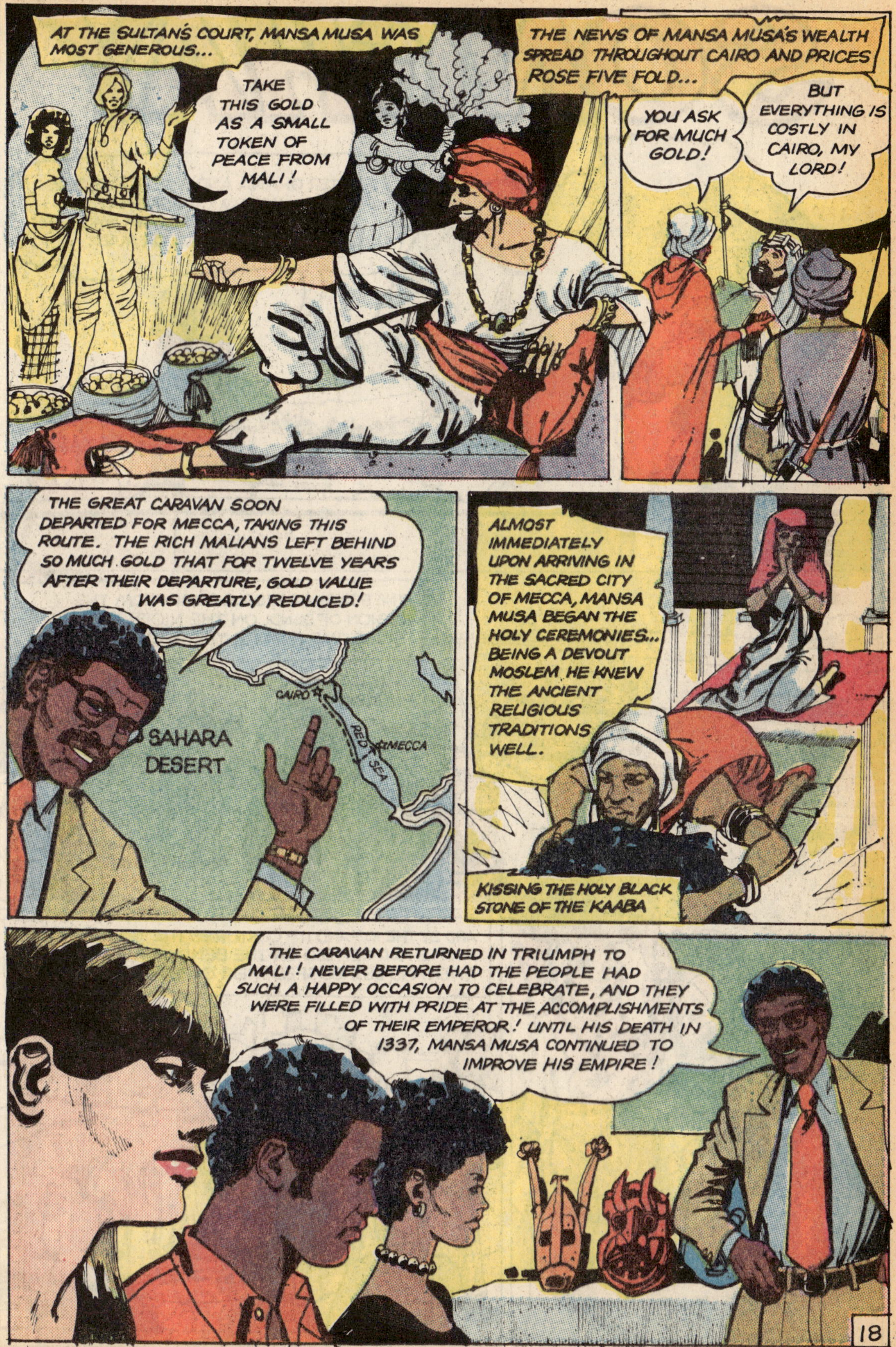

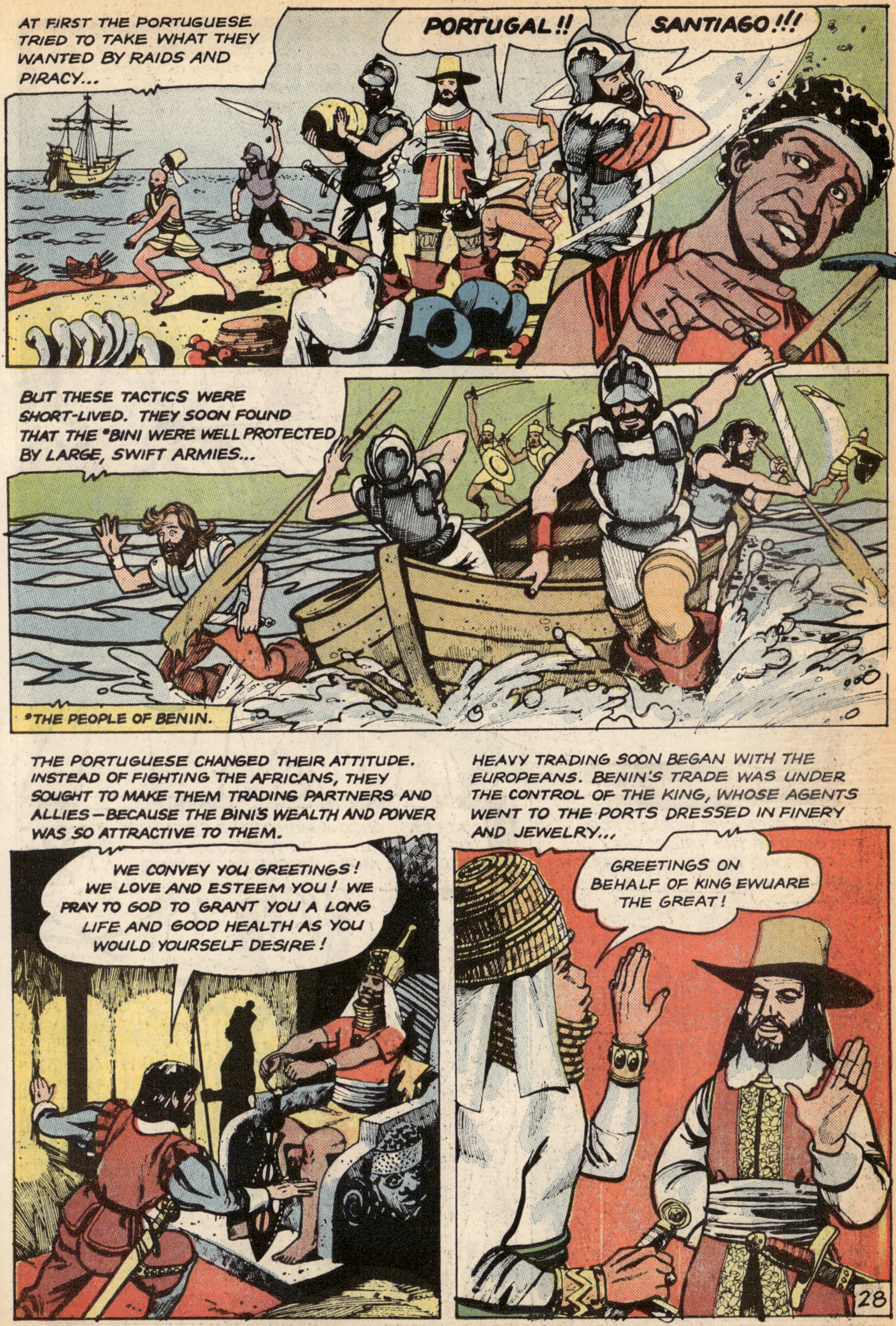

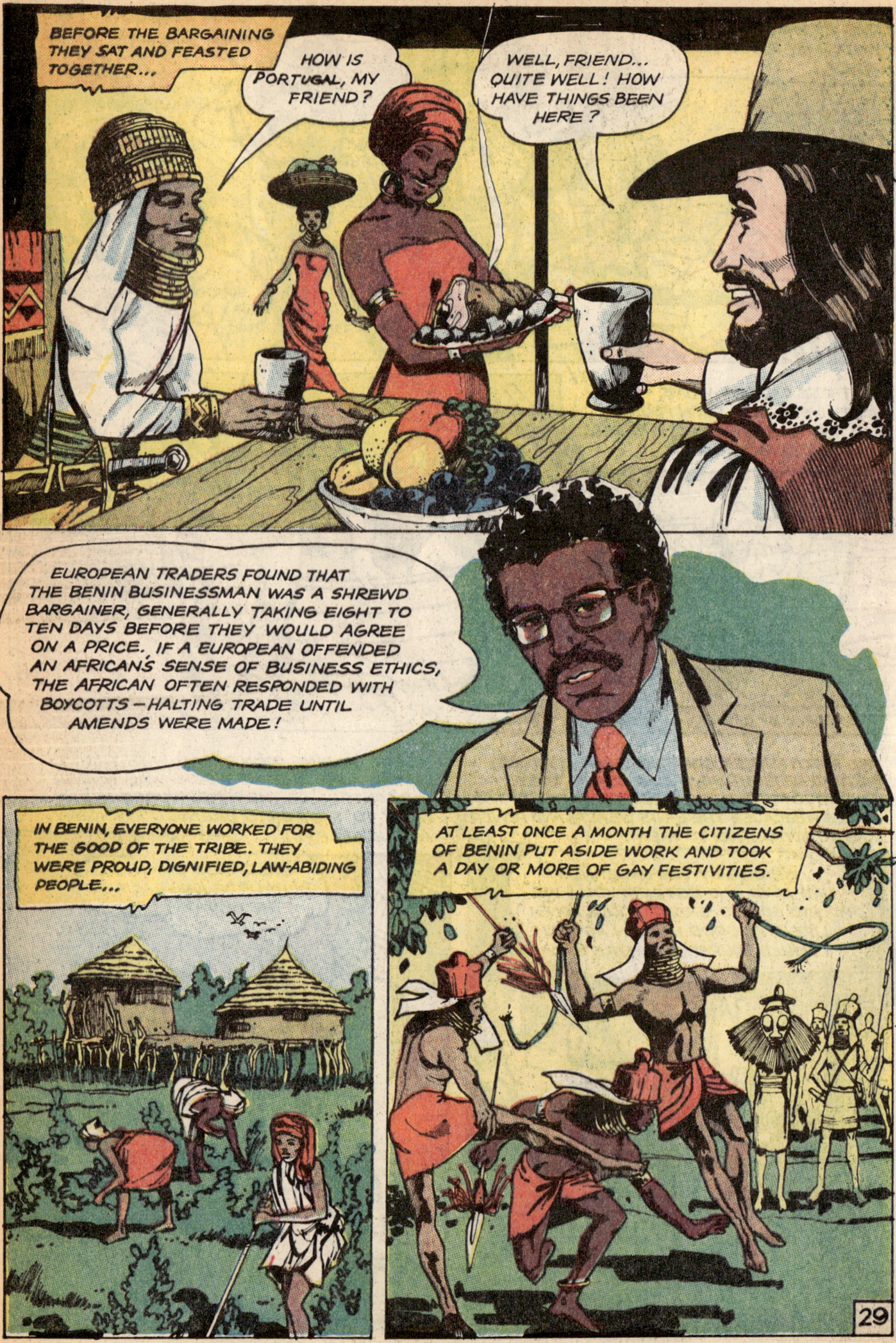

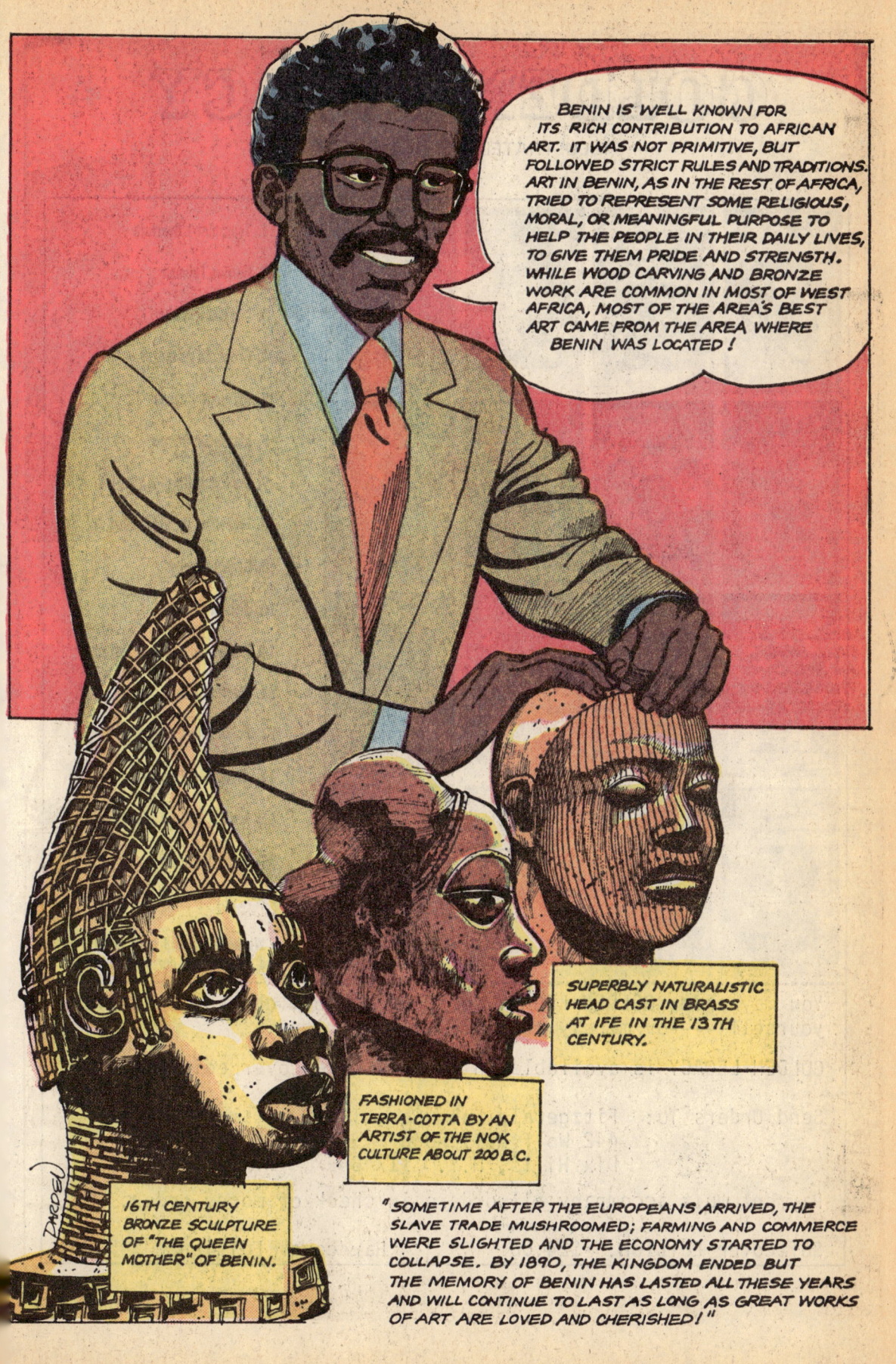

GOLDEN LEGACY
ILLUSTRATED HISTORY SERIES

1. Toussaint L'Overture
2. Harriet Tubman
3. Crispus Attucks
4. Benjamin Banneker
5. Matthew Henson
6. Alexander Dumas
7. Frederick Douglass Part I
8. Frederick Douglass Part II
9. Robert Smalls
10. Joseph Cinque
11. White, Wilkins & Marshall
12. Black Cowboys
13. Dr. Martin Luther King
14. Alexander Pushkin
15. Ancient African Kingdoms
16. Black Inventors

"We hope you will read, enjoy and benefit from our endeavors."

You may order GOLDEN LEGACY for your school, church, relatives, yourself-----or merely as a gift for a friend!

GOLDEN LEGACY is available in soft or hard cover editions.

Send Orders To: Fitzgerald Pub. Co., Inc.
                  442 Wolf Hill Road
                  Dix Hills, N.Y. 11746

Payment must accompany all orders in check or money order.

Softcover Edition: $24.00   Hardcover Edition: $45.00

GOLDEN LEGACY
ILLUSTRATED HISTORY MAGAZINE

THE BLACK INVENTORS LATIMER & WOODS

Vol. 16

© FITZGERALD PUB. Co. Inc. 1976

DRAFTSMAN   ENGINEER   INVENTOR

Lewis Howard LATIMER

Pioneer of the ELECTRIC LIGHTING INDUSTRY

I WAS ONE OF THE PIONEERS OF THE ELECTRIC LIGHTING INDUSTRY FROM ITS CREATION UNTIL IT HAD BECOME WORLDWIDE.
— Lewis H. Latimer

ILLUSTRATED by Leo CARTY

THE TELEPHONE SYSTEM, AS WE KNOW IT, IS THE PRODUCT OF MANY, MANY MINDS, TO WHOM HONOR SHOULD BE GIVEN...
— Alexander Graham Bell

Research and Text by Bertram Fitzgerald

THE LATIMER STORY REALLY BEGINS WITH HIS FATHER'S ESCAPE FROM SLAVERY IN VIRGINIA...

....AND ARRIVAL IN BOSTON IN 1831, WHERE HE LATER MET AND MARRIED ANOTHER RUNAWAY SLAVE FROM VIRGINIA.

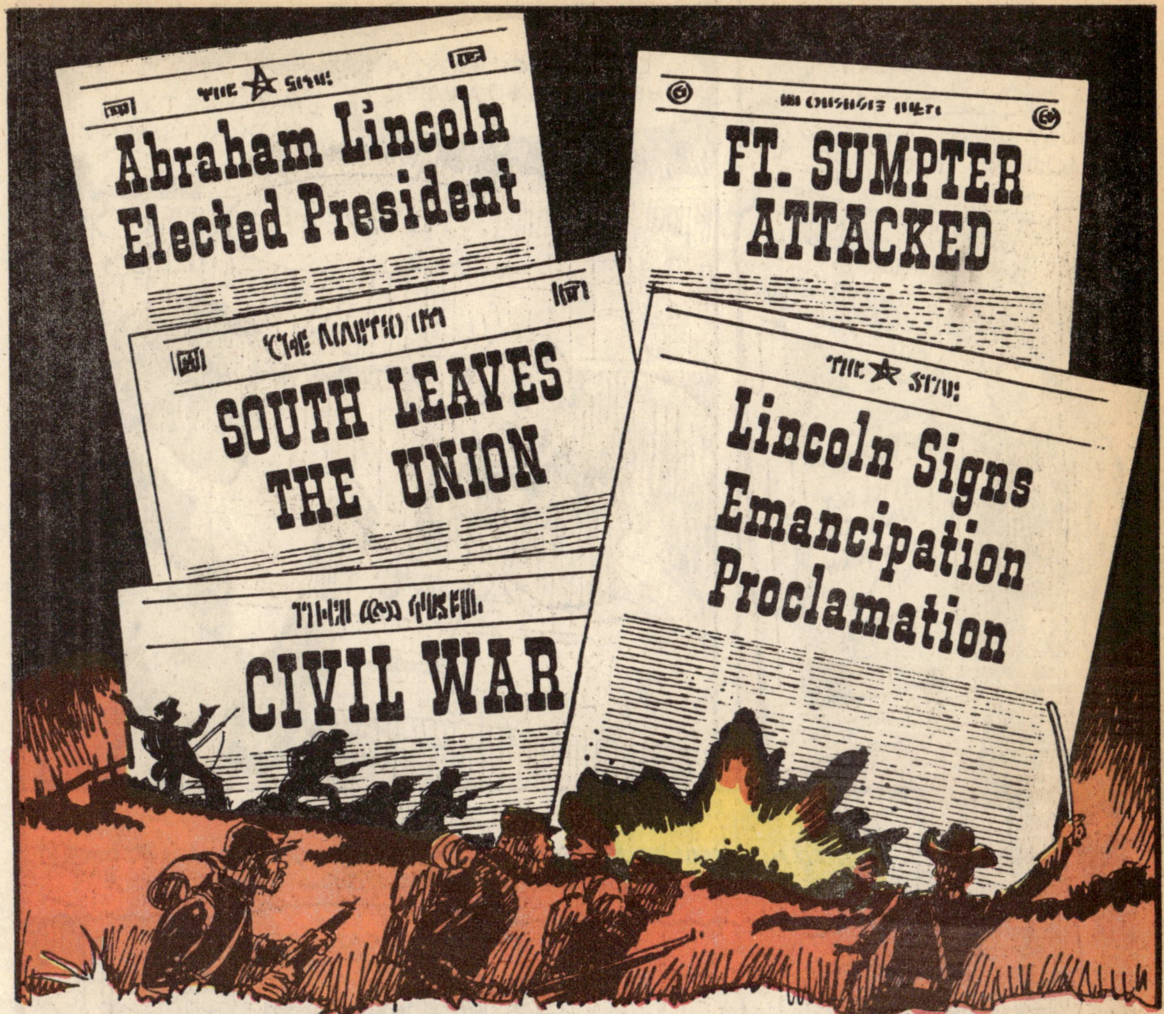

Abraham Lincoln Elected President

FT. SUMPTER ATTACKED

SOUTH LEAVES THE UNION

Lincoln Signs Emancipation Proclamation

CIVIL WAR

LATIMER'S TWO BROTHERS JOINED THE UNION ARMY, LEWIS WAS TOO YOUNG... BUT WANTED TO HELP FREE HIS PEOPLE...

SLAVERY WON'T END UNLESS THE WAR IS WON!

SO HE RAISED HIS AGE AND JOINED THE NAVY.

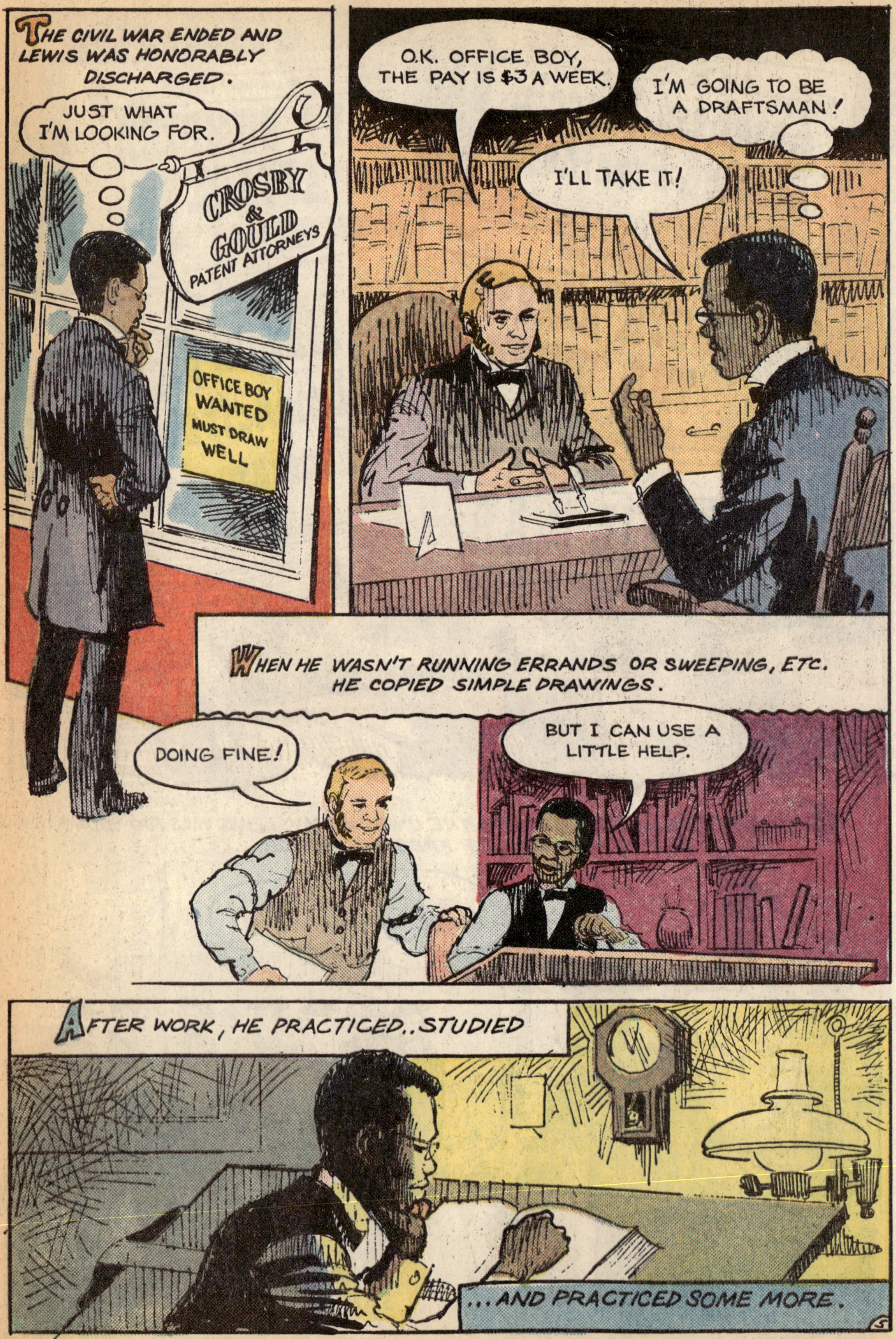

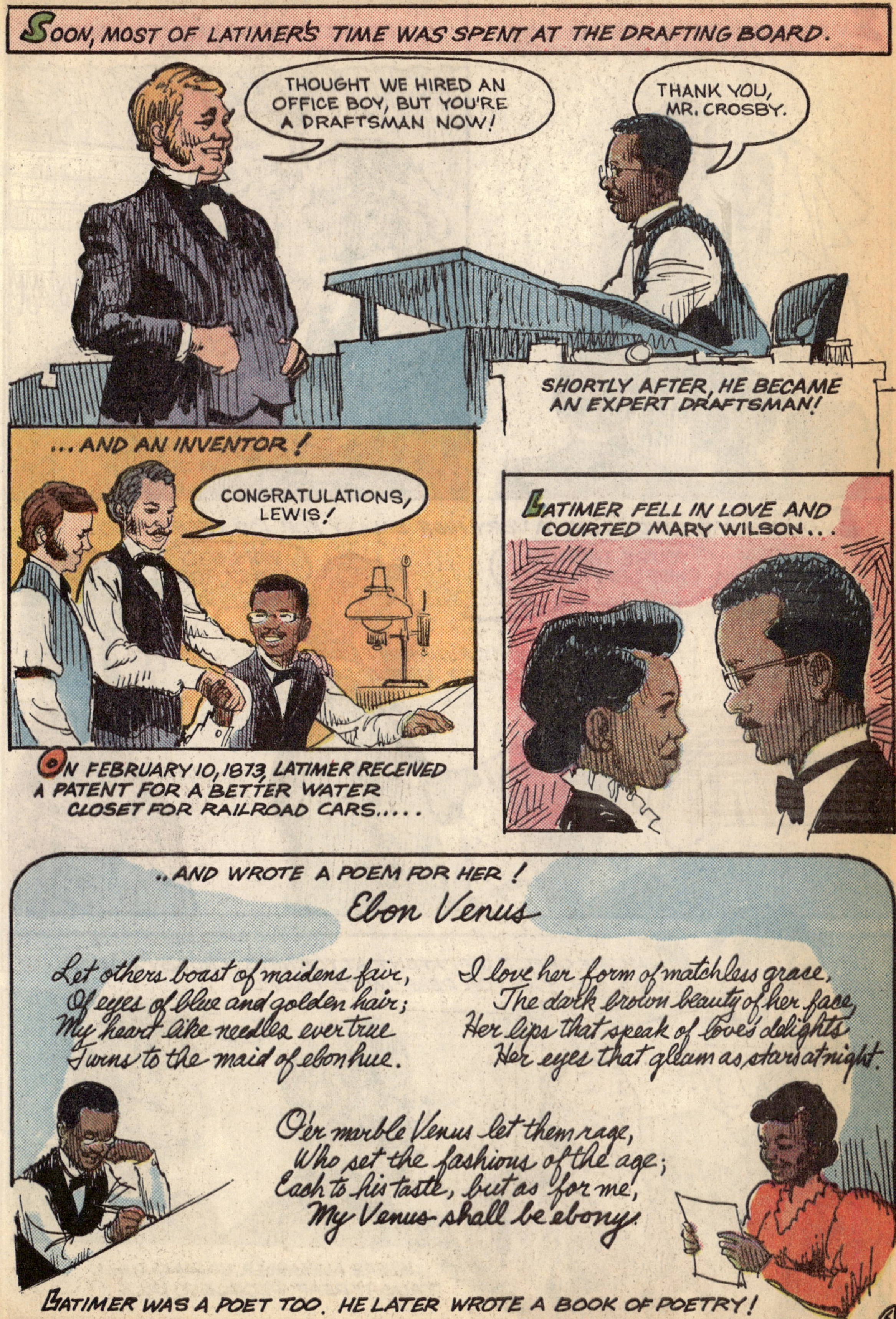

LATIMER WAS NOW CHIEF ENGINEER OF THE U.S. ELECTRIC LIGHTING COMPANY AND IN CHARGE OF INSTALLING ELECTRIC LIGHTING PLANTS IN...

NEW YORK

PHILADELPHIA

CANADA

BONJOUR, MONSIEUR.

IN THOSE DAYS, STREET LIGHTS WERE WIRED ON A SERIES CIRCUIT...

LATIMER WIRED STREET LIGHTS WITH A PARALLEL CIRCUIT....

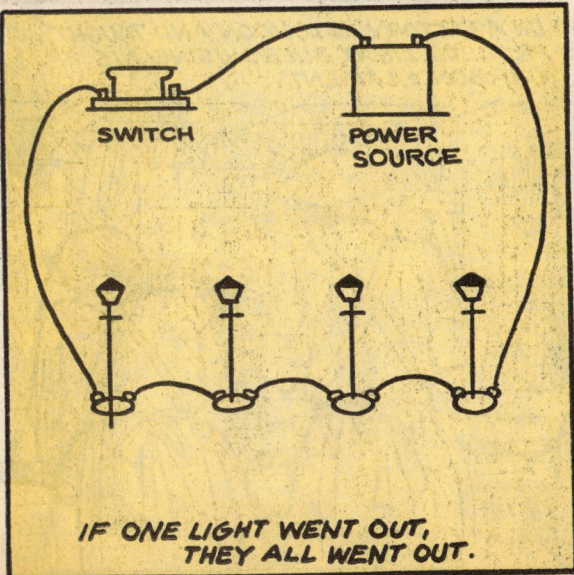

IF ONE LIGHT WENT OUT, THEY ALL WENT OUT.

IF ONE LIGHT WENT OUT, THE OTHERS STAYED ON!

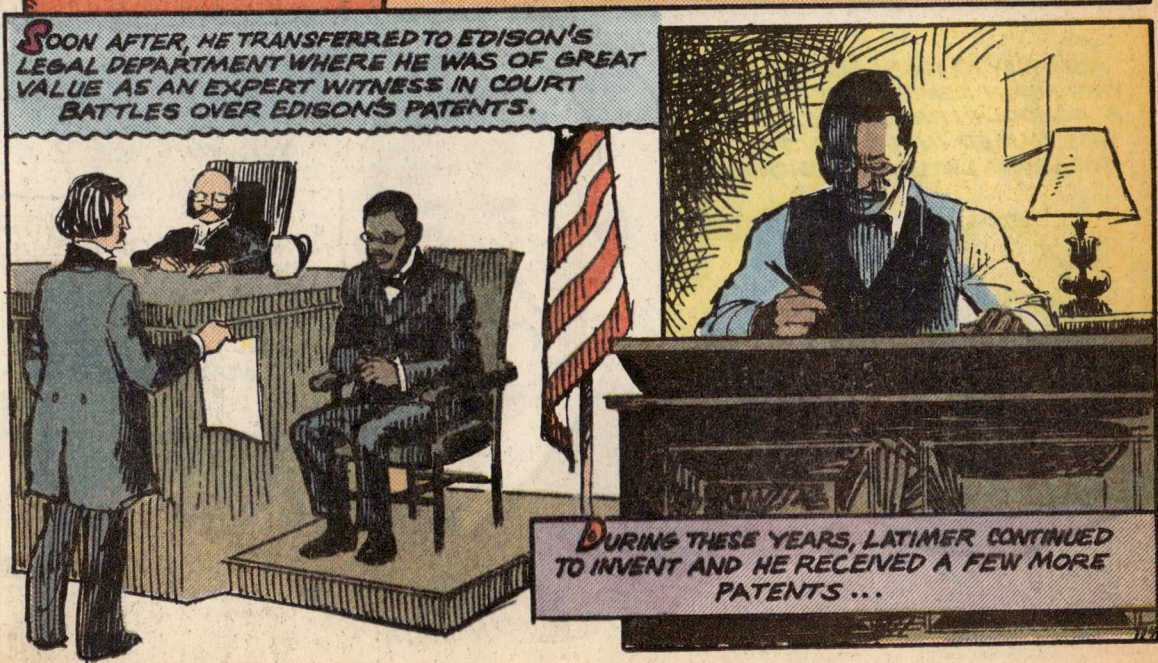

In 1918, an important group of inventors and scientists that worked closely with Edison formed **THE EDISON PIONEERS!**

...and Lewis Latimer was a member of this famous group from its beginning!

On December 11, 1928, Lewis Howard Latimer died at the age of 80 and the Edison Pioneers published this statement:

"We hardly mourn his going so much as we rejoice in pleasant memory at having been associated with him in a great work for all people under a great man ...Mr. Latimer was a full member, and an esteemed one, of the Edison Pioneers"

On May 10, 1968, Lewis Latimer was again remembered when a school in Brooklyn, N.Y. was named in his honor, **The Lewis Latimer School.**

"I was one of the pioneers in the electric light industry from its creation until it had become worldwide."

JAN E. MATZELIGER
1852 — 1889
INVENTOR OF THE SHOE LASTING MACHINE

MATZELIGER WAS BORN IN SURINAM, SO. AMERICA AND CAME TO AMERICA AT THE AGE OF 18 YEARS. HE LIVED IN LYNN, MASSACHUSETTS.

BY AGE 30, HE HAD INVENTED THE SHOE LASTING MACHINE! IT WAS THE FIRST MACHINE TO COMPLETE SEVERAL OF THE OPERATIONS REQUIRED TO MAKE A SHOE, AND ALL IN ONE MINUTE.

MATZELIGER'S LASTING MACHINE REDUCED THE COST OF SHOES BY ONE-HALF, DOUBLED THE WORKERS WAGES AND HELPED LYNN, MASS. BECOME THE SHOE CAPITAL OF THE WORLD.

ELIJAH McCOY 1844-1928
INVENTOR OF AUTOMATIC LUBRICATING DEVICES.

McCOY, THE SON OF A RUNAWAY SLAVE, WAS BORN IN CANADA AND EDUCATED AS A MECHANICAL ENGINEER IN SCOTLAND.

AFTER THE CIVIL WAR, McCOY MOVED TO DETROIT, MICHIGAN, WHERE HE INVENTED AUTOMATIC LUBRICATING DEVICES THAT MADE IT UNNECESSARY TO STOP MACHINERY TO BE OILED.

THE EXPRESSION "THE REAL McCOY" BECAME FAMOUS BECAUSE OF REMARKS MADE ABOUT HIS INVENTIONS. HE RECEIVED 57 PATENTS.

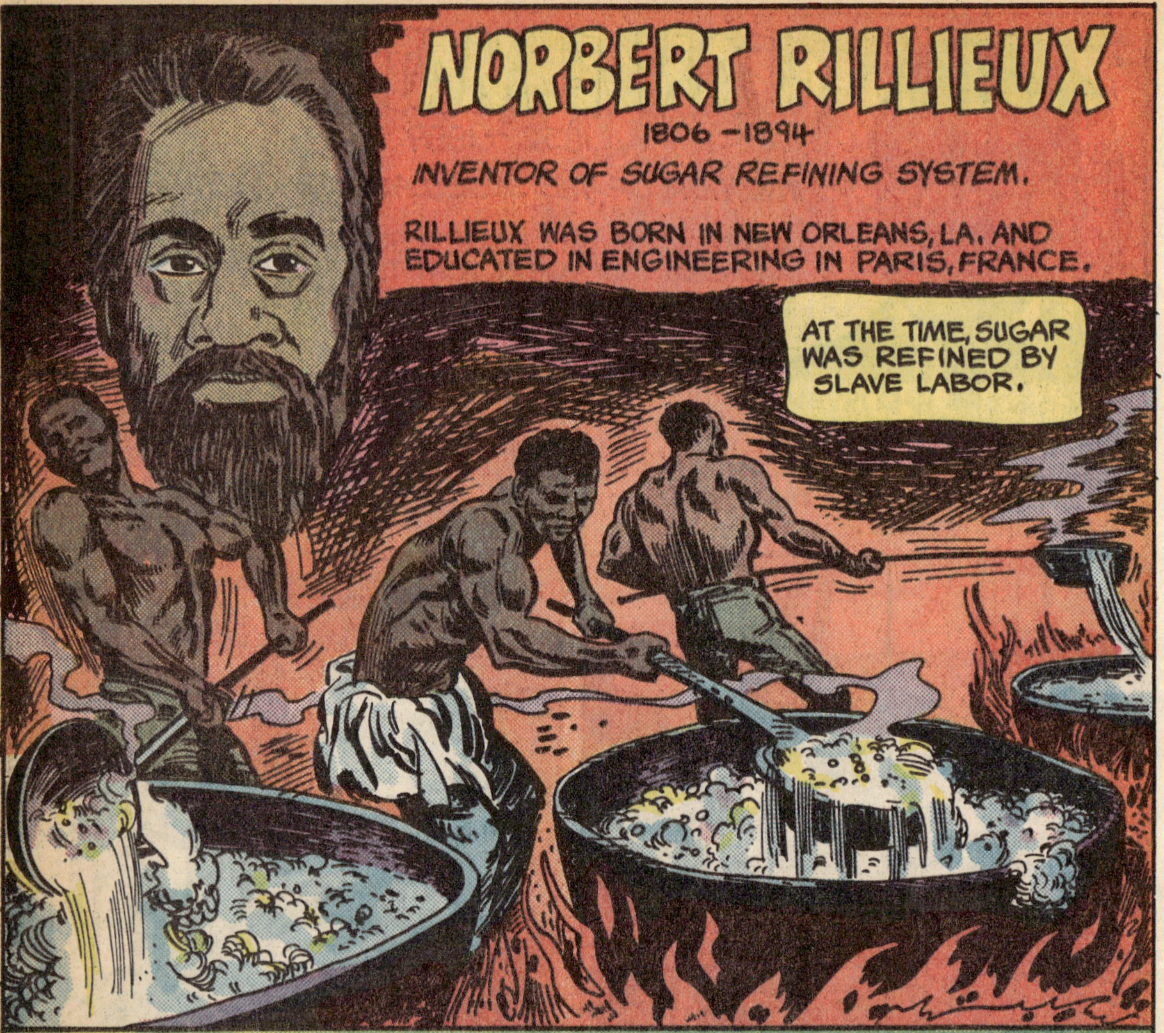

GRANVILLE T. WOODS
ENGINEER — INVENTOR

GRANVILLE T. WOODS WAS BORN ON APRIL 23, 1856 IN COLUMBUS, OHIO... AT THAT TIME IN AMERICA, MOST BLACKS WERE SLAVES BUT GRANVILLE'S PARENTS WERE FREE! THEY WERE VERY, VERY POOR BUT THEY WERE *FREE!*

AND THEY SENT GRANVILLE TO SCHOOL AS OFTEN AS THEY COULD AFFORD TO...

RECEIVED PATENTS FOR MORE THAN 50 INVENTIONS. HE WAS OFTEN CALLED THE BLACK EDISON

WHEN...
SORRY, SON, BUT WE NEED YOUR HELP. YOU'LL HAVE TO LEAVE SCHOOL!
I'LL FIND A JOB, DAD.

LITTLE GRANVILLE WAS LUCKY THAT HE FOUND A JOB IN A RAILROAD MACHINE SHOP DOING HARD AND UNSKILLED LABOR...
...INSTEAD OF FARM WORK OR ODD JOBS.

STILL EAGER TO LEARN, HE TAUGHT HIMSELF MANY OF THE JOBS THERE...

I'LL GIVE YOU HALF MY PAY EACH WEEK IF YOU'LL TEACH ME MECHANICS.

MUCH LATER...
YOU'VE LEARNED ALL I KNOW, WHAT'S NEXT?

AT 20, WOODS TRAVELED TO NEW YORK WHERE HE WORKED 7 DAYS A WEEK...

..AND ATTENDED SCHOOL IN THE EVENINGS STUDYING ELECTRICAL AND MECHANICAL ENGINEERING FOR TWO YEARS...

AFTER COMPLETING HIS COURSE... HE SAW THE WORLD AS AN ENGINEER ON A BRITISH STEAMSHIP.

THEN BACK TO THE RAILROADS AS AN ENGINEER ON THE DANVILLE-SOUTHERN LINE.

BUT WOODS WAS NOT PROMOTED ON SEVERAL JOBS BECAUSE HE WAS BLACK, SO HE STARTED HIS OWN BUSINESS...

...MAKING TELEPHONE, TELEGRAPH AND ELECTRICAL EQUIPMENT.

WOODS SOON BEGAN TO THINK OF OTHER THINGS...STEAM POWER.

HIS INTEREST IN STEAM POWERED ENGINES LED TO HIS...

BECOMING GRANVILLE T. WOODS, THE INVENTOR!

YOU'VE INVENTED A BETTER STEAM BOILER FURNACE!

GOT THE PATENT FOR IT TOO!

ELECTRIC STREET CARS OFTEN STOPPED OR BROKE DOWN BECAUSE OF POOR CONTACT WITH THE OVERHEAD POWER WIRES.

WOODS INVENTED THE "TROLLER". IT PROVIDED PERFECT CONTACT BETWEEN THE STREET CAR AND THE POWER WIRES.

BECAUSE OF WOODS' INVENTION, ELECTRIC STREET CARS ALMOST NEVER BROKE DOWN AND WERE LATER CALLED "TROLLEY" CARS.

ELECTRIC STREET CARS (TROLLEY CARS) WERE VERY DANGEROUS. MANY LARGE BULKY COILS WERE USED ON THE ELECTRIC MOTOR TO ADJUST ITS POWER AND CHANGE THE CARS SPEED.

THE COILS BECAME RED HOT AND OFTEN CAUSED FIRES.

WOODS SOLVED THAT PROBLEM TOO... HE INVENTED A COMBINATION OF AN ELECTRIC MOTOR AND GENERATOR THAT WAS SAFE AND DID NOT OVERHEAT.

IT ALSO CONTROLLED THE MOTOR'S POWER, SPEED, PROVIDED A SMOOTHER RIDE AND SAVED 40% OF THE ELECTRIC POWER.

WOODS MADE A SIMILAR INVENTION THAT PREVENTED THEATER FIRES THAT WERE OFTEN CAUSED BY AN OVERLOAD OF ELECTRIC POWER WHEN THE LIGHTS WERE DIMMED.

SERIOUS ACCIDENTS HAPPEN AT NIGHT AND IN HEAVY FOG, OR IN TUNNELS. SIGNALS DON'T ALWAYS WORK.

THERE WAS NO SURE WAY OF PREVENTING ONE TRAIN FROM CRASHING INTO ANOTHER.

WOODS CAME TO THE RESCUE WITH A GREAT INVENTION — THE INDUCTION TELEGRAPH SYSTEM!

IT'S A WAY TO TELEPHONE OR TELEGRAPH MESSAGES TO AND FROM A MOVING TRAIN.

ALSO BETWEEN MOVING TRAINS.

TRAINS AVOIDED ACCIDENTS BY INFORMING EACH OTHER OF THEIR LOCATIONS.

THE RAILWAY DISPATCHER WAS ALSO ABLE TO LOCATE ANY TRAIN AT A GLANCE.

THOMAS EDISON AND OTHER INVENTORS CLAIMED THIS INVENTION. THEY TOOK WOODS TO COURT BUT WOODS WON AFTER A VERY LONG LEGAL BATTLE.

I'D LIKE TO BUY YOUR COMPANY, MR. WOODS, AND HAVE YOU COME TO WORK FOR US.

THANK YOU, MR. EDISON, BUT NO!

MANY BIG CITIES HAVE SUBWAYS AND ELEVATED TRAIN SYSTEMS THAT ARE OPERATED BY ELECTRICAL POWER. TRAIN YARDS NEAR OR WITHIN CITIES OFTEN USE ELECTRICAL POWER TO MOVE THE TRAINS INTO AND AROUND THE YARDS.

GRANVILLE T. WOODS INVENTED AN ELECTRICAL RAILWAY POWER SYSTEM THAT, TODAY, IS KNOWN AS "THE THIRD RAIL"*!

* IT RUNS ALONG ONE SIDE OF THE TRACKS AND IS THE SOURCE OF ELECTRICAL POWER THAT MOVES THE TRAIN.

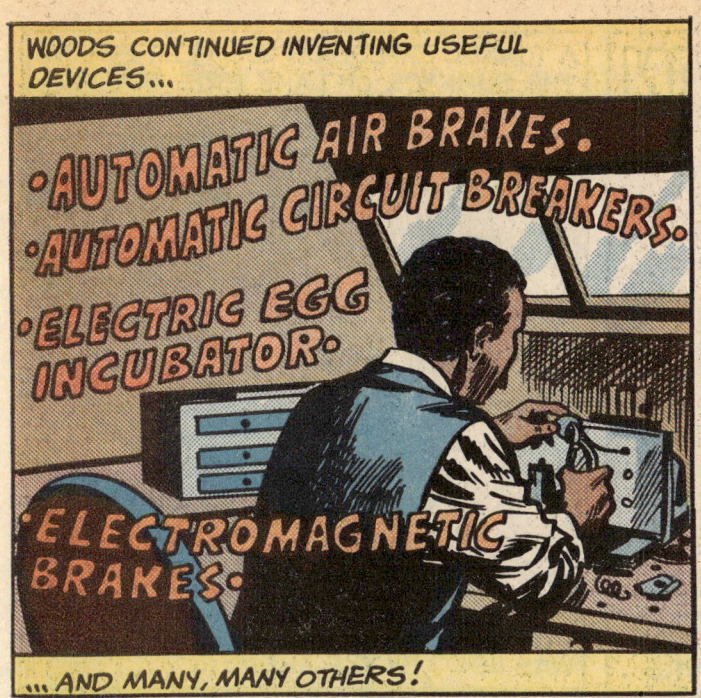

WOODS CONTINUED INVENTING USEFUL DEVICES...
- AUTOMATIC AIR BRAKES.
- AUTOMATIC CIRCUIT BREAKERS.
- ELECTRIC EGG INCUBATOR.
- ELECTROMAGNETIC BRAKES.

...AND MANY, MANY OTHERS!

SEVERAL MAJOR CORPORATIONS PURCHASED MANY OF HIS INVENTIONS... AMERICAN TELEPHONE & TELEGRAPH — WESTINGHOUSE — GENERAL ELECTRIC — AMERICAN ENGINEERING COMPANY.

WHEN GRANVILLE T. WOODS DIED ON JANUARY 30, 1910, HIS INVENTIVE IDEAS HAD IMPROVED ALL OF OUR LIVES AND ADVANCED OUR COMMUNICATION, TRANSPORTATION AND ELECTRICAL APPLIANCE INDUSTRIES.

THE END

GOLDEN LEGACY
ILLUSTRATED HISTORY SERIES

1. Toussaint L'Overture
2. Harriet Tubman
3. Crispus Attucks
4. Benjamin Banneker
5. Matthew Henson
6. Alexander Dumas
7. Frederick Douglass Part I
8. Frederick Douglass Part II
9. Robert Smalls
10. Joseph Cinque
11. White, Wilkins & Marshall
12. Black Cowboys
13. Dr. Martin Luther King
14. Alexander Pushkin
15. Ancient African Kingdoms
16. Black Inventors

"We hope you will read, enjoy and benefit from our endeavors."

You may order GOLDEN LEGACY for your school, church, relatives, yourself-----or merely as a gift for a friend!

GOLDEN LEGACY is available in soft or hard cover editions.

Send Orders To: Fitzgerald Pub. Co., Inc.
442 Wolf Hill Road
Dix Hills, N.Y. 11746

Payment must accompany all orders in check or money order.

Softcover Edition: $24.00   Hardcover Edition: $45.00